Silent Revolution

'*Silent Revolution* explains how best to enrich the rich and impoverish the poor with maximum speed and efficiency. Combining theoretical clarity with you-are-there reportorial detail, the author brings home both the inanity and the extraordinary power of the neo-liberal doctrine which is systematically destroying countless lives and communities – and not just in Latin America. Naively, I believed that on the whole I knew what was worth knowing about the debt crisis, the impact of structural adjustment and the enthusiastic participation of local elites in the economic enslavement of their own countries. Duncan Green has disabused me: he has written an informative book, but also a salutary, fascinating and necessary one.'

Susan George, Associate Director, Transnational Institute and author of *Faith and Credit: The World Bank's Secular Empire* (1994)

'*Silent Revolution* is a provocative counterweight to the story that Latin America is a testimony to the success of laissez-faire – and a salutary warning to the rest of the world about its capacity to marry growth and social well being.'

Will Hutton, Economics Editor of *The Guardian* and author of *The State We're In* (1995)

'*Silent Revolution* is a superb guide to the neo-liberal revolution in Latin America, taking us from its bloody birth in the Chilean coup of 1973 to its spectacular unravelling during the Mexican financial crisis of 1995. Combining unassailable analysis with a thorough grasp of economic and political trends, Duncan Green convincingly argues that the region is headed for even greater tragedy unless people put an end to their leaders' dangerous obsession with the market and move toward more equitable and ecologically sustainable models of economic development.'

Walden Bello, University of the Philippines, author of *Dark Victory: the United States, Structural Adjustment and Global Poverty* (1994)

Silent Revolution

The Rise of
Market Economics
in Latin America

Duncan Green

CASSELL

For Catherine, Calum and Finlay

Cassell
Wellington House
125 Strand
London WC2R 0BB

First published 1995

Reprinted 1996

Published in association with
Latin America Bureau (Research and Action) Ltd
1 Amwell Street
London

Distributed in North America by Monthly Review Press
122 West 27 Street
New York, NY 10001, USA

British Library Cataloguing-in-Publication Data

Green, Duncan
  Silent Revolution: Rise of Market Economics in Latin America
  Economics in Latin America
  I. Title
  330.98

ISBN   0-304-33455-3 (hardback)
        0-304-33456-1 (paperback)

Cover photograph of La Paz ©Tony Morrison/South American Pictures
Typeset by Ben Cracknell

Printed and bound in Great Britain by Biddles Ltd, Guildford and King's Lynn

Contents

Books from the Latin America Bureau

The Latin America Bureau (LAB) publishes books on contemporary issues in Latin America and the Caribbean.

Current titles include:

- Introductions to Latin American and Caribbean society and culture, economics and politics

- Country guides – Bolivia, Venezuela, Jamaica and Cuba are the first in the series

- A series on Latin American women's lives and experiences

- Latin American authors in translation: from street children to salsa, from rubber tappers to guerrilla radio stations

LAB is also publisher of Duncan Green's bestselling *Faces of Latin America*, an exploration of the people and processes that have shaped modern Latin America.

Faces of Latin America celebrates the vibrant culture of its peoples and looks at the key actors in the region's turbulent politics, with chapters on the military, democracy, the guerrillas, indigenous peoples, the Church and the women's movement.

> *'a clear, lively and most informative survey of Latin America, illustrated by good vignettes of people and places, drawn from [Duncan Green's] wide experience'*
>
> **Literary Review**

> *'an indispensable introduction and source of reference'*
>
> **New Statesman and Society**

For a free 20-page LAB Books catalogue, write to LAB, Dept SR, 1 Amwell Street, London EC1R 1UL, or call 0171-278-2829.

LAB Books are distributed in North America by Monthly Review Press, 122 West 27 Street, New York, NY 10001 (Tel: 212-691-2555).

Introduction

From the ninth floor of the World Bank building in La Paz, the marchers look more like ants than people. Over the hum of the air-conditioner and the computers, the bangs of firecrackers and chanted slogans can barely be heard. 'Bolivia will never belong to the gringos' drifts up, tinny and weak through the megaphones.

The sun is setting, catching the snowy peak of Mount Illimani high above the city, glowing on skyscraper and slum alike. 'These people can't be allowed to win', mutters the Bolivian yuppie in the striped shirt, and goes back to talking up the economy.

Much more than nine floors separate the World Bank's Juan Carlos Aguilar from the protesters far below. Juan Carlos is fired with crusading zeal. This sleek, impossibly young technocrat thinks that only his free-market panacea can enable Bolivia to leave behind 500 years of poverty and inequality. To his eyes the demonstrators are a relic from Bolivia's revolutionary past, an obstacle to future prosperity that must be side-stepped if they are not to divert politicians from the path of economic righteousness.

Success is in the eye of the beholder. The silver-tongued Juan Carlos spins a seductive web of statistics, speaking purely in abstract economic variables – growth, trade, inflation. Bolivia's hungry masses – un-employed tin-miners and factory-workers, street-sellers, vagrants and hungry peasant farmers – talk instead about trying to feed their families, grappling with the crumbling health service and their desperate search for some kind of paid job. All are supposedly discussing the well-being of the same nation, yet often there seems almost no connection between their different worlds.

There are Juan Carlos clones throughout Latin America, young, smartly dressed men and women speaking perfect English thanks to their post-graduate degrees from US universities. They run the booming stock exchanges, subsidiaries of transnational corporations, economy ministries and offices of multilateral organizations like the World Bank. They, and

1

their friends in Washington, London and Frankfurt, share a common vision and awesome self-belief. They know what is wrong with Latin America, and they know how to put it right. In 1990, *Newsweek* described the scene:

> The Latin techno-Yuppies are easy to pick out of a crowd. Still in their late 30s or early 40s, they are old enough to appreciate the Beatles and young enough to regard themselves as standing against the traditional Latin establishment. They fondly recall their student days in the United States (they regard Cambridge, Massachusetts, as practically an honorary Latin capital). In Mexico City – a bastion of the movement – the techno-car of choice is a spanking new Nissan or Mercedes; at dinner time, the techno-Yuppies dine at the expensive outdoor cafés and Italian-style trattorie found in the Polanco neighbourhood. Their power suits carry Armani or Christian Dior labels.[1]

Latin America's techno-Yuppies are the avant-garde of a 'silent revolution' which has been going on in the region since the early 1980s. It is a revolution which has gone largely unreported outside Latin America, except in the pages of the *Financial Times* and other media catering to foreign investors. As in any revolution, the old order is being turned upside down, but this economic transformation does not aspire to create a socialist utopia. Instead, it is enshrining market forces at the heart of the region's economy.

What is neo-liberalism?

In Latin America, the new thinking is known as neo-liberalism, but even the name is confusing. Outside the region, the word 'liberal' often describes people who support civil rights and a stronger sense of community values, but in this case, the liberalism is economic, not political. The overriding freedom in the neo-liberal canon is that of the 'free' market, and where freeing the market is incompatible with freeing the people, the market usually takes precedence. The notorious Chilean dictator General Pinochet was a crusading neo-liberal.

The 'neo' prefix is needed because after the 1930s liberalism went out of fashion in Latin America, dropped in favour of an economic model known by the unlovely name of Import Substituting Industrialization, or 'import substitution' for short. Import substitution changed the economic face of the continent through a strategy of state-led development of domestic industry, but for the neo-liberals, it was a big mistake. Their diagnosis of Latin America's economic ills is simple: too much state, too much regulation, too much government spending and not enough emphasis on the private sector and foreign trade. In Britain it would be more accurately termed neo-conservatism, for it is a close relative to what Latin Americans sometimes call *Thatcherismo*.

The neo-liberals draw their inspiration from the great classical traditions of economic thought. The bible of classical economics is Adam Smith's *An Inquiry into the Nature and Causes of the Wealth of Nations*, published in 1776. Smith's work reflects the rise of a new entrepreneurial class in the early years of Britain's Industrial Revolution, and many of its themes have remained central to economic debate ever since.

Refined in succeeding generations by other great economic thinkers such as David Ricardo (1772–1823), Thomas Malthus (1766–1834), and John Stuart Mill (1806–73), Smith's book endeavoured, in contemporary language, to explain the origins of economic growth. He found them in the unhindered operation of the market, which he memorably described as an 'invisible hand', working to maximize economic growth and human happiness. Smith and his followers fiercely criticized any attempt by government to interfere with the benign workings of the market as likely to damage the prospects for growth.[2] Subsequently, Ricardo extended such ideas to trade between nations and wages, arguing that 'like all other contracts, wages should be left to the fair and free competition of the market, and should never be controlled by the interference of the legislature'.[3]

The second strand of neo-liberalism is monetarism, essentially the theory that a change in the money supply leads to a corresponding change in the overall level of prices, but does not affect output or employment. This theory is said by one author to be 'at least 500 years old and . . . sometimes claimed to date from Confucius'.[4] The theory was formalized by Irving Fisher (1867–1947) as the quantity theory of money, which was revived by Milton Friedman (born 1912) in the 1960s, following the successful challenge launched by Keynes's *General Theory* in 1936.[5] Monetarism underlies the monetary approach to the balance of payments which forms the theoretical basis for IMF programmes.

Classical economics provided the intellectual foundations for the *laissez-faire* capitalism of the Victorian age. The trauma of the Great Depression in the 1930s convinced many people that the untrammelled workings of the market were anything but benign, and the classical school suffered a temporary eclipse in favour of the ideas of its two greatest adversaries, Karl Marx, who challenged the supremacy of the market, and John Maynard Keynes, who challenged monetarism. Both men argued for a far more central role for the state in economic management. As the state-led models of these two thinkers ran into trouble in the 1960s, a new generation of economists and politicians were once again drawn to the attractive simplicity of Smith's view of the world.

The neo-liberal recipe has evolved as the silent revolution has unfolded, and not all countries have followed every recommendation, but the core message, sometimes known as the Washington Consensus, is unvarying. The solution to the region's under-development lies in a three-stage economic transformation: stabilization, structural adjustment and export-led growth.

Stabilization
Stabilization means curbing inflation, seen as the single greatest obstacle to economic recovery. In neo-liberal eyes, the way to fight inflation is the monetarist path of reducing the growth in the money supply by cutting public spending and raising interest rates. Wage controls are also used to reduce demand in the economy. In practice, usually under IMF tutelage, stabilization pursues a second, often-contradictory, objective – making sure the country does not default on its debt repayments to the northern commercial banks, the IMF and the World Bank. This usually entails a large devaluation to generate a trade surplus with which to keep up its debt repayments.

Structural adjustment
In the longer term, stabilization should coincide with or be swiftly followed by 'structural adjustment'. The aim here is to implant a functioning market economy in the country by 'getting the prices right', removing artificial distortions such as price controls or trade tariffs, allowing the unregulated market to determine the most efficient allocation of resources. Because of its role in distorting prices and generally interfering with the free operation of the market, the state is seen as part of the problem, not part of the solution, and the economy has to be restructured to reduce the state's role and unleash the private sector. This means privatizing state firms and the broader deregulation of trade and investment. Deregulation should also remove 'structural rigidities' in the workforce. In practice this often means cutting labour costs by making it easier to hire and fire employees, restricting trade union activities and encouraging greater 'flexibility' through short-term contracts and subcontracting. Like stabilization, structural adjustment supports eliminating government spending deficits, which are seen as inflationary, but adjustment differs in that it more frequently involves closing the deficit by enhancing revenue as well as cutting spending. This is usually achieved by a mixture of privatization proceeds and raising sales taxes such as VAT.

Export-led growth
Structural adjustment paves the way for an export-led economic recovery.

The government should give priority to exports, encouraging the private sector to diversify and find new markets for its products. This sometimes involves suppressing domestic demand (which diverts goods away from exports to local consumption). Removing all trade barriers (on both imports and exports) will, argue the neo-liberals, ensure that resources are allocated efficiently, and that exports are made more competitive because their producers will be able to cut costs by importing the cheapest inputs available, whether fertilizers and pesticides for agro-exports or manufactured inputs for industry. Export-led growth generally means encouraging foreign investors to bring in new technology and capital.

Bolivia: the neo-liberal showcase

For the international sales reps of the silent revolution, Bolivia is a success story. 'No other area in the world is taking so many initiatives to open and integrate its economies with world markets,' enthuses Shahid Hussain, the World Bank's Vice President for Latin America and the Caribbean.[6]

In mid-1985 a new government took power at a time of acute economic crisis. Inflation, driven by a massive fiscal deficit, was running at an almost inconceivable annualized rate of over 23,000 per cent, the national economy had been shrinking for five consecutive years[7] and real wages had fallen by 30 per cent since 1981.[8] The country had been unable to keep up with the repayments on its foreign debt since March 1984.[9]

The foundations of what was christened the New Economic Policy were laid with presidential decree 21060 in August 1985. The decree was drawn up by Harvard professor Jeffrey Sachs following discussions with the IMF and World Bank and was designed to win IMF approval, which in turn would enable Bolivia to reschedule its debt payments to western governments and commercial banks. In Bolivia the decree is known merely by its number – one enterprising radio taxi company in Cochabamba had the brainwave of buying a 21060 telephone line, guaranteeing that its customers would never forget it.

The main measures contained in the decree were:[10]

- *removal of restrictions on imports and exports;*
- *establishment of a single, flexible exchange rate;*
- *public-sector wages frozen for four months (later reduced to three);*
- *an end to fixed prices on most goods and services;*
- *state companies given one month to present programmes for 'rationalizing' (i.e. sacking) staff;*
- *'free contracting' introduced in all firms, allowing management to hire and fire at will.*

After the initial stabilization, subsequent decrees tried to reactivate the economy by stimulating exports and encouraging both foreign and local investment.

The harsh medicine duly won approval from the IMF, which in June 1986 announced $57m in new credits, while the World Bank started lending again after a three-year gap and creditor nations agreed to reschedule debt repayments on favourable terms.[11] Further IMF aid for structural adjustment followed in the years to come.

Professor Sachs has since exported the model to Poland and other Eastern European economies, but as he himself admits, there are severe limitations to the Bolivian 'miracle'.

> I always told the Bolivians, from the very beginning, that what you have here is a miserable, poor economy with hyperinflation; if you are brave, if you are gutsy, if you do everything right, you will end up with a miserable, poor economy with stable prices.[12]

Which is a pretty accurate description of what has happened. On the positive side, the shock therapy rapidly stabilized the economy, as inflation fell to 66 per cent in 1986, and just 11 per cent in 1987.[13] Moreover, the stabilization was achieved without a severe recession; since 1987 the economy has been growing again, albeit slowly in per capita terms. Despite the near-collapse of the world market for Bolivia's main export, tin, total exports have increased steadily, largely thanks to new non-traditional crops such as soya beans and coffee. A tax reform has greatly increased government revenues.

A job creation programme, known as the Emergency Social Fund, was set up in 1987 with World Bank support to mitigate the social impact of the measures. The ESF spent a total of $194m, creating 76,000 jobs over its four-year life span and winning world-wide praise for its speed and efficiency.[14] However a closer look shows that the Fund generally ended up helping the better-off, while virtually ignoring the poorest rural communities.[15]

But the bad news far outweighs the good. Above all, the model has exacted a tragic human cost discernible in the statistics of falling wages and rising inequality, but more powerfully apparent to any casual observer of Bolivia's streets and farms.

At regular intervals along the empty country roads, children stand all day holding out imploring cupped hands in the vain hope of a coin or two tossed from the occasional passing car. According to local aid workers, the practice only started in the late 1980s. One study by the UN's International Fund for Agricultural Development[16] revealed that 97 per cent of the rural population live below the poverty line – the highest level of rural poverty in the world. Structural adjustment has worsened the crisis in peasant agriculture by giving the lion's share of credit and investment to big agribusiness farms producing for export, while lowering barriers to cheap food imports. As a result, Bolivian peasants find themselves unable to sell their crops.

'I've seen far more serious malnutrition in children since '85,' says Dr Ana María Aguilar of the Children's Hospital in La Paz. Tuberculosis, a poverty-related disease, is also on the rise. In the early years of structural adjustment, from 1987 to 1991, government figures show the percentage of Bolivian families below the poverty line rising from 74.6 per cent to 80.1 per cent.[17] In El Alto, the slum city on the outskirts of La Paz, 96 per cent of babies have birth weights of less than the international standard for low birth weight, 5½lb.[18] By way of comparison, the figure for Ethiopia in 1990 was just 16 per cent.[19] In one of Dr Aguilar's wards, a 13-year-old boy stands protectively over the motionless form of his sister, whose brain is being attacked by TB-meningitis. 'She can't say anything, but she knows I'm here,' he says quietly.

In the cities that fearful euphemism 'rationalization' has spawned wave upon wave of redundancy notices. Often the managers used the 'shake-out' to get rid of the trouble-makers first. The man shining tourists' shoes at his little stall on La Paz's main street is Selvestre Hiladi, aged 51. Until 1988 he was the trade union general secretary in a factory making plastic shoes. Since then his working week has gone from 40 to about 65 hours, and his wife has had to go out selling clothes on the street. He had no choice, he says. 'We old ones have to do whatever we can, you have to swallow your pride. The customers treat you like shit and you just have to take it.' For 10 minutes' work, he charges the equivalent of 18 cents. Meanwhile, Selvestre says, the factory owners are doing fine. After they broke the union, they sacked the whole workforce and hired new people at lower wages.[20]

As protection was stripped away, cheap imports bankrupted over 120 of Bolivia's factories, reversing decades of gradual industrialization.[21] Many of those sacked have no option but to join the 'informal sector' where over 60 per cent of Bolivia's urban population now scrape a living as best they can among the overcrowded ranks of street sellers, self-employed artisans and others engaged in desperate forms of hand-to-mouth existence.[22] A man in the prime of life spends his entire day trying to hawk a handful of wooden coat hangers to indifferent passers-by; Indian women sit motionless in shawls and bowler hats, guarding tiny heaps of shrunken fruit. Too many sellers, not enough customers to go round. According to social scientist Silvia Escobar, by 1991 there was a street seller for every three families in Bolivia's cities.[23]

Those who have clung on to a paid job have lost many rights as the neo-liberal crusade to 'remove rigidities in the labour market' has effectively abolished the minimum wage and eight-hour day. Since 1985 the number of children leaving school early to support their family has increased by almost half.[24]

Even in the safely distanced realm of macroeconomic statistics preferred by the neo-liberal pundits, Bolivia's structural adjustment has been a mixed bag. Stability has failed to bring investment, either from domestic or foreign sources; the country remains highly dependent on large doses of foreign aid which, along with the inflow of cocaine dollars, has played a key, if unacknowledged, role in cushioning the population against some of the worst effects of adjustment. By 1993, the privatization of state enterprises had made almost no progress, largely because no one wanted to buy them. Instead, large parts of the state sector, notably the mining company Comibol, were run down and allowed to wither away.

Furthermore, at least part of the credit for the government's success in stabilizing the economy must go to an unlikely ally – the cocaine trade, which boomed in the early years of the adjustment. Cocadollars generated foreign exchange and jobs, thereby cushioning the social impact of the measures and allowing the government to maintain a relatively high level of imports. The government's no-questions-asked approach to money laundering ensured that, at its peak, as much as $20m a month entered the private banking system, staving off an economic collapse.[25]

From the comfort of his office, Juan Carlos may paint Bolivia's silent revolution as a stunning success but Richard Ardaya, a textile worker sacked as a result of decree 21060, is even more damning about the stabilization programme than Professor Sachs: 'What's stabilized here is poverty – it's permanent.'[26]

About this book

Silent Revolution shows the all-encompassing nature of the transformations under way in Latin America. Outside the region, public discussion has concentrated almost exclusively on the region's debt crisis and the role of the international financial institutions, in particular the IMF, normally cast by its critics as the neo-colonial villain of the piece. While the debt crisis was undoubtedly an extraordinary exercise in financial pillage of the South by the powerful northern countries, that has now largely ceased, revealing its more lasting legacy as the catalyst for a profound restructuring of the region's economy, a process that is still under way throughout the continent.

Central to the restructuring was the belief that the state's role in the economy should be reduced. This book looks at the successes and failures of state and market in Latin America's recent past and contrasts the recent failings of state involvement in the region with the booming Asian economies such as Taiwan and South Korea, which rely on a hands-on role for the state that is anathema to neo-liberal orthodoxy.

From the earliest days of the debt crisis the IMF and, increasingly, the World Bank were key players in persuading or forcing Latin American policy-makers to adopt the neo-liberal agenda. *Silent Revolution* explores the structure, thinking, power and policies of the IMF and the Bank. It also analyses the real extent of their policy changes since the late 1980s, made in response to a rising chorus of criticism over the human costs of their policies.

Most information on this phenomenon, arguably the most important political and economic issue facing the region today, is written in impenetrable language designed by and for professional or apprentice economists. This book aims to tell the story in plain English. Although this will doubtless run the risk of oversimplifying complex processes, losing some 'shades of grey' along the way, the exercise will be worthwhile if it helps a wider audience grasp the human and economic impact of the silent revolution.

The abstraction of most economic debate on the issue also tends to downplay the impact of economic change on those whom it is supposed to benefit – ordinary Latin Americans. While examining neo-liberalism's macroeconomic record at regional and national level, *Silent Revolution* also reveals the human costs of the region's experiment in market economics and talks to some of the ordinary men and women whose jobs and lives have been changed for ever by structural adjustment. In doing so, this book tries to answer two central questions: is the region's economy better off after 13 years of adjustment, and are Latin Americans themselves leading better lives as a result?

One of the central assumptions of the silent revolution is that free trade will enhance prosperity for all those who participate in it. This book analyses Latin America's position in a changing global economy and shows how countries are increasingly forced into adopting free trade policies by a combination of technological change and the growing political influence of international lenders and powerful nations. It explores the impact of trade liberalization on the region's workforce. This book also surveys the recent flurry of Regional Trade Agreements which have become an essential part of the region's economic hopes.

Change does not occur in a political vacuum, and change as profound as that currently taking place requires powerful support. Once the doctrine of military dictators, neo-liberalism has now become the accepted wisdom among politicians over much of the spectrum. *Silent Revolution* examines the kind of political systems that have proved most successful in implementing change and asks the question, is neo-liberalism popular?

Most criticisms of structural adjustment are written by dissident economists from the North, who then offer up their own alternatives with scant recognition for the opinions of those suffering adjustment's impact in the South. *Silent Revolution* shows how Latin Americans are themselves actively involved in the search either for more effective versions of market-led growth, or for a completely different model of 'people-centred development' and analyses the political constraints on the changes they propose.

The power of language

In any debate over the costs and benefits of neo-liberalism, its supporters start out with a distinct advantage, for the silent revolution has managed to get language on its side. Calling unregulated commerce 'free trade' and unfettered capitalism 'the free market' automatically confers legitimacy on the ideas. Likewise, 'removing trade barriers', 'enhancing efficiency/competitivity', 'getting the prices right' and 'improving growth' sound essentially positive, even if the listener is vague on the details, and even vaguer on the consequences. Critics are forced to choose between adopting neo-liberal terminology which automatically works against them (usually reducing them to strewing dozens of inverted commas around words like 'free trade' and 'efficiency') or trying to frame an entirely different language for the debate, which inevitably means that they are written off as more concerned with political correctness than the real world.

Neo-liberalism's advocates are also adept at the use of euphemism and obfuscation. 'Protection' might sound like something positive (after all, a mother protects her children), but call it *protectionism* and there is nothing to stop free-market *machismo* from stigmatizing it as a sign of weakness. A recent linguistic sleight-of-hand has seen US politicians and policy-makers talking of Washington's determination to support 'market democracies'. Democracy is clearly something no one can oppose, and Washington's push to spread market forces into every corner of the world economy wins public support on its coat-tails.

In massacring language and baffling almost any non-economist, the IMF is unsurpassed: loans become 'arrangements' or 'facilities', part payments are 'tranche disbursements'. In his book, *The Money Lenders*, Anthony Sampson decoded a sample of IMF-speak from the Fund's 1979 Annual Report: '"There are of course circumstances in which the application of credit tranche conditionality would not be appropriate", they explained, meaning "We cannot always impose conditions on new loans".'[27] The IMF's 'stabilization programmes' frequently achieve exactly the opposite. The queen of all euphemisms is undoubtedly 'structural adjustment', a stunningly bland name for the process that lies at the heart of the silent revolution.

Such incomprehensible or mind-numbing language acts as a convenient form of bureaucratic camouflage – what investigative journalist is going to try and convince an editor to take a story about the iniquities of something called 'the International Monetary Fund's Enhanced Structural Adjustment Facility'?

Rather than trying to invent a whole new vocabulary, this author chooses to debate on the linguistic terrain of the free-marketeers in an effort both to demystify the language, and to show that, even on its own terms and in its own words, after thirteen years of near-total ideological dominance, neo-liberalism can claim remarkably few successes in return for far too many failures in both human and economic terms.

Notes

1 '10,000 men of Harvard', *Newsweek* (New York), 10 December 1990, p.42.

2 William J. Barber, *A History of Economic Thought* (London, 1967), p.48.

3 David Ricardo, *On the Principles of Political Economy and Taxation*, in Piero Sraffa (ed.), *The Works and Correspondence of David Ricardo*, Vol. 1 (Cambridge, 1951), p.105.

4 David Begg, Stanley Fischer and Rudiger Dornbusch, *Economics* (Maidenhead, Berks, 1991), p.498.

5 John Maynard Keynes, *The General Theory of Employment, Interest and Money* (Cambridge, 1974), p.383.

6 *Guardian* (London), 25 June 1991.

7 Economist Intelligence Unit, *Bolivia Country Profile 1989/90* (London), p.6.

8 Sophia Tickell and Richard Burge, *Bolivia Case Study* (mimeo) (London: Christian Aid, 21 May 1993), p.2.

9 *Ibid.*, p.2.

10 Cedoin, *Informe 'R'* (La Paz, August 1985), p.2.

11 EIU, *op. cit.*, p.25.

12 *NACLA Report on the Americas* (New York, July 1991), p.28.

13 CEPAL, *Balance Preliminar de la Economía de América Latina 1994* (Santiago, 1994), p.43.

14 Oxfam, *The Experience of the Bolivian Emergency Social Fund* (mimeo) (Oxford, 1992).

15 Frances Stewart, 'The Many Faces of Adjustment', *World Development* Vol. 19, No. 12 (Oxford, 1991), p. 1860.

16 *Latinamerica Press* (Lima), 18 November 1993, p.3.

17 CEDLA (La Paz, 1993), based on INE, *Encuesta de Hogares*.

18 Ministerio de Previsión Social y Salud Pública, *Subsistema Nacional de Información de Salud 1991-92* (La Paz).

19 UNICEF, *The State of the World's Children* (Oxford, 1994).

20. Interview with author (La Paz, October 1993).

21 *NACLA Report on the Americas*, *op. cit.*, p.25.

22 *Ibid.*, p.22.

23 Interview with author (La Paz, October 1993).

24 Cedoin, *Bolivia Bulletin* (La Paz, February 1991), p.3.

25 James Painter, *Bolivia and Coca: A Study in Dependency* (Boulder, CO, 1994), p.54.

26 Interview with author (La Paz, October 1993).

27 Anthony Sampson, *The Money Lenders* (New York, 1982), p.104.

SIERRA MADRE

MEXICO

ATLANTIC OCEAN

Havana
CUBA
Mexico City •
DOMINICAN REPUBLIC
Santo Domingo
JAMAICA
Kingston
PUERTO RICO
BELIZE
Belmopan
CARIBBEAN SEA
HONDURAS
GUATEMALA
Tegucigalpa
Guatemala City
TRINIDAD & TOBAGO
EL SALVADOR
Port of Spain
San Salvador
Managua
Panama
NICARAGUA
City
Caracas
GUYANA
COSTA RICA
Georgetown
San José
VENEZUELA
Paramaribo
SURINAME
PANAMA
Cayenne
FRENCH GUIANA
Bogotá
COLOMBIA
Quito
ECUADOR
Amazon

C O R D I L L E R A

PERU
BRAZIL
Lima •
MATO GROSSO
Brasilia •
La Paz
BOLIVIA
PARAGUAY
Rio de Janeiro
São Paulo
Asunción

PACIFIC OCEAN

CHILE
Santiago •
URUGUAY
Montevideo
Buenos Aires
ARGENTINA
Paraná

L O S   A N D E S

LATIN AMERICA
Peters Projection

CHAPTER 1

State versus Market

The Rise and Fall of Import Substitution

Anybody who has ever used a Brazilian disposable nappy (diaper) will probably have first-hand experience of how import substitution failed the consumer. They didn't work. Until recently, Brazil's nappies were treacherous things, liable to leak or spring open with disastrous consequences for your carpet. The tale of the Brazilian disposable is a microcosm of what went wrong with much of Brazil's industry, stemming from the flawed model for economic development adopted in Latin America after the 1930s.

The offending items were made by Brazilian workers in a Brazilian factory. They were protected by import taxes against competition from better-quality foreign varieties. The taxes were originally designed to encourage the development of a Brazilian nappy industry, thereby reducing the economy's reliance on manufactured imports. However, protection also absolved the manufacturer from having to worry about quality or keeping prices down.

This is particularly true because the market is so small in Brazil. Only one Brazilian baby in forty wears disposables[1] – the poor majority can't afford them, and many of the rich prefer to pay the poor to wash their babies' cloth nappies rather than buy disposables. Consequently, there was little room in the market for more than a few producers, who could fix prices between themselves to prevent competition. The consumer was the loser.

Like many of the beneficiaries of Brazilian protectionism, the producer was a transnational company, Johnson & Johnson. It had built a factory in Brazil in 1975, 'tariff hopping' to take advantage of the protected market, where it had an effective monopoly. It could undoubtedly have invested to upgrade the quality, but in the absence of competition, why bother? When the Brazilian government tried to open up the economy to imports, Johnson & Johnson did their utmost to prevent it:

> *The Argentine nappies on sale in Mappins, one of the country's largest store chains, at half the price of Brazilian ones, required a long battle.*

When Mappins began the imports, trucks were held up on the border while Johnson & Johnson, which monopolises the Brazilian nappy market, found a helpful bureaucrat with an ancient regulation classifying nappies as pharmaceutical products which could be imported only if accompanied by a qualified pharmacist, transported and kept in cold storage.[2]

Faced with a small local market, Johnson & Johnson might have tried to cut costs by exporting to other countries. This would allow them to increase output, bringing economies of scale which would lower the unit cost. But who would buy an over-priced, substandard Brazilian nappy? The problem recurs throughout Brazilian industry. A 1990 study of the performance of 220 São Paulo companies showed them to be 'generally dozens or hundreds of times worse than that necessary to compete on world markets'.[3]

Yet even in Brazil, routinely branded by the financial press as the laggard of the silent revolution, times are changing. The imports from Argentina eventually got past the bureaucratic hurdles and broke Johnson & Johnson's monopoly. In the years that followed, a number of competitors got in on the act, both importing and producing locally. By late 1993 prices were down to about a third of their former levels and Johnson & Johnson had been driven into third place in the nappy market, behind brands such as Procter & Gamble's Pampers.[4] The quality of life (and carpet) of a small number of disposable-dependent foreigners and wealthy Brazilians undoubtedly improved, lending further support to the arguments in favour of the switch from import substitution to the free market.

Brazil was something of a late convert to the merits of the market. In the rest of Latin America the state-versus-market pendulum, which had swung so completely to the side of the state in the 1950s, reached the opposite extreme in the early 1980s, in the first days of the debt crisis. Free marketeers in the US and Latin America hailed the demise of import substitution as proof that the state should stay out of running the economy. Governments were inherently bureaucratic, inefficient and corrupt and always put short-term political advantage before long-term economic prosperity, they argued. The only way forward was the standard IMF recipe of deregulation, privatization and free trade, which would free the region from the dead hand of statism and let Adam Smith's 'invisible hand' of the market lead it to a golden dawn of prosperity and growth.

One of the strongest cards in neo-liberalism's hand is its self-belief. Its diagnosis and cure are presented as common sense: the market is obviously more efficient than the state; free trade has to be better for growth than protectionism; the state should not spend more than it earns. As one US critic complained, 'So completely do the free market ideas of neo-liberalism dominate the current Latin American debate that opposing ideas are increasingly treated with the bemused condescension usually reserved for astrological charts and flat-earth manifestos.'[5] At a seminar in London's Institute of Latin American Studies, Paul Luke of Morgan Grenfell Debt Arbitrage and Trading (a man introduced as 'the leading City analyst on Latin America') caused barely a stir when he informed his audience in urbane tones of absolute certainty that 'protectionism is obviously bad for growth' (Japan? Taiwan?) and that in Latin America only those of 'low IQ' (among whom he included the recently elected Venezuelan president Rafael Caldera) dissented from the basic neo-liberal recipe. Like Mrs Thatcher's grocer's shop analogy of the British economy, the arguments convince because they are simple and endlessly repeated. But are they right? Furthermore, if they are so obvious, why did Latin America (or the US or Europe) ever opt for anything else?

Since independence in the early nineteenth century, debt crises have scourged Latin America at roughly 50-year intervals – the 1820s, 1870s, 1930s and 1980s.[6] Each crisis has swept away the previous economic model and laid the basis for the next 50-year experiment. Each birth has been painful and each model has entailed more losers than winners in Latin America's historic search for the road to long-term development. After the crisis of the 1820s, Latin America chose an export-led model based on selling raw materials (commodities) to North America and Europe. After the second crisis in the 1870s, the larger republics began some modern manufacturing. The disastrous world depression of the 1930s set Latin America on the path of vigorous import substitution which duly came unstuck in the 'lost decade' of the 1980s. At the beginning of each change of direction, successive generations of economists and politicians were just as convinced as Juan Carlos Aguilar in his office in La Paz that their way was the only way; it was just 'common sense'.

Up until the 1930s Latin America's economy depended on exporting raw materials to the industrialized world in order to earn hard currency with which to buy manufactured products. Following the Wall Street Crash of 1929 and the ensuing depression in Europe and North America, this classic free-trade model fell apart. World coffee prices fell by two-thirds, cutting Brazil's exports from $446m in 1929 to just $181m by 1932.[7] In El Salvador the coffee slump drove impoverished workers to rebel in 1932, ending in an army massacre of 30,000 peasants which virtually wiped out the country's Indian population. Most of Latin America in the 1930s experienced growing poverty, social unrest, repression, economic recession and defaults on the foreign debt. Latin America's export markets disappeared, and economies starved of hard currency had drastically to curtail imports.

Import substitution

What began as emergency measures to produce goods which could no longer be bought abroad eventually grew into the fully-fledged model of import substitution, which became the unchallenged economic gospel in Latin America after the Second World War. Import substitution's theoretical foundations were mainly laid by the UN's Economic Commission for Latin America and the Caribbean (known by its Spanish acronym, CEPAL). Free trade had failed the region, and 'common sense' dictated that the state should intervene to encourage national industry and protect its citizens from the cold winds of the world market.

Import substitution built on the ideas of John Maynard Keynes, whose arguments for state management of the economy had inspired New Deal economics in the US and the creation of the welfare state in Britain. At its height, import substitution's brand of state-led development was the unquestioned orthodoxy of the age. 'In the 1960s the economics department taught you Keynes and *Cepalismo*', says Humberto Vega, Chile's donnish chief of the Treasury. 'Classical economics was only taught in economic history! The role of the state was obvious, no one argued with it, not even the right, which was very protectionist.'[8] Soviet industrialization and the heavily state-led revival of the European economy after the Second World War had further established the centrality of the state in successful economic planning.

The state stepped in with a 'big push' to redirect the economy away from its dependence on primary exports and kickstart it into producing manufactured goods for the domestic market. To achieve this, it:

- *invested heavily in the kind of infrastructure required by industry, such as new roads, water and electricity supplies;*
- *kept labour costs down in urban areas by subsidizing basic foods and imposing price controls;*
- *protected local industries against foreign competition by imposing import taxes and 'non-tariff barriers' such as import quotas;*
- *nationalized key industries such as oil, utilities and iron and steel, and established new ones. This produced a large state sector, intended to play a leading role in developing the economy;*
- *supported an overvalued exchange rate, making Latin America's exports expensive and imports cheap. This hurt exports, but helped industry by reducing the price of imported machinery and inputs, while tariff and non-tariff barriers ensured that the relative cheapness of imports did not*

*undercut their products. An overvalued exchange rate also kept inflation
down by ensuring cheaper imports.*

The new economic model went hand in hand with the political phenomenon known as populism. Charismatic leaders such as Juan
Domingo Perón (Argentina), Lázaro Cárdenas (Mexico) or Getulio
Vargas (Brazil) preached a message of nationalist development and
became the darlings of the new urban masses. Such men made brilliant
leaders, but poor economists. They avoided politically divisive decisions
over how to distribute wealth, prefering to print enough money to keep
everyone happy in the short term. They bequeathed an inflationary legacy with which the region is still grappling.

Although now widely derided by the new generation of liberal economists, import substitution transformed the region's economy. By the
early 1960s, domestic industry supplied 95 per cent of Mexico's and 98
per cent of Brazil's consumer goods.[9] From 1950 to 1980 Latin America's
industrial output went up six times, keeping well ahead of population
growth. Infant mortality fell from 107 per 1000 live births in 1960 to 69
per 1000 in 1980;[10] life expectancy rose from 52 to 64 years. In the mid-
1950s, Latin America's economies were growing faster than those of the
industrialized West.

Industrialization transformed the continent's economy. In what had
previously been a predominantly rural, peasant society, great cities sprang
up in an unplanned sprawl of cheap concrete tower blocks, dirty factories, flyovers and congestion. Rich, smart central districts with luxury
shopping malls and mirror-glass skyscrapers were dwarfed by the vast
shanty towns of the poor which ring all the major cities, epitomizing the
sharp inequalities of wealth in the region. Convinced by their own
boom-time, we-can-do-anything rhetoric, the Brazilian military
embarked on huge road and dam-building sprees. In 1968 and 1970
Mexico City hosted the Olympics and the World Cup to announce its
arrival as an international capital. The state played the pivotal role in
achieving this transformation.

Import substitution also changed the political face of the continent, as
leaders like Perón and Vargas built their support on the burgeoning
urban working class. Especially in its earlier phase (before the Brazilian
military coup of 1964), this broadened political participation to new areas
of society, building up a strong trade union movement (albeit often with
an unhealthily close relationship with the state) and greatly strengthening
democratic politics.

Brazil and Mexico were the success stories of import substitution.
Between 1960 and 1979 they increased their share of Latin America's

industrial output from 50 per cent to over 60 per cent and attracted over 70 per cent of foreign direct investment over the same period.[11] Brazil, whose industrial output per person went up over fourfold between 1950 and 1970,[12] became Latin America's economic giant, producing a third of the regional GDP by 1981,[13] making it the seventh largest industrial producer in the world.[14]

Yet the cracks were already beginning to show by the late 1950s. Industrialization was capital-intensive, and failed to generate the expected number of new jobs for the region's unemployed masses. Transnational companies proved particularly ineffective in creating new jobs. The result was a two-tier labour force, a small 'aristocracy of labour' employed in the modern industrial sector of the economy, and a mass of un- or under-employed workers elsewhere.

Sheltered by tariff barriers, industries became inefficient, producing shoddy and expensive goods for consumers who had no choice. In 1969 the Chilean domestic prices of electric sewing machines, bicycles and home refrigerators were respectively three, five and six times higher than international prices.[15] The small domestic markets for such goods were usually dominated by a few companies, who established 'oligopolies', fixing prices between themselves and thereby avoiding the pressures of competition which might have forced them to invest more and produce better quality goods. 'Before it was easy to be a businessman in Argentina, with subsidies, speculation and protection,' says the country's president and leading neo-liberal crusader, Carlos Menem. 'This was a country of rich businessmen and poor companies.'[16] Local middle classes soon came to equate local manufacture with low standards. When Argentina liberalized imports in the late 1970s, the shops of Buenos Aires would plaster their windows with signs saying *todo importado*, 'everything imported', to attract customers.

Although import substitution successfully ended the need to import some goods, especially consumer durables like cars and TVs, it merely replaced that dependence with a new kind, stemming from industry's reliance on imported capital goods such as heavy machinery, turbines and cranes. This meant that Latin America did not solve its trade deficit. The overvalued exchange rates and priority given by government to producing for the domestic market made matters worse, as neglected and uncompetitive exports failed to keep up with booming imports.

Countries undergoing import substitution were dogged by the economic consequences of inequality, which the model further exacerbated. Only a small proportion of the people in most Latin American republics actually functioned as consumers for the new industries – the great majority were too poor to buy anything. In all but the largest countries, such as Brazil and Mexico, the domestic market was therefore too small for fledgling industries to achieve the necessary economies of scale. Foreign companies were particularly reluctant to invest outside the big economies for this reason. Few governments were willing to undertake the kind of fundamental redistribution of wealth required to create a sizeable domestic market. Instead, they opted for regional free trade agreements, hoping that by grouping the middle classes of, for example, all the Central American countries, they could reach the market size required for industrial take-off. In practice, these agreements soon foundered, as they worked to the benefit of the stronger economies, and the weaker ones quickly pulled out.

Knowing that the government would always bail them out in the end, many (though not all) state industries proved inefficient producers, saddling the treasury with large operating losses. The widespread subsidies and increased state spending on social services as well as state investment further contributed to chronic government spending deficits. When governments covered these by printing money, inflation started to gather pace.

Import substitution was particularly disastrous for the countryside, which was starved of public investment and social services as the government gave priority to urban areas. Peasants selling their harvests suffered when price controls were imposed on their crops, while import substitution's overvalued exchange rates also encouraged a flood of cheap food imports which undercut local farmers. The deepening misery in the countryside, coupled with the industrial boom in the cities, provoked a massive spate of migration. Between 1950 and 1980, 27 million people left their farms and villages and joined the great exodus to the cities.[17]

Other aspects of government policy benefited rural areas, however. In the wake of the Cuban revolution, the US promoted land reform throughout the region via President Kennedy's Alliance for Progress. Limited amounts of land were distributed, and credit provided for small farmers through the state banking system in countries such as Chile, Colombia and Venezuela.

The neglect of the countryside, where most of Latin America's poorest people live, along with the failure to generate jobs, meant that import substitution had a negative effect on income distribution. The region became increasingly polarized between rich and poor, the worst offender being Brazil, where from 1960 to 1970 every social class increased its income, but the bulk of the increase went to the rich. The richest 10 per cent of Brazilians increased their share of total income from 28 per cent to 48 per cent.[18] Today, according to admittedly patchy UN figures, Brazil is the second most unequal country in the world (after Botswana);

the richest fifth of the population earns 32 times more than the poorest fifth.[19] Modern Brazil is a country of extraordinary contrasts, from the blighted rural north-east, where conditions are as bad as many of the poorest parts of Africa, to the high-rise opulence of downtown Rio or São Paulo.

Import substitution also deepened Latin America's love-hate relationship with transnational companies. Although nationalists objected to the transnationals' repatriation of profits and the limited benefits they brought to the rest of the economy, Latin America's leaders saw them as a vital source of technology and capital, both in short supply in the region. Especially from the 1960s, transnationals extended their grip on the most dynamic sectors of the economy, leaving the more sluggish industries to local capital. The stranglehold exerted by the transnationals allowed the state to neglect spending on research and development (R&D), leading to a growing technology gap between Latin America and the North. This gap made it even more difficult for Latin American-owned companies to break into the fastest growing areas of world trade, such as electronics and pharmaceuticals, which are also the areas of most rapidly developing technology.

As the flaws in the model became apparent, governments modified their policies. From the late 1960s onwards, countries such as Brazil and Mexico gave increased priority to manufactured exports to try and fill their growing trade gaps. Although Mexico's sudden oil bonanza in the late 1970s meant it temporarily lost interest in industrial exports, Brazil achieved some extraordinary results. Following the military coup of 1964, a combination of devaluation (to increase exports' competitivity) and the army's ruthless suppression of labour to bring down wages, led to the 'economic miracle' of 1967–73; manufacturing exports tripled in the three years to 1973. Having already built factories in Latin America to produce for the protected local markets, transnational companies were best placed to turn their attention to exports, and dominated the export boom in Mexico and Brazil. In the region as a whole, manufactured exports increased forty-fold from 1967 to 1980,[20] but even then they represented only a fifth of industrial output, which remained predominantly directed at the local market, and the continued reliance on imported capital goods meant that the trade gap in manufactures continued to grow.[21]

The debt crisis

The final decline of import substitution began with the sudden rise in world oil prices in 1973. The billions of 'petrodollars' which OPEC countries recycled onto the world's financial markets had to go somewhere, and western banks fell over themselves to lend to Third World governments. The banks fell into the trap of believing, in the words of Citicorp chairman Walter Wriston, that 'a country does not go bankrupt'[22] as a private company could. Understandably, the Latin American governments flocked to borrow at the low or even negative real interest rates being offered by the banks. They believed such rates would be permanent, enabling them both to grow their way out of poverty and pay off their debts. Almost everyone had a good reason to borrow: Brazil was faced with an acute foreign exchange crisis and as its oil import bill soared, it chose to borrow abroad to keep importing the oil, machinery and inputs it needed for its industrial growth. The economy kept on growing, but so did Brazil's foreign debt. By 1978 its debt service took up 64 per cent of its export income.

[From 1978–82] Brazil borrowed $63.4bn, well over half of its total gross foreign debt, in a frenzied, and eventually useless attempt to avoid default. Almost all of this money did not even enter Brazil, but stayed with the foreign banks ($60.9bn) … [Brazil was forced to] contract a huge paper debt that it would later be forced to honour through the export of real goods. It was a financial con trick on an unprecedented scale.[23]

In other oil-importing countries such as Chile and Argentina, the neo-liberals made their first appearance on the scene following bloody military coups in 1973 and 1976 respectively. The military governments chose not to try and grow their way out of trouble, opting instead for an end to import substitution and the sudden removal of import barriers. The results were catastrophic, as both countries went through a swift de-industrialization involving a spate of bankruptcies and job losses. The Argentine military opted for a particularly spectacular form of industrial suicide by removing import controls and tariffs at the same time as leaving the peso massively overvalued; the result was a flood of artificially cheap imports. Argentina's consumer goods imports increased over five times between 1975 and 1981, while local industrial output fell by 3 per cent a year over the same period.[24] Since the import boom had to be paid for with foreign borrowing, the Argentine and Chilean debts rose just like the Brazilian one, but without the benefit of industrialization.

In Mexico, the advent of the OPEC price rise just as massive new oil finds came on stream ought to have been good news. But the government borrowed massively to build up the oil industry. Pemex, the state oil giant, ran up a company debt of $15bn by the early 1980s.[25]

Although some of the proceeds from aid and oil exports went into building up heavy and export industries, far more was spirited out of the country into US banks as capital flight. As loans poured in, dollars also poured out, as government officials or business leaders siphoned as much as possible into US bank accounts. In many cases this involved corruption, such as taking kickbacks on government contracts, but in Venezuela and Mexico, for example, it was quite legal to export dollars into a US account. Estimates of the extent of capital flight vary wildly, but according to one World Bank report: 'Between 1979-82, $19.2bn left Argentina, $26.5bn left Mexico and $22bn left Venezuela: 64 per cent, 48 per cent and a staggering 137 per cent respectively of the gross capital inflows to those countries.' The Bank concluded, 'Much of the money being borrowed from abroad was funnelled straight out again.'[26] Even in 1986, at the height of austerity, one banker confessed that his bank regularly 'sends a guy with two empty suitcases' to Mexico City to pick up dollar deposits.[27]

The 'dance of the millions', as the influx of petrodollars became known, also coincided with a period of military rule in Latin America; from 1972–82 arms imports grew at an annual rate of 13 per cent. In 1986, the Peruvian Foreign Minister estimated that Latin America's total defence spending over the previous 10 years came to over $114bn, roughly half the region's entire foreign debt.[28]

It seemed that whatever a Latin American government's policies, the temptation of cheap foreign capital seduced it into running up huge debts in the 1970s. One of the few exceptions was Colombia, which refused to be sucked into the borrowing frenzy and consequently, in economic terms at least, was an island of growth and falling poverty and inequality throughout the 1980s. Even Chile's first attempt at neo-liberal reform under Pinochet foundered under the weight of debt – Chile's economy was actually worse hit than any other by the initial shock of the debt crisis. Brazil, Mexico and Argentina became the Third World's top three debtors. The flood of foreign borrowing allowed Latin America to stave off the collapse of import substitution for a few more years, but the delay proved expensive in both financial and human terms.

Outside the region, the world economy and political thinking had changed radically since the days of Keynesian consensus in the 1950s. In the late 1960s, the unprecedented global economic boom of the postwar years began to run into trouble, and both Keynesianism and import substitution came under academic siege from a new generation of economic liberals. The resurgent free marketeers argued for a sharp cut in the state's role in the economy, and took over the commanding heights of the world economy with the elections of Margaret Thatcher (1979) and Ronald Reagan (1980). The monetarist obsession with reducing inflation supplanted Keynesian concerns with full employment and the welfare state. In just twenty years, the roles had been reversed: neo-liberalism had become the common sense of the day, and statism consigned to the junkyard of history.

For Latin America the problems began with the second big oil price rise of 1979. A new generation of First World conservative leaders reacted to rising global inflation by raising interest rates. The move prompted a deep recession in their own economies, which formed the main markets for Latin American exports. Latin America had to pay higher interest rates just as its exports began to fall; the sums no longer added up. In August 1982, the crash finally came when Mexico announced it was unable to meet its debt repayment obligations. Latin America's 'lost decade' had begun.

The debt crisis which broke over the continent in August 1982 brought in its wake recession and hardship for millions of Latin Americans. But for Sir William Ryrie, a top World Bank official, it was 'a blessing in disguise'.[29] The debt crisis forced Latin America into a constant round of debt negotiations, providing the Reagan government, along with the IMF and the other international financial institutions with all the leverage they needed to overhaul the region's economy, in alliance with northern commercial creditor banks and the region's home-grown free-marketeers. Latin America was ripe for a free-market revolution.

Winning the argument

Ideas are powerful, as Keynes observed:

> The ideas of economists and political philosophers, both when they are right and when they are wrong, are more powerful than is commonly understood ... I am sure that the power of vested interests is vastly exaggerated compared with the gradual encroachment of ideas ... Soon or late, it is ideas, not vested interests, which are dangerous, for good or evil.[30]

Critics of neo-liberalism often talk as if Washington, the IMF and the World Bank have single-handedly imposed neo-liberalism on a uniformly reluctant continent. While the Fund has undoubtedly played an important role, it would never have been possible without the support of local economists and politicians, the pre-existing crisis in import substitution and the perceived lack of alternatives. A sizeable élite in Latin America, perhaps 20 to 30 per cent of the population, have stood to gain from access to First World consumer goods, jobs with international companies and the opportunities brought by deregulation and increased trade. As one veteran Central American intellectual observed, 'Neo-liberalism has united the élites of the South with those of the North and created the biggest convergence of financial, technological and military power in history.'[31] By the time the debt crisis swept away the remnants of import substitution in the early 1980s, neo-liberalism enjoyed an unstoppable coalition of influential supporters and potential beneficiaries both inside and outside the region, and had the intellectual high ground to itself.

Ideological shifts are partly generational. The young men and (occasionally) women who end up as policy-makers grow up, go to school and usually university, read the newspapers, argue and debate the new ideas of the time, and often go on to post-graduate studies. By the time they leave university for their first job, their mental frameworks are well established and do not easily change in later years, barring the occasional road-to-Damascus style conversion. For the academic generals grooming new generations of ideological warriors for the fray, the message is, get them young.

Fresh from university, the eager, young, would-be policy-makers join up for the war of ideas, where the battalions from the university economics departments, private think tanks, government ministries, banks and international institutions meet and argue their case in a global merry-go-round of conferences and seminars. To the winners, the spoils: jobs in universities, government departments, international agencies and eventually, perhaps, Minister of Finance or one of the other key posts in the economic cabinet. With them, the chance to change the nature of the economy and influence the fate of millions of citizens, followed by a well-paid directorship or two after leaving office. For the losers, unless they switch sides, years in the intellectual wilderness, trying to build up a critique and an alternative model that will eventually drive the pendulum back in their direction. In this world, the big institutions like the World Bank and IMF command enormous influence; when it comes to the broad issue of 'development', their huge research budgets decide what is researched and by whom, both by their own staff and an army of thousands of consultants. The arrangement has been described by one scholar as an 'intellectual-financial complex',[32] enabling the Bretton Woods institutions to set the parameters, and to some extent conclusions of the debate on world development.

Chile provides a good example of the connections between academic research, institutional power and the harsh realities of politics. There, the first steps in the neo-liberal counter-attack against the state took place almost 20 years before General Pinochet seized power. In the mid-1950s the Economics Faculty in the far-off University of Chicago was nurturing the flame of liberalism at a time when Keynes's thinking was the orthodoxy of the age. In their academic redoubt, the high priests of Chicago, Friedrich von Hayek, Milton Friedman and Arnold Harberger, laid the intellectual foundations for the liberal crusade which swept the world in the 1970s.

Friedman and Harberger were the economists, specializing in fierce critiques of state intervention and laying the theoretical basis of monetarism. Von Hayek was the philosopher, expanding liberal ideas to include the social and political arguments for 'taking the politics out of politics': using an authoritarian state to prevent pressure groups such as trade unions and political parties from interfering with a government's ability to make decisions free from immediate political pressures.[33] Such interference, they argued, could only inhibit the efficiency-maximizing role of the market and hinder growth. The combination of reducing the state's role in the economy, while greatly strengthening its powers to undermine trade unions and other potential opponents became the hallmark of neo-liberal rulers from General Pinochet to Mrs Thatcher.

Taking note of CEPAL's growing influence, Chicago decided to launch a counter-attack on its doorstep. In 1955 Professor Theodore W. Shultz, President of the Department of Economics, visited the Catholic University of Chile to set up a scholarship system for a select group of Chilean post-graduate students.[34] Between 1956 and 1961 at least 150 promising Chilean students received US government-sponsored fellowships to study economics at Chicago.[35] It was money well spent. Many of the students went back to academic posts in the Catholic University, which became the intellectual powerhouse for neo-liberal ideas as Chile's statist experiment ended in spectacular economic collapse (helped by Washington's destabilization programme and other forms of sabotage) during the years of Salvador Allende.

In 1973 General Augusto Pinochet overthrew Allende in a military coup. Within three months, the army had killed at least 1500 people in a savage assault on trade unionists and political activists.[36] Whatever their feelings about the massacre, the coup was a golden opportunity for the neo-liberals. The inexperienced technocrats faced initial scepticism from both the military and Chile's business community until March 1975, when they flew in Milton Friedman and Arnold Harberger for a high-profile lobbying effort. A month later Pinochet ditched his initially cautious economic team and put the 'Chicago Boys' in charge.[37] Chile has never been the same since.

Ever since the Chicago Boys arrived, the running of the Chilean economy has remained firmly in the hands of the technocrats. After 1973, a mirror image of the rise of the Chicago Boys got under way as a new generation of anti-Pinochet technocrats began to assemble in the wings. Many were driven into exile and had little option but to enrol in post-graduate studies in order to earn a living. In Chile, intellectual opponents of Pinochet set up private think tanks, often with funding from international aid agencies. By 1985 there were 30 private research institutes in Chile working in the social sciences, employing 543 researchers. Of these, 30 per cent held MA or PhD degrees from foreign universities.[38] Academic rigour in their work was essential to fend off accusations that the new think tanks were mere front organizations for proscribed left-wing political parties, and as a result their analyses and opinions won widespread respect.

In the libraries and cafes of exile, and later back in Chile after the early 1980s, Chile's intellectuals endlessly argued over the reasons for the collapse of the Allende government, the world's first elected Marxist government. The failure of Allende's economic programme could not wholly be blamed on the saboteurs, and a radical rethink gathered pace, further fuelled after 1985 by the swift growth of the Chilean economy under Pinochet and the startling collapse of statist systems in Eastern Europe.

By the time General Pinochet left power in 1990, the opposition had accepted many of the Chicago Boys' ideas: the state should be kept out of economic management where possible; foreign investment and economic stability, including low inflation, are essential for growth; the government should not spend its way into a deficit. However, the 'CIEPLAN monks' as they became known (named after one of the leading think tanks) took a more pragmatic approach to economic planning, and believed the benefits of growth had to be more fairly distributed than during the Pinochet years which had seen a sharp increase in inequality within Chile. This also involved a real commitment to democratic government.

As the soldiers retired to their barracks, a new generation of technocrats moved smoothly from think tanks to ministries and Chile's economy continued to grow with scarcely a blip. They were still almost all postgraduates from US and European universities, but fewer of them came from Chicago. Within weeks of their defeat, General Pinochet's leading economists were busily setting up a new series of think tanks in which to lick their wounds before mounting an eventual counter-offensive.

On economics and economists
The rise of Latin America's technocrats is part of a world-wide phenomenon in recent decades, the exaltation of economists as the natural leaders of the world order.

Since the days of Newton, physics has been a role model for other disciplines because of its elegance, simplicity and above all, its ability to predict events in the real world. Physics moves from hypothesis to prediction using mathematics, then checks the prediction against reality. Other sciences, such as biology, concentrate on description, emphasizing change and empirical observation rather than theoretical abstraction.

Unfortunately, economics wants to be like physics. Over the years, what started off as a fairly empirical discipline has been drawn towards the seductive certainties of mathematics. Some pure (if politically suspect) mathematicians pour scorn on the whole idea:

> *Just as primitive peoples adopt the Western mode of denationalised clothing and of parliamentarism out of a vague feeling that these magic rites and vestments will at once put them abreast of modern culture and technique, so the economists have developed the habit of dressing up their rather imprecise ideas in the language of calculus ... Any pretence of applying precise formulae is a sham and a waste of time.[39]*

Academic prestige (including the lion's share of Nobel laureates) within the economics establishment increasingly stems from mathematical wizardry, not from engaging with real world events or people. As one economist admitted, 'I must confess to an instinctive conviction that what cannot be measured may not exist.'[40] So much for human happiness, job satisfaction, anxiety and stress at the workplace.

To enable mathematics to be applied, a series of assumptions must be made to simplify the real world into a model fit for the computer. Wassily Leontieff, a Nobel prize-winning mathematical economist, poured scorn on the whole idea:

> *Page after page of professional economic journals are filled with mathematical formulas leading the reader from sets of more or less plausible, but entirely arbitrary assumptions to precisely stated but irrelevant theoretical conclusions.[41]*

At the cutting edge, neo-liberal practitioners like the World Bank's Lawrence Summers prefer to be seen as engineers rather than physicists. In a speech to delegates at the joint IMF–World Bank meeting in Bangkok in 1991, Summers revealed the origins of his self-belief:

> *The laws of economics, it's often forgotten, are like the laws of engineering. There's only one set of laws and they work everywhere.[42]*

At that time Summers was the Bank's Chief Economist and Vice-President for Development Economics. In 1993 he became President Clinton's Under-Secretary to the Treasury.

The most basic assumption of all is Homo Economicus,[43] an abstraction of the human being. Homo Economicus has no friends, family, community nor any other non-economic links. S/he has an insatiable urge to acquire goods and his/her happiness is directly proportional to consumption. A person with ten cars is ten times happier than a person with one. S/he acts purely on the basis of short-term self-interest. With assumptions like these, it is small wonder that the end result – neo-classical economics – leads to a society that is strong on materialism and fails miserably on issues like justice, inequality or quality of life. Small wonder that Thomas Carlyle famously labelled the discipline 'that Dismal Science'.[44]

The variables used by economists to describe the world around them are themselves open to question. Most governments and commentators measure a country's economic performance in terms of Gross Domestic Product (GDP), the sum of all the goods and services produced by a country. Yet as an indicator of well-being or misery, GDP leaves out almost as much as it describes:[45]

- *it excludes important areas of activity that lie outside the money economy, such as unpaid domestic labour, thereby ignoring a large part of women's contribution to the economy. If women are forced out to work and end up paying for their childcare, GDP goes up for both the job, and the paid childcare, distorting the picture as well as ignoring the impact of a 'double day' on women's lives;*
- *it excludes issues of wealth or income distribution within a country (although other standard, if rarely used, indicators can fill in the gap);*
- *GDP assumes nature is infinitely bountiful, and excludes the exhaustion of natural resources. 'Costa Rica between 1970 and 1990 lost natural capital (such as soils and forests) amounting to more than 6 per cent of its total GDP in that period. Yet the national accounts were silent on this continuing haemorrhage.'[46] GDP also fails to allow for depletion of natural capital caused by using nature as a 'sink' for dumping waste. In fact, waste disposal is classed as a productive activity and therefore contributes positively to growth.*
- *GDP compares different countries by converting at the official exchange rate, even though this can be massively over- or undervalued. This weakness is now widely recognized, and the United Nations Development Program produces annual estimates of per capita GDP at 'purchasing power parity' which attempt to compensate for exchange rate distortions. To date, however, the World Bank has largely insisted on using conventional measures of GDP.*

Unfortunately, no one has yet come up with a better alternative. For the time being, whatever its flaws, GDP growth will continue to be used as the yardstick of economic success and this book will be forced to talk in terms of free markets, free trade and GDP, despite serious reservations as to their value as objective and useful concepts.

A further myth arising from the mathematical pretensions of the discipline is that of objectivity. Many economists genuinely believe that theirs is an impartial, scientific trade. As one of Pinochet's economic aides recalled, 'I never dealt with politics; I was only perfecting economic laws. President Pinochet created compartments: the cavalry, the artillery, the economists.'[47] In fact, economists are highly political animals, and their assumptions are usually a pretty clear guide to their personal beliefs. Take Deepak Lal, for instance, World Bank analyst and one of the fathers of neo-liberalism, writing about the special interest groups created under import substitution: 'A courageous, ruthless and perhaps undemocratic government is required to ride roughshod over these newly-created special interest groups.'[48]

A political choice is implicit in any technical debate over the rival merits of state and market. States are, to some degree, accountable and representative. Markets are not. Whatever the flaws of the Latin American state, many grassroots organizations and other pressure groups have spent decades learning how to pressure it into listening to their needs and demands. Replacing the state with the market disenfranchises them, unless they are to acquire genuine influence over the decisions of transnational corporations, large local companies and others, an implausible scenario which the technocrats seek to avoid at all costs in the name of economic efficiency. Some critics believe that the central purpose of neo-liberalism is political rather than economic:

> The aim of the last generation of free market thinkers, notably Hayek and his followers, was less to build a robust view of what actually happens in a market economy than a model that could compete with Marxism. The aim was ideological and required all kinds of contortions to produce the desired result. As a source of inspiration in a battle of ideas which the West needed to win, it worked; as a source of policy recommendations, millions have reason to curse the theory for the avoidable suffering exacted in its name.[49]

The division of the academic world into disciplines has driven economics ever further into abstraction, creating an aloof élite who frequently dismiss the views of non-economists. As Paul Samuelson (another Nobel prize-winner) said in a presidential address to the American Economic Association, 'In the long run, the economic scholar works for the only coin worth having – our own applause.'[50]

Such matters would be of little concern if the rise of the technocracy had not given economists such enormous (and growing) influence over the way governments decide policy. Things can go disastrously wrong when academics are invited to take theories developed in the closed world of the economics faculty and apply them remorselessly to millions of their fellow citizens. In extreme cases, as in Pinochet's Chile, the economic cabinet can end up resembling Aztec high priests, sacrificing thousands of lives on the altars of the unfathomable gods of monetarism or structural adjustment.

Notes

1 *Folha de São Paulo* (São Paulo), 22 November 1993.

2 *Financial Times* (London), 14 August 1990.

3 *Ibid*.

4 *Folha de São Paulo, op. cit.*

5 *NACLA Report on the Americas* (New York, February 1993), p.16.

6 Victor Bulmer-Thomas, *Life after Debt – The New Economic Trajectory in Latin America* (mimeo) (London, March 1992), p.1.

7 Werner Baer, *The Brazilian Economy: Growth and Development* (New York, 1989), p.36.

8 Interview with author (Santiago, September 1993).

9 Duncan Green, *Faces of Latin America* (London, 1991), p.70.

10 Eliana Cardoso and Ann Helwege, *Latin America's Economy: Diversity, Trends and Conflicts* (Cambridge, MA, 1992), p.8.

11 Oxford Analytica, *Latin America in Perspective* (Boston, MA, 1991), p.185.

12 Carlos Fortin, 'Rise and decline of industrialisation in Latin America', in CEDLA, *Eight Essays on the Crisis of Development in Latin America* (Amsterdam, 1991), p.57.

13 CEPAL, *Anuario Estadístico de América Latina y el Caribe 1993* (Santiago, 1994), p.188.

14 World Bank, *World Development Report 1983* (New York, 1983), p.161.

15 Cardoso and Helwege, *op. cit.*, p.95.

16 *Financial Times* (London), 30 December 1991.

17 Green, *op. cit.*, p.56.

18 Cardoso and Helwege, *op. cit.*, p.240.

19 United Nations Development Programme, *Human Development Report 1994* (New York, 1994), pp. 164 and 196.

20 Green, *op. cit.*, p.73.

21 Oxford Analytica, *op. cit.*, p.183.

22 Quoted in Bernard Nossiter, *The Global Struggle for More* (New York, 1987), p.6.

23 Jackie Roddick, *The Dance of the Millions: Latin America and the Debt Crisis* (London, 1988), p.138.

24 Fortin, *op. cit.*, p.65.

25 Green, *op. cit.*, p.73.

26 Roddick, *op. cit.*, p.65.

27 Karen Lissakers, 'Money in flight: bankers drive the getaway cars' *International Herald Tribune* (New York), 7 March 1986.

28 Green, *op. cit.*, p.74.

29 William Ryrie, 'Latin America: A changing region' *IFC Investment Review* (Washington, DC, Spring 1992), pp.4–5.

30 John Maynard Keynes, *The General Theory of Employment, Interest and Money* (Cambridge, 1974), p.383.

31 Xavier Gorostiaga, *Latinamerica Press* (Lima), 6 May 1993, p.6.

32 Joel Samoff, 'The intellectual–financial complex of foreign aid', *Review of African Political Economy* (Sheffield, March 1992), pp. 60-75.

33 Von Hayek's ideas are expounded in *The Road to Serfdom* (London, 1944) and *Constitition of Liberty* (Chicago, 1960).

34 Patricio Silva, 'Technocrats and politics in Chile: From the Chicago Boys to the CIEPLAN monks', *Journal of Latin American Studies* (London, May 1991), p.390.

35 Pamela Constable and Arturo Valenzuela, *A Nation of Enemies: Chile under Pinochet* (New York, 1991), p.168.

36 *Ibid.*, p.20.

37 Patricio Silva, *op. cit.*, p.392.

38 *Ibid.*, p.400.

39 Norbert Weiner, quoted in Herman E. Daly and John B. Cobb, Jr, *For the Common Good* (London, 1990) p.31.

40 *Ibid.*, p.31.

41 *Ibid.*, p.32.

42 Susan George and Fabrizio Sabelli, *Faith and Credit: The World Bank's Secular Empire* (London, 1994), p.106.

43 See Daly and Cobb, *op. cit.*, Chapter 4.

44 Thomas Carlyle, *Latter-Day Pamphlets, No. 1* (London, 1899), p.44.

45 Victor Anderson, *Alternative Economic Indicators* (London, 1991), Chapter 3.

46 United Nations Development Programme, *Human Development Report 1993* (New York, 1993), p.30.

47 Constable and Valenzuela, *op. cit.*, p.81.

48 Deepak Lal, *The Poverty of Development Economics* (London, 1983), p.33.

49 Will Hutton, 'New economics hits at market orthodoxy', *Guardian* (London), 19 April 1993.

50 Daly and Cobb, *op. cit.*, p.34.

CHAPTER 2

Poverty Brokers

The International Monetary Fund and the World Bank

The acronyms of faceless international organizations do not usually start riots, but the three letters IMF (International Monetary Fund) provoke explosive reactions throughout Latin America. Since 1982 and the start of the debt crisis, 'IMF riots' have periodically ravaged the region's cities from Buenos Aires to Caracas, leaving hundreds of dead and wounded and losses of millions of dollars in damaged and looted property.

The riots have been a response to the IMF's role in orchestrating (some say imposing) a neo-liberal response to the region's debt crisis through austerity measures enshrined in 'stabilization programmes'. Since the mid-1980s, other institutions, notably the World Bank, have joined the IMF in moving the region's silent revolution forward from stabilization to the broader goal of structural adjustment, aimed at opening up Latin America's economy to trade and foreign investment. Critics charge that such policies have failed to produce a return to sustained growth, while exacerbating poverty and inequality. Such claims have led to a growing international clamour for the reform of the two institutions and their policies, but so far their behaviour on the ground suggests that little has changed.

One of the most bloody IMF riots took place in 1984 in the Dominican Republic, which shares a troubled island with Haiti in the Caribbean. After a year of wrangling over the Dominican government's failure to fulfil its promises to the Fund, the IMF retaliated with a virtual financial blockade of the country. On 19 April 1984 the Dominican government caved in and announced that food and medicine prices would be 'liberalized'. Overnight, medicines went up by 200 per cent, while milk, rice and cooking oil all doubled. Four days later riots started in the capital, Santo Domingo, then spread to thirty other towns. By the night of the 25th, 112 civilians were dead and 500 wounded.[1]

The hunger and carnage in Santo Domingo and Caracas (300 to 1500 dead in IMF riots in 1989, depending on whom you believe) are a far cry from the gleaming opulence of the joint annual meeting of the Fund and its sister organization, the World Bank. Every September, 10,000 or so well-groomed delegates jet in from the world's capitals for a week of speeches, big-time financial wheeling and dealing, and spectacular over-eating.

> A single formal dinner catered by Ridgewells costs $200 per person. Guests began with crab cakes, caviare, crème fraiche, smoked salmon and mini beef Wellingtons. The fish course was lobster with corn rounds followed by citrus sorbet. The entrée was duck with lime sauce, served with artichoke bottoms filled with baby carrots. A hearts of palm salad was offered accompanied by sage cheese soufflés with a port wine dressing. Dessert was a German chocolate turnip sauced with raspberry coulis, ice-cream bonbons and flaming coffee royale.[2]

When not sleeping off such blow-outs, the delegates discuss the IMF and World Bank's efforts to manage the world economy. According to its founding articles, the IMF's purposes include:[3]

- to 'promote international monetary cooperation';
- to encourage the 'growth of international trade';
- to 'promote exchange stability' and 'avoid competitive exchange depreciation';
- to help eliminate foreign exchange restrictions 'which hamper the growth of world trade';
- to provide members with loans 'under adequate safeguards' when they get into balance of payments difficulties;
- to lessen and shorten imbalances in the international balance of payments of member countries.

At first sight, such apparently laudable aims make the IMF sound like a philanthropic institution, smoothing the path of world trade and lending a helping hand to members who get into difficulties. It hardly seems the stuff to provoke mayhem and bloodshed on the streets of the Third World. But the IMF's enormously increased power after the onset of the debt crisis in 1982, coupled to its hard-line interpretation of its role in 'adjusting' troubled economies, has turned it into an 'Institute of Misery and Famine' in the eyes of much of the developing world. In the words of two respected British development agencies, 'They set out as pioneers and builders, [but] they have become the South's policemen and (at best) ambulance service.'[4]

Like the United Nations, the IMF and its sister organization, the World Bank, were born at the end of the Second World War as part of an attempt by the victorious western powers to prevent a repeat of the trade disputes of the Great Depression, which had sown the seeds of war.

While constitutionally they are part of the UN system, in practice the structure and role of the giant multilateral organizations demonstrate two radically opposed approaches. While the UN and its organizations largely subscribe to a 'one country, one vote' principle (at least in the General Assembly), decisions at the IMF and World Bank are taken on the basis of 'one dollar, one vote', guaranteeing the dominance of both by the US government.

With Europe largely reduced to rubble, the US emerged from the war as the world's economic superpower, able to dictate the rules of the game. At the IMF and World Bank's founding conference in Bretton Woods, New Hampshire, in July 1944, the US delegation swiftly quashed the suggestions of John Maynard Keynes, the illustrious economist who headed the British delegation, and imposed Washington's blueprint for the post-war world economy and the institutions that would guide it. Half a century later, the Third World (which at the time was still emerging from colonial rule) is still paying the price for that fateful clash between a triumphant US and a bankrupt Britain.

Bretton Woods established the US dollar as the international currency, although Keynes had argued for a new, neutral world currency. The arrangement simplified US investment overseas, allowing the US government to fund both investment and military spending by printing dollars as required. At the same time in the third Bretton Woods institution, the General Agreement on Tariffs and Trade (GATT), founded in 1947, a body was created to press for fewer restrictions on world trade.

The IMF and World Bank, officially named the International Bank for Reconstruction and Development, at first confined their attentions to rebuilding Europe with loans to Denmark, France and Holland. As Europe began to recover, the Bretton Woods institutions began to look further afield. The Bank's first loan to a developing country went to Chile in 1948.[5]

Bretton Woods enshrined 'might is right' at the heart of global economic management. Voting power at the international financial institutions, as the IMF and World Bank are known, is determined by contribution to working capital. As of 1994 the USA had 17.81 per cent of the vote,[6] just sufficient to guarantee it the right to a veto over IMF policy decisions, which requires a 15 per cent block of votes.[7] In contrast, no other country has more than 6 per cent of the voting rights. In the real world, US economic supremacy has long since crumbled, but the IMF has frozen the 1944 balance of power and Washington's veto into its voting system. As a sop to European sensibilities, the Managing Director of the IMF has traditionally been a European (currently Michel Camdessus from France), while the World Bank President has always been an

American (since 1995, James Wolfensohn, an international investment banker whose firm advises 30 major international corporations).

The US government even won the symbolic squabble over where to locate the offices of the international financial institutions, which ended up in Washington, under the wing of the US government and well away from the UN headquarters in New York. Locating the global financial institutions in the US political capital, rather than its financial centre, further underlined the political importance Washington attached to the international financial institutions' role in building a new global economic order along US guidelines.

The IMF

In theory, the IMF concerns itself with short-term stabilization, while the World Bank deals with longer-term issues like project funding and structural adjustment. In practice, the distinction has become increasingly blurred in recent years. Starting operations with 44 member governments,[8] the IMF's membership had expanded to 177 by 1993,[9] swollen by the rapidly escalating number of Eastern European republics desperate to rejoin the capitalist fold.

In normal times, the IMF oversees members' economic performance with regular visits to discuss policies and put pressure on member governments to observe Fund rules on issues like free trade and capital transfers. In such periods of tranquility, the IMF does not need to impose sanctions, but does have considerable influence over the weaker economies, not least through its gamut of 'technical aid' services, including conferences, training and the secondment of economic advisers to member governments.

However, the Fund only really comes into its own as a 'lender of last resort', when a member gets into balance of payments difficulties – which usually means it cannot borrow sufficient money abroad to cover its trade deficit *and* keep up with debt service payments. In these circumstances, a member government can approach the IMF for a loan to bridge the financial gap, a procedure known as a 'Stand-by Arrangement'. In return for the loan, the Fund imposes conditions on the borrower, intended to make it pursue policies which will eliminate the balance of payments problem. The borrower's promises are enshrined in a 'letter of intent' to the IMF, usually kept secret from the public both in the US and the country concerned. The letter is almost invariably drafted by IMF officials, leaving the government to try to negotiate modifications to the document.[10] Once the letter is 'received' by the Fund, it releases ('disburses') the loan in staggered instalments ('tranches'). If at any point the country fails to comply with the promises and targets ('performance criteria') laid out in the letter of intent, the Fund can suspend payments. Stand-by Arrangements usually run from 12-18 months, and can then be renewed if the balance of payments problem has not been solved. It frequently is not – confirmed addicts like Jamaica, Costa Rica and Ecuador are now into their second decade of almost continuous IMF loans.

In the first years of the debt crisis, the IMF worked closely with creditor banks, which embarked on a seemingly endless round of negotiations to reschedule the debts of most Latin American nations. Rescheduling postponed a debtor's repayments (often at the cost of increasing a country's overall debt), and saved the commercial banks from having to write off their Latin American loans, which would have spelt disaster for their image on their home stock markets. For each debtor country, the banks formed advisory committees of creditors who undertook negotiations with individual debtors on a 'case-by-case' basis. In the language of the school playground, the banks ganged up on the debtors, using divide and rule to prevent any chance of a debtors' cartel forming. The advisory committees agreed tactics with IMF officials also engaged in negotiations with the government, creating what one critic[11] has called 'The Consortium' of commercial banks, northern governments and international financial institutions which spoke with one all-powerful voice to the financially crippled nations of the South.

It is its role as a leading agency in the Consortium that gives the Fund its real power, for the amounts of money it loans are often small compared to capital flows in and out of the third world. From 1989–93, it actually received $9.3bn more in loan repayments from Latin America than it lent in new money[12] (countries may default on commercial bank or bilateral loans, but IMF repayments are normally sacrosanct). Instead, its clout stems from its role as international financial policeman. Most other potential lenders, such as the World Bank and the governments and banks of the rich industrialized world, usually make their loans conditional on an agreement with the IMF. International investors also see an IMF deal as a clean bill of financial health. The equation is simple: no Stand-by Arrangement, no cash. For any debtor country, the Fund is thus able to turn the taps of world finance off and on at will, turning it into 'the most powerful international organisation of the 20th century, decisively influencing the well-being of the majority of the world's population'.[13]

This was particularly the case in the first years of the debt crisis, when most other sources of capital dried up. Since private capital flows surged back into the larger economies of Latin America in the early 1990s, the IMF's supremacy has declined somewhat, though since foreign investors and the Fund frequently share the same view of what constitute 'sound policies' in Latin America, the impact of this change has been limited. Many of the smaller economies, however, remain starved of capital and almost as dependent on the IMF as ever.

The IMF's elaborate strategy of carrots and sticks was not devised at Bretton Woods. Conditions were not attached to the European borrowers in the international financial institutions' initial phase of post-war reconstruction. Conditionality, as it is known, began in the 1950s and has grown steadily more stringent and all-pervasive ever since. In the aftermath of the debt crisis, the IMF and later World Bank's use of conditionality allowed the powerful industrialized nations to revamp one Third World economy after another along free-market lines. Critics believe that in the process, the IMF has systematically put the powerful nations' self-interest before the welfare of the Third World poor, allowing Washington, London and Frankfurt to exert huge leverage over other countries at arm's length through the mechanism of a 'deniable' and nominally impartial international organization. In the words of one US Deputy Trade Secretary on the virtues of the Bank's role in the Philippines:

> We have not been particularly successful ourselves in winning policy reforms from the Philippines. Because it is something of a disinterested party, however, the World Bank has been enormously successful in negotiating important policy changes which we strongly support.[14]

The fewer the options open to the bankrupt government, the greater the Fund's ability to dictate terms. With few exceptions (such as when the British Labour government was forced to go to the IMF in 1976), the IMF is unable to influence the policies of the powerful nations, despite their often outrageous double standards and has not lent to a developed country since Australia and Iceland in 1982. The powerful patrons of the international financial institutions rarely practise what they preach. Throughout the debt crisis, the US was running up the world's largest trade and fiscal deficits and a national debt far greater than that of the whole Third World put together, yet the IMF was powerless to make its most powerful and out-of-control member take a dose of its own neoliberal medicine. Looking back on his achievements, Eddie Bernstein, the key US negotiator at Bretton Woods, reflected that US double standards had damaged the credibility of the IMF: 'It suffers from having never been able to discipline its principal member, the United States.'[15]

Many believe the US was right to avoid following the IMF recipe. As Arthur Schlesinger, the US historian who later worked for President Kennedy, pointed out:

> *If the criteria of the International Monetary Fund had governed the
> United States in the 19th century, our own economic development would
> have taken a good deal longer. In preaching fiscal orthodoxy to developing
> nations, we were somewhat in the position of the prostitute who, having
> retired on her earnings, believes that public virtue requires the closing down
> of the red-light district.[16]*

Since its first loan to Chile in 1948, the IMF had periodically been
involved in Latin America. When the debt crisis broke in August 1982
this occasional involvement rapidly escalated. During 1982 and 1983, 17
Latin American governments signed IMF agreements, the only significant exceptions being Venezuela, Colombia, Paraguay and Nicaragua,[17]
which throughout the period of Sandinista rule was effectively boycotted
by the international financial institutions under political pressure from
Washington. By the mid-1980s, the Fund was involved in almost every
country in the region (see Table 2.1 opposite).

How the Fund thinks

The IMF was created to help countries sort out occasional balance of
payments problems, which occur when a country's foreign exchange
receipts (through both export income and capital inflows) are no longer
sufficient to cover its expenditure (on imports and capital outflows such
as debt repayments). The Fund sees balance of payments problems as
stemming from what it calls 'excessive demand' – a diagnosis that, whatever its technical merits, must sound perverse to the poverty-stricken
masses of the South. In IMF eyes, too much demand is chasing too few
goods. This sucks in imports, creating a trade deficit which then feeds the
balance of payments crisis.

Excess demand also forces up prices, and the IMF believes that inflation also adds to the balance of payments problem. Since the causal connection between inflation and a balance of payments deficit is at first sight
not at all obvious, it is worth spending some time to understand the
IMF's reasoning.

Inflation at home erodes the real value of the national currency. If the
government is to ensure that goods produced inside the country are to
remain competitive with imports and competing exports from elsewhere, the exchange rate must fall by the same amount, but this rarely
happens since exchange rates are seldom completely free to float.

To illustrate this, imagine that a sack of home-grown beans costs ten
pesos in a Latin American country, or ten dollars to buy on the international market and that the exchange rate is 1:1. For a bean purchaser, the
prices of imported or domestically produced beans will be equal. If

Table 2.1: Adjustment-related loans by the World Bank and IMF to Latin American and Caribbean countries 1981–94

The entries in the table are for IMF loans, the World Bank's Structural Adjustment Loans (SALs) and loans for Brady Plan debt reductions, and for adjustment loans from the World Bank's 'Soft Loan' body, the International Development Association (IDA), which lends only to the poorest countries in the region.

The IMF's fiscal year runs to 30 April, while that of the World Bank ends on 30 June. For reasons of space, the table does not include many other World Bank loans which are an essential part of their support for adjustment, such as Sectoral Adjustment Loans (SECALs). The various kinds of IMF loan are:[70]

Stand-By Arrangement (SBA): The traditional short-term loan described in the text. Covers from one to two years.

Extended Fund Facility (EFF): A medium-term loan, usually for three years, with annual reviews to assess compliance with performance criteria and to 'spell out' policies for the next year.

Structural Adjustment Facility (SAF): A concessional medium-term loan for low-income countries, usually for a three year period.

Enhanced Structural Adjustment Facility (ESAF): Similar to the SAF in terms of objectives and conditions for eligibility, but differs 'in the scope and strength of structural policies'.

Date of inception	Amount (m SDRs/US$[1])	Type of loan	Date of inception	Amount (m SDRs/US$[1])	Type of loan
Argentina			*Costa Rica*		
1983	1,500	SBA	1981	276.75	EFF[2]
1984	1,419	SBA	1982	92.25	SBA
1987	947.5	SBA	1985	54	SBA
1992	2,483.15	EFF	1985	80	WB SAL
1993	450	WB Debt & Debt Service Reduction Loan (Brady Plan)	1987	40	SBA
			1988	100	WB SAL
			1989	42	SBA
			1991	33.64	SBA
			1993	21.04	SBA
Barbados			1993	100	WB SAL
1982	31.88	SBA	*Cuba*		
Belize			*Dominica*		
1984	7.13	SBA	1981	8.55	EFF
Bolivia			1984	1.4	SBA
1986	50	SBA	1986	2.8	SAF
1986	63.49	SAF	1987	3	WB SAL
1988	136.05	ESAF	*Dominican Republic*		
1991	27.21	2-year extension to ESAF	1983	371.25	EFF
			1985	78.5	SBA
			1991	39.24	SBA
1991	50.4	IDA SAP	1993	31.8	SBA
Brazil			*Ecuador*		
1983	4,239	EFF	1983	157.5	SBA
1988	1,096	SBA	1985	105.5	SBA
1992	1,500	SBA	1986	75.4	SBA
Chile			1988	75.35	SBA
1983	500	SBA	1989	109.9	SBA
1985	750	EFF	1991	75	SBA
1985	250	WB SAL	*El Salvador*		
1986	250	WB SAL	1982	43	SBA
1987	250	WB SAL	1990	35.6	SBA
1988	75	1-year extension of EFF	1991	75	WB SAL
			1992	41.5	SBA
1989	64	SBA	1993	47.1	SBA
Colombia			1994	50	WB SAL

Date of inception	Amount (m SDRs/US$[1])	Type of loan
Grenada		
1981	3.43	SBA
1983	13.5	EFF
Guatemala		
1981	19.1	SBA
1983	114.75	SBA
1988	54	SBA
1992	54	SBA
Guyana		
1990	78	IDA SAP
1990	49.5	SBA
1990	81.52	ESAF
Haiti		
1982	34.5	SBA
1983	60	SBA
1986	28	SAF
1989	21	SBA
Honduras		
1982	76.5	SBA
1988	50	WB SAL
1990	30.5	SBA
1990	90	WB SAL
1991	20	IDA SAL (supplement)
1992	40.68	ESAF
Jamaica		
1981	477.7	EFF
1983	76.2	WB SAL
1983	60.2	WB SAL
1984	64	SBA
1984	55	WB SAL
1985	115	SBA
1987	85	SBA
1988	82	SBA
1990	82	SBA
1991	43.65	SBA
1992	109.13	EFF
Mexico		
1983	3,410.63	EFF
1986	1,400	SBA
1989	3,263.4	EFF
1990	1,260	WB Debt & Debt Service Reduction (Brady Plan)
1992	466.2	1-year extension to EFF

Date of inception	Amount (m SDRs/US$[1])	Type of loan
Nicaragua		
1991	40.86	SBA
1994	67.6	IDA SAL
Panama		
1982	29.7	SBA
1983	150	SBA
1984	60.2	WB SAL
1985	90	SBA
1986	100	WB SAL
1992	93.68	SBA
Paraguay		
Peru		
1982	650	EFF[2]
1984	250	SBA
1992	300	WB SAL
1992	150	WB SAL (supplement)
1993	1,018.1	EFF
Suriname		
Trinidad & Tobago		
1989	99	SBA
1990	85	SBA
1990	40	WB SAL I
Uruguay		
1981	31.5	SBA
1983	378	SBA
1985	122.85	SBA
1987	80	WB SAL I
1989	140	WB SAL II
1990	94.8	SBA
1984	55	WB SAL
1991	65	WB Debt and Debt Service Reduction (Brady Plan)
1992	50	SBA
Venezuela		
1989	402	WB SAL I
1989	3,857.1	EFF
1990	150	WB interest support for debt reduction (Brady Plan)
1992	–	9 month extension of EFF

Sources: IMF *Annual Report*, Washington, 1988, 1990, 1991, 1993, 1994; Margaret Garritsen de Vries, *Balance of Payments Adjustment, 1945–1986: The IMF experience*, Washington, 1987; World Bank, *Annual Report*, Washington, 1982–94.

[1] World Bank and IDA loans are given in US dollars while IMF loans are measured in Special Drawing Rights (SDRs), the Fund's international unit of account. As of February 1995, one SDR was worth about $1.50.

[2] Cancelled following year and replaced by SBA.

inflation then pushes the domestic price of a sack of local beans up to twenty pesos, the government should devalue the peso to two pesos to the dollar, if it wants the prices of imported and local beans to remain equal. If it does not, what economists call a 'distortion in relative prices' will occur, and it becomes cheaper to import beans than to produce them locally. If the beans were originally destined for export, where the price in dollars is usually fixed by the world market, currency appreciation will make their crops less and less profitable. Over the whole economy, the process will thus encourage imports and deter exports, exacerbating the balance of payments deficit. Price distortions generally contribute to inefficiency in the economy, by skewing the way producers and consumers make decisions.

Over-valuation also contributes to the balance of payments problem by encouraging capital flight, as peso holders try to convert them into dollars and get them out of the country before the impending devaluation reduces their value. The general mood of uncertainty and instability created by inflation and devaluation also discourages foreign investors, who will be reluctant to convert their dollars into depreciating pesos.

Inflation has other bad side-effects. The delay between assessing and collecting taxes means that inflation can erode government revenues, worsening the budget deficit and reducing the government's capacity to buy dollars to pay off the foreign debt. The Fund also rightly claims that inflation is a tax on the poor, since they are worst hit by price rises and have no means of defending their income levels, whereas better-off wage earners can usually index their incomes to inflation, or convert them into dollars. High inflation often provides rich pickings for investors able to play the financial system, for example by jumping between different interest-bearing accounts and currencies to take advantage of the short-term distortions that inflation produces.

In the aftermath of the debt crisis, an obvious way for Latin American countries to ease their balance of payments problems would have been to declare a moratorium on their escalating debt service payments, but the IMF used all its influence to prevent this occurring, arguing that countries that defaulted would become international financial pariahs who would be unable to borrow in the future. Instead, the Fund argued for a further reduction in demand and devaluation, this time to cut imports and diversify the economy's efforts to exports, in order to generate a trade surplus with which to pay the debt service. The result was a 'double whammy', driving Latin America into an acute recession in the years after the debt crisis.

Beyond the immediate objective of correcting a balance of payments deficit, the IMF clearly has a much broader agenda, namely imposing a neo-liberal economic model on the country concerned. A successful IMF programme promises to enable a country to move smoothly from 'stabilization', through 'structural adjustment' to achieve the final nirvana of 'export-led growth'. IMF conditions demand a smaller role for government, a switch in power and resources to the private sector, the privatization and deregulation of industry, and the opening up of the economy to foreign trade and investment.

What the Fund does

In the short term, rather than increasing supply to bring supply and demand into balance, the Fund proposes a swift, but painful cure of recession and reduced demand, provoking two otherwise sober econom- ists to write, 'To many people who have witnessed the consequences of IMF programs on the poor, this cure seems about as sensible as the idea of bleeding a feverish patient.'[18]

The Fund's measures can broadly be divided into two groups, those aimed at achieving short-term stabilization, and those concerned with longer-term structural adjustment. Stabilization aims to control inflation and rapidly create a large trade surplus with which to continue debt ser- vice payments. Measures include:

- *cutting consumer spending power by raising interest rates to limit domes- tic credit. High interest rates also discourage capital flight and encourage inward investment. In practice, the Fund is also willing to accept wage controls as a means of controlling inflation, though it claims to disap- prove;*
- *curtailing the fiscal deficit by cutting government spending. This involves removing state subsidies on food, fuel and public transport and reducing social spending on health, housing and education, measures which also help cut demand in the economy as a whole. Measures can also include raising government revenue by increasing charges on state-run utilities such as electricity and water.*
- *devaluing the currency to encourage exports and discourage imports (which since they are priced in dollars, become more expensive in terms of the local currency).*

Structural adjustment is a more profound and longer-term process, through which the international financial institutions try to implant a functioning free-market economy in the country concerned. Controls on prices, wages, interest rates, investment, trade and exchange rates are removed since the IMF believes in letting the unregulated market decide prices to maximize the efficient allocation of resources. Governments are forced to cut back on state investment in the economy, as part of the effort to reduce state spending, but also in the belief that the state 'crowds out' private-sector investment by soaking up the available credit. The full repertoire of structural adjustment measures did not come into force until the late 1980s, once the World Bank had become fully immersed in the adjustment process.

The World Bank

From the Mexican default in August 1982 until mid-1985, the IMF and its short-term stabilization approach dominated the response to the debt crisis. The continent was forced to cut back on imports and use the dollars it saved to pay debt service, and to go through a fierce recession to curb inflation. The scheme saved the banks and northern financial markets from collapse, but at huge social cost in the South.

By 1985, it had become obvious that the commercial banks had no intention of renewing lending to Latin America, and resistance was growing among debtor countries who saw no point in squeezing their people to pay endless tribute to the rich nations while receiving nothing in return. In the second half of 1985, Peru's President, Alan García, defied the IMF by announcing that 'Peru's main debtors are its people'[19] and unilaterally limited debt repayments to 10 per cent of the value of Peru's exports, calling on other Latin American debtors to join him. Peru was duly punished for its presumption, but the West realised that a change of tack was needed to prevent its whole debt strategy from crashing.

US Treasury Secretary James Baker retook the initiative within months of García's move. In October 1985, at the annual IMF–World Bank meeting in Seoul, South Korea, he unveiled his 'Baker Plan' for shifting from recessive to growth-oriented adjustment. The plan, which applied only to the 15 largest debtors, entailed asking the private banks to renew lending to the South (a request they largely ignored). It also gave the World Bank and regional development banks like the InterAmerican Development Bank (IDB) a greatly increased role in lending and overseeing longer-term structural adjustment.

The World Bank, the second of the Bretton Woods 'heavenly twins' has traditionally played the role of Mr Nice Guy in contrast to the IMF's Mr Scrooge. It has also proved far more of a chameleon, regularly changing its stated aims and policies during its 50 years of operation in accordance with the prevailing political wind. Most recently, it has 'gone green' and rediscovered poverty (its main theme in the 1970s), although the impact of the new rhetoric on its policies on the ground remains debatable.

The Bank played a minor role in European reconstruction, lending for large infrastructure projects, then adopted the same 'big is best' philosophy in the South. Until shortly before the debt crisis, the Bank remained a project lender, concentrating on giant projects such as road and dam building. By backing such 'mega-projects' it has become notorious among environmentalists for its role in deforestation, flooding out indigenous communities and supplanting peasant agriculture with large agribusiness schemes. Such projects still constitute the bulk of the Bank's loans, a vast global enterprise which churned out over $2.5m an hour in 1993.[20]

The onset of the debt crisis saw the Bank's role shift from project-based lending to structural adjustment, a process which accelerated sharply with the Baker Plan. In 1980 the World Bank created a new credit line of Structural Adjustment Loans (SALs) to support economic reform programmes. SALs remained a minor part of the World Bank's loans portfolio until the Baker Plan was announced, but by 1987 they and other forms of policy-based lending had risen to 20 per cent of the Bank's loans to Latin America.[21]

1987 also saw a massive internal shake-out, known inside the Bank simply as 'the Reorganization'. Under pressure from the Reagan administration, the incoming president of the Bank, Barber Conable, oversaw a top-to-bottom overhaul of the organization, designed to make the Bank more effective in its new role as global enforcer of structural adjustment. All staff, except those at the very top, were suspended in a forced mass resignation, then each tier chose its subordinates in a cascade system. Loyalty was rewarded, dissidence flushed out. About 10 per cent of the Bank's staff were 'terminated'. It was brutal, but effective, as even the Bank's critics concede:

> It took the Church several hundred years to convert only a part of humanity to Christianity. It took the Bank little more than a decade to impose structural adjustment worldwide, or very nearly. In the single year 1987 it was able to reorganize itself from top to bottom the better to serve this recent but all-pervading doctrine. By any standards, this is a stunning performance. The Bank is without contest the premier policy institution deciding how the South and East are to be organized. Nobody else even comes close.[22]

SALs come with a new checklist of conditions and performance targets attached. The Bank usually makes SALs conditional on countries having already put in place an 'appropriate macro-economic framework'. In practice, this usually means having agreed a stabilization programme with the IMF.[23] The phenomenon of 'cross-conditionality' was born, whereby a country had simultaneously to satisfy two different sets of conditions from the IMF and World Bank. Were it to break either set, the result could be a suspension of the programme and an economic boy-cott by world capital markets. While the Fund's conditions tend to be quantified and precise, the Bank's are more qualitative and negotiable. The result is an administrative nightmare, as local government officials spend more time trying to satisfy the international financial institutions' endless requirements than on running their own economies.

Despite its image as a philanthropic aid-provider, the World Bank, like the IMF, has actually become a drain on the Latin American economy. From 1990–94 Latin America paid the Bank $11bn more in repayments and interest than it received in new loans.[24]

The debt crisis has accelerated the convergence of the two institutions. In the years following Bretton Woods, there was a clear division of roles: the IMF was placed in charge of finding short-term, economy-wide solutions to balance of payments crises; the World Bank promoted long-term development via project funding. Since the early 1970s, this division of labour has become increasingly blurred. In 1974 the IMF moved into medium-term lending with its EFF (Extended Fund Facility). Later it added SAFs (Structural Adjustment Facilities) and ESAFs (Enhanced Structural Adjustment Facilities), new kinds of concessional loans geared even more directly to structural adjustment policies.

At the same time, the shift to SALs has brought the World Bank into apparent competition with the Fund on short-term, economy-wide reform. With the creation of Sectoral Adjustment Loans (SECALs) in 1983, the Bank further increased its ability to intervene in Third World economies by lending in return for reforms in specific sectors, such as privatization, 'rationalization' or stimulating exports.[25] The Bank can now throw its weight around in the economies of the South to manage the fine detail of policy in a far more all-pervasive way than the IMF's efforts, which are restricted to macro-economic targets like the fiscal deficit or exchange rate. It has become a more effective neo-liberal bat-tering ram, while its more sensitive handling of publicity and its own image have so far allowed it to escape the IMF's global notoriety.

The Baker Plan failed to rekindle lending from the private banks; bank lending to the Third World actually fell in the first year of the Plan. However, it triggered a new phase in the neo-liberal restructuring of Latin America's economy as the emphasis switched from the short-term stabilization programmes of the early 1980s, to longer-term neo-liberal transformation of the economy. SALs encourage very specific reforms, such as:

- *deregulating foreign trade. The international financial institutions believe that protectionism spawns inefficiency, so import taxes and quotas are removed as part of the wider effort to 'get the prices right'. The market can then allocate resources more efficiently and comparative advantage becomes the basis for a country's trade;*

- *privatizing state-owned companies. This has proved an extremely attractive option to both governments and the international financial institutions from the mid-1980s onward, since it sheds loss-making companies which contribute to the fiscal deficit, while the proceeds from sales create a one-off boost to government revenue (not to mention plentiful opportunities for corruption). The international financial institutions also believed that privatization would lead to a more efficient economy, since it would encourage the private sector (especially transnational companies) to inject new capital and technology, and 'muscular management', free from political considerations, could sack staff deemed surplus to requirements;*
- *deregulating the labour market. This involved making it easier for employers to hire and fire at whim, an assault on the power of trade unions which enabled employers to cut salaries, reducing 'red tape' such as health and safety legislation which pushes up employers' costs, and encouraging a range of 'flexible practices' such as sub-contracting, self-employment and part-time work, all of which increase business competitivity, while reducing workers' wages and job security;*
- *tax reform and higher charges for state-produced goods like electricity and water were both introduced as a means of balancing government budgets. Most tax reforms involved increasing sales taxes, such as VAT, which proportionally hit the poor hardest.*

Just as with the initial stage of IMF-run stabilization, the Baker Plan may have failed to fulfil its stated aims, but the World Bank's plunge into structurally adjusting the South proved remarkably successful in opening up the Latin American economy to the traders and investors of the rich nations, and reforming it along neo-liberal lines, while further eroding Latin America's economic sovereignty.

The IDB

A lesser-known international financial institution, the Inter-American Development Bank (IDB), also plays a leading role in the region's adjustment process. Founded in 1959, the IDB has stuck closer than the World Bank to its original role in providing finance for specific projects. During its first 20 years it concentrated on agriculture and social sector projects, leaving the World Bank to its obsession with infrastructural 'mega-projects' such as giant dams and roads. With the onset of the debt crisis, it lost favour with Washington, as structural adjustment ousted project lending, but since the late 1980s it has made a comeback and gained new funding for its lending. To get the new funds from the US, it was forced to clamber aboard the structural adjustment bandwagon, but opposition from Latin America ensured that adjustment-oriented sectoral loans should be limited to a quarter of total lending,[26] which came to $6bn in 1993.[27] This was actually more than gross disbursements to the region by the World Bank, which came to $5.2bn in that year.[28]

As with the IMF and World Bank, the US government exerts a high level of control over the IDB, which is suitably headquartered in Washington. The US has just enough votes (34.61 per cent)[29] to veto loans financed through the Fund for Special Operations, IDB's 'soft window' for concessional loans. Nevertheless, the IDB, led by its Uruguayan president, Enrique Iglesias, has been at the forefront of the policy rethink within the international financial institutions, calling for a renewed emphasis on poverty reduction, improved education, health care and redistribution of wealth.

Criticisms of structural adjustment

The human and economic impact of structural adjustment is examined in detail in subsequent chapters. The Bretton Woods institutions argue their case on the basis of 'no pain, no gain'. Although the model invariably produces the pain through increased poverty, inequality and unemployment, the gains have so far proven more elusive. The Fund and Bank still avow that they will be proved right in the long run, but as Keynes acerbically remarked, 'In the long run, we are all dead.'[30]

The model can be criticized at several levels. Even in its own terms, its dual aims of short-term stabilization and long-term export-led growth often appear incompatible. While attacking inflation is supposed to be the underlying purpose of the exercise, the devaluation which almost invariably accompanies an IMF agreement leads to a surge in prices as imports suddenly rise in price. These kinds of policy plunged much of Latin America into a 'stagflation' cycle of recession and high inflation during the 1980s.

Although the initial impact of recession and devaluation produced a large trade surplus in the early years of the debt crisis, nearly all of the surplus promptly left Latin America as debt service payments rather than being invested in the region's future. Moreover, the Fund and Bank's insistence that Latin American countries should remove protection against imports led to a flood of cheap imports from the late 1980s, turning a regional trade surplus of $29.3bn in 1989 into a deficit of $18.2bn in 1994.[31] Of the 19 Latin American republics for which figures are available from the UN, only Brazil, Ecuador and Venezuela still had a trade surplus by 1993. The chief offender was Mexico, hailed as a triumph of structural adjustment, which was running an annual $20bn trade deficit by 1992. Critics point out that the goal of export promotion need not automatically require total import liberalization, which wipes out vulnerable industries and burns up the foreign exchange acquired from improved exports.

In the Third World as a whole, the international institutions ignore what is known as the 'fallacy of composition'. In dealing with each country separately, they assume the rest of the world economy remains unchanged so that devaluing and boosting both traditional and non-traditional exports will improve a country's trading performance. But if the whole Third World follows the same policies, it risks flooding the market with new agricultural products, with the inevitable impact on prices; if Kenya, Zimbabwe and Guatemala all decide to compete in exporting coffee or non-traditionals such as mange-tout (snow peas), it may be good news for shoppers in the North's supermarkets, but it spells falling incomes for their own farmers. Under Washington's tutelage, Third World economies were forced to run just to stand still, as their terms of trade continued to deteriorate.

One authoritative analysis by Britain's Overseas Development Institute came to damning conclusions on the IMF's record.[32] IMF programmes have a 'muted effect on economic growth'; they often 'result in substantially reduced investment levels'; 'the urban labour force commonly suffers reduced real earnings'; and 'programmes often fail to trigger additional inflows of capital from the rest of the world'.

Perhaps most startling of all, the study showed that two-thirds of IMF programmes had broken down in recent years, but that it did not seem to make any difference to the eventual outcome! It concluded that any balance of payments improvements were more the result of the government focusing its mind on macro-economic management, than anything to do with the direct involvement of the IMF.

There are numerous other ways to approach the problem of balance of payments deficits besides the Fund's exclusive focus on reducing demand. The experience of the newly industrialized countries (NICs) of South-East Asia shows that vigorous state intervention and selective protection of local industry can play a vital role in creating a dynamic export sector and generating a trade surplus. Such 'protectionist' policies are, however, anathema to the Bretton Woods institutions, which argue, in defiance of the history of just about every successful economy in the world, that protectionism inevitably leads to inefficient and unsuccessful economies.

The Bank's insistence on such ill-conceived dogma stung the normally reticent Japanese government into a comprehensive rebuttal of Bank thinking. A report issued in 1991 by Japan's Overseas Economic

Cooperation Fund found the Bank 'too optimistic' when it expected that 'industries that sustain the economy of the next generation will sprout automatically through the activities of the private sector'; the Bank's view of trade was erroneously based on 'static comparative advantage'. The Japanese also believed, 'Different conditions of individual countries have to be carefully taken into account. Unfortunately, the World Bank focus seems to be almost the same for all countries.' The report also disagreed with the Bank's 'idea that the private sector has to be treated in the same manner whether it be national or foreign'. For the OECF, 'The notion of transferring basic industries to foreign capital is an extremely grave and serious affair.' The Bank, however:

> seems to lack a long-term vision of how to develop [export] industries, perhaps because it supposes that the activities of the private sector alone will be enough to reach that goal. This lack of vision is truly lamentable.[33]

During the Reagan-Bush years, the Bretton Woods institutions' stubborn belief in the free-market panacea was echoed in the White House. Under Bill Clinton, however, many US policy-makers have come to accept the need for a more hands-on role for the state, but this shift in thinking has yet to penetrate the Fund and the Bank, which risk becoming in the words of one Mexican commentator, 'the last redoubt of the conservative paradigm'.[34] In *Faith and Credit: The World Bank's Secular Empire*, an excellent, and highly critical, portrait of the Bank, Susan George and Fabrizio Sabelli lay out some of the reasons for its inability to change with the times. Likening the Bank to the Vatican, the authors portray a hermetic, arrogant institutional culture, convinced that it holds the keys to earthly salvation:

> this supranational, non-democratic institution functions very much like the Church, in fact the medieval Church. It has a doctrine, a rigidly structured hierarchy preaching and imposing this doctrine, and a quasi-religious mode of self-justification.[35]

The authors believe that the Bank can only get away with continuing to impose an outdated doctrine on the South because, in the post-Cold War world, other global institutions and northern governments no longer care what happens there.

> Since the North no longer even seems to be bothering to articulate a policy towards the South, the Bank's own policies are filling the void ... In the empty space, devoid of leadership and ideas, whatever the Bank wants to do, it can do. By default, structural adjustment plus Bank projects are northern policy with regard to the poorer countries, the only policy on offer. [emphasis in the original][36]

George and Sabelli condemn the Bretton Woods institutions for their erosion of national sovereignty. Although the official fiction maintains that countries themselves decide their policies, after which the Fund (or Bank) decides whether they merit financial support, in practice the international financial institutions have held such power (especially in the early 1980s) that they can effectively dictate much of a country's economic policy. Each new condition imposed in return for a loan chips away at a country's ability to determine its own economic path. By the mid-1980s one of the World Bank's Structural Adjustment Loans resembled an enormous shopping list of economic reforms, with anything up to a hundred separate policy conditions.[37] They conclude:

> With the engineered decline of national sovereignty in the former Second World and the Third, unelected technocrats will play a growing international political role, however much their rhetoric may try to disguise it. In this world-order scenario, leadership remains in the hands of the G-7 countries. GATT or its successor World Trade Organization is in line to become the International Ministry of Trade. The IMF will press its claim to be the International Ministry of Finance. The way history is moving, the way the institution is playing its cards, the Bank is the prime candidate for the Ministry of Everything Else.[38]

The Fund and the Bank's standard policy packages take little account of local political or economic conditions. As one local expert complains, 'Even before they arrive in a given Latin American country, the experts of the IMF know better than Latin American economists how to tackle the problem.'[39] Typically, macro-economists from Washington fly in for three weeks with a blueprint for the country's future economic policy already in their briefcases. Once in the country, they negotiate with local technocrats from the Finance Ministry, often themselves former IMF or World Bank employees, but they do not consult other bodies like the Agriculture Ministry, or the UN Food and Agriculture Organisation, who have a far better understanding of how the Fund's economic prescriptions will affect people on the ground.[40]

In a hundred-page open letter of resignation from his job as senior economist with the IMF, Grenadian economist Davison L. Budhoo lambasted the IMF mentality in the 1980s:

> Let us remove all elements of recipient discretion from our programs. Let us state explicitly and unequivocally what the Third World blighters must be made to do, and when and how they must be made to do it ... Let us give the countries of the South specific things to do in specific months, and even during specific weeks of specific months. Let us finally put a particular cut-

off point for completing our task of effecting Reaganomics and Thatcheromics in the South.[41]

The politics of adjustment

The motive for Budhoo's resignation was one of the most serious claims of fraud and bad faith levelled at the Fund in recent years. Budhoo worked for the IMF between 1985–87, evaluating the state of Trinidad and Tobago's economy. He later resigned, charging that he had uncovered evidence that the Fund deliberately distorted the state of the country's economy in order to force it to adopt stronger adjustment measures. This included more than doubling the figures for Trinidad's fiscal deficit, vastly inflating the figures for the rises in the country's labour costs, and giving a distorted picture of the real exchange rate to strengthen its argument for devaluation of the local currency. Budhoo claimed that when he pointed out the mistakes, he was ignored, forcing him to conclude that the distortions were 'premeditated and systematic' frauds.[42]

The Bretton Woods institutions invariably present their policy packages as an 'objective' solution to a country's internal problems, yet self-interest is clearly involved, since powerful interests in the North reap rich rewards from structural adjustment, which opens up the economies of the South to First World traders and investors. In the massive privatizations of the late 1980s and early 1990s US and European transnational corporations were able to snap up the pick of Latin America's airlines and telecommunications companies and also moved in on its oil sector. Structural adjustment's emphasis on export-led growth, along with its tendency to de-industrialize Third World economies, leads to more abundant, and therefore cheaper, supplies of raw materials for the industrialized economies, locking much of the South into a neo-colonial economic relationship with the North. Given the control by those same rich countries of the Fund and the Bank, it is hard to believe that this is pure coincidence.

But in the North, as in the South, adjustment creates both winners and losers, while individuals at different points in the social pyramid usually experience both costs and benefits from the adjustment process. The recession and import suppression in Latin America in the 1980s undoubtedly destroyed jobs in northern export industries, while the debt crisis forced northern governments to bail out their own banks with taxpayers' money at a time when government budgets were already under severe pressure. More generally, adjustment's damaging impact on the environment has accelerated global warming and the depletion of natural resources. These negative factors may outweigh the benefits to northern consumers from cheaper commodities, or the retention of low productivity jobs in northern factories, achieved by the virtual destruction of many areas of Latin American industry in the past 13 years.[43]

Often, however, it is impossible to disentangle political from economic criteria. The IMF and World Bank believe in the market and will not fund a government which rejects their ideas in favour of a more progressive agenda such as redistributing wealth or building up national industry through some measure of protection, although by the mid-1990s even the IMF was prepared to accept limited government support for 'safety nets' to ease the worst impact of adjustment. Staff at the Bretton Woods institutions probably *do* believe that their decisions are based purely on economic grounds, but in practice, they promote the US agenda for the Third World. Washington certainly sees it that way, according to one US official who advised, 'We must counter, both in the UN and within the framework of the North–South dialogue, any discussion of global problems which questions the validity of the free market and of free enterprise in the countries of the Third World.'[44]

The US has regularly used the Fund and the Bank to reward its allies, however undeserving, and punish its enemies, however strong their case for a loan. In 1993, Mexico, emerging from a decade of neo-liberal shock treatment, duly reaped its reward when it took over from India as the World Bank's all-time largest borrower.[45] A few years earlier, a leaked memo from the British Foreign Office provided a revealing account of political interference in the World Bank, at a time when Britain was faithfully toeing Washington's hard line against Nicaragua at the height of the Contra war. Stamped 'Confidential', the memo stated, 'There is no need to amend our voting policy towards Nicaragua for the time being. The problem of explaining it in public will, however, persist and we shall need to stick to our present line of claiming that our opposition is based on technical grounds.' Underneath this paragraph, an exasperated civil servant had scribbled 'If we can find them!'[46]

In all this there is a danger in over-simplifying what is going on. Many critics of structural adjustment talk as if the international financial institutions are solely responsible for imposing structural adjustment from outside on a passive Latin America. In many ways, this view resembles the over-simplifications of the 'dependency school' of development economics of the 1960s and 1970s which tended to place all Latin America's economic ills at the door of the rich countries, blaming them for having locked the region into an endless cycle of commodity dependence and poverty.

But adjustment also has powerful allies within Latin America, not least among the business groups who have made fortunes out of privatization and deregulation. Even among those who do not stand directly to gain, the collapse of the import substitution model, and the failure in the mid-1980s of many of the attempts to find a less painful 'heterodox' way of stabilizing the economy led to the widespread adoption of the 'there is no alternative' attitude. In 1988, even the Sandinistas in Nicaragua turned to a more or less neo-liberal package to stabilize an economy riven by hyper-inflation. There was also a much higher level of consensus over the need for longer-term export-led growth, than over how to stabilize the economy in the first years of the silent revolution. Furthermore, those doing the adjusting found the IMF an ideal scapegoat for policies which they may well have wanted to introduce anyway. For any Latin American politician, an IMF riot is infinitely preferable to an anti-government revolution. (The politics of the silent revolution are discussed in Chapter 7.)

Changing the international financial institutions

The international financial institutions and the governments who control them are not entirely impervious to criticism or public pressure, and as the end of the decade approached, attacks on the international financial institutions' impact in the debtor countries rained down from all sides.

Of the two big Bretton Woods institutions, the Bank has proved more responsive to public pressure than the IMF, and by the late 1980s was acknowledging the need for action on issues such as environmental destruction and poverty. Unfortunately, as Susan George observes, 'Every time the Bank is effectively criticized, it has responded by expanding.'[47] New 'units' are promptly created on issues such as women, the environment or the role of NGOs, often employing some of the Bank's most effective critics, dissipating their energies in an exhausting bureaucratic battle to change the system from within. The number of environmental specialists rose from 5 to 200 in the eight years to 1993, but the most powerful men in the Bank, as Lawrence Summers showed (see p. 108), still ignore their findings.

Most environmental criticism has focused on the Bank's project loans, but governments and non-governmental organizations (NGOs) in the South, supported by development agencies in the North, have also mobilized public opinion on the social impact of adjustment. Several UN agencies, notably UNICEF, have conducted an impressive lobbying effort while always treating the IMF with 'an appropriate degree of professional deference'.[48] UNICEF's publication *Adjustment with a Human Face*[49] has come to be seen as a landmark critique of the international financial institutions' policies in the South. One of its principal findings was that, although structural adjustment had greatly increased poverty in the region, the international financial institutions' lending policies and conditions had paid 'almost no attention to the special problems of the poor' by the late 1980s.[50] One high-ranking World Bank economist confessed, 'We did not think that the human costs of these programmes could be so great, and the economic gains so slow in coming.'[51]

In 1990 the Bank responded to such criticisms by adopting poverty alleviation as its main objective, formalizing its new commitment in that year's *World Development Report*. World Bank President Lewis Preston described sustainable poverty reduction as 'the over-arching objective of the World Bank. It is the benchmark by which our performance as a development institution will be measured.'[52] The new strategy aimed

> To reduce poverty through broadly-based labour-intensive growth to gener-
> ate jobs and income for the poor; social investment to improve poor people's
> access to education, nutrition, health care and other social services and social
> safety nets to protect the poorest and most vulnerable sections of society.[53]

Even the IMF has taken steps to adapt to the new climate. Since 1988 IMF country missions have been obliged to report on the poverty implications of its programmes, while an IMF survey in 1989 confessed that 'It would be morally, politically and economically unacceptable to wait for resumed growth alone to reduce poverty.'[54]

But such fine rhetoric has a way of placing the blame, as well as the onus for change, on Latin American governments. With each new twist and turn in international financial institution policy, further conditions have been placed on the recipient governments. First the IMF's broad macro-economic targets, then the World Bank's more detailed demands – privatization, public-sector redundancies and sectoral adjustment. Now a new layer of 'social conditions' has been added, telling the governments how to run their health and education systems. The steady encroachment by the multilateral organizations and their rich sponsors on the sovereignty of the indebted nations of the South seems inexorable.

Despite such moves, criticism has continued to mount over the gap between the new rhetoric and the reality on the ground. 'The World Bank has successfully integrated poverty as a first order priority in its reports, but *not* in its actual lending practice', concluded a study by one respected economist.[55] Protests and calls for reform reached a head at the IMF and World Bank's fiftieth birthday jamboree in Madrid in October 1994. What was supposed to be an occasion for pomp and self-congratulation turned into a public relations disaster as both Bretton Woods institutions came under a barrage of criticism, ranging across the political spectrum from the banners, barracking and stunts which punctuated the conference to sweeping calls for reform from the infinitely respectable Bretton Woods Commission. To compound the embarass-ment, the IMF managing director, Michel Camdessus, got involved in a public wrangle with his major funders over a new issue of Special Drawing Rights – the argument boiled down to whether the funders or staff were actually in charge of the organization.

NGOs critical of the Bretton Woods institutions tend to be divided over whether to propose abolition or reform, but they coincide in many of their criticisms of the IMF and World Bank as presently constituted. In two highly critical reports[56] published to coincide with the Madrid con-ference, Oxfam gave a forceful presentation of such views. It lamented the fact that 'repackaging and public relations have triumphed over seri-ous reflection and self-criticism'.[57] The British development agency argued that the new approach was centrally flawed because it failed 'to introduce the redistributive reforms and protection of basic rights neces-sary to tackle the root causes of poverty and inequality'.[58] Despite its pro-fessed aims, the World Bank's new strategy actually made poverty worse, since 'The promotion of labour-intensive growth is premised on dismant-ling of workers' rights and the erosion of wages, which will further exacerbate economic insecurity and inequality.'[59] Oxfam criticized the Bank for failing to recognize that income redistribution should be an essential part of any poverty-reduction strategy and argued that 'Simply bolting-on social welfare provision to wider adjustment policies which are themselves exacerbating poverty does not amount to a poverty-reduction strategy.'[60] Oxfam concluded, 'Fundamental reforms will be required to structural adjustment programmes before the World Bank can truly claim to be on the side of the poor.'[61]

The reports also highlighted the underlying unfairness of the interna-tional financial institutions, namely their 'profoundly undemocratic char-acter',[62] adding:

> *In Oxfam's view it is not acceptable for Northern governments to demand greater accountability on the part of governments in the South, when these same governments are effectively transferring economic policy sovereignty to remote, unaccountable institutions in Washington, controlled by the North.*[63]

The World Bank is accustomed to criticism from the NGOs, although at Madrid it was stung into, by its own standards, an unusually abusive reply to the Oxfam reports cited above. However, calls for reform also came from insiders, in the shape of the Bretton Woods Commission, a gathering of the great and good of international finance, chaired by Paul Volcker, former head of the US Federal Reserve. While broadly sup-portive, Volcker's commission concluded that the IMF should stop behaving as a development institution and concentrate on managing the chaotic global monetary system, while the World Bank should focus on promoting development through the private sector and 'speeding the transformation from state to market', while cutting back on its own bureaucracy and waste.[64]

Unloved and fifty years old, the Bretton Woods institutions seem headed for a profound mid-life crisis. But a seasoned Bank-watcher like Susan George is sceptical about the likelihood of change.

> *Perhaps the Bank's world-view has become about as relevant to today's context and to late twentieth-century problems as that of the schoolmen or of the Flat Earth Society; but this does not mean it will disappear just because it is outmoded or wrong. We may recall that the Catholic Church only got around to rehabilitating Galileo in 1992 although it first condemned his views in 1633.*[65]

Postscript: the IMF in Nicaragua 1994; plus ça change?

In April 1994 the Nicaraguan government signed a letter of intent with the IMF which showed how little the Fund's approach had changed since the early days of the debt crisis. The agreement was for a three-year Enhanced Structural Adjustment Facility. The deal opened the way to some $400m in aid from the US and other sources, while the World Bank promised to provide a further $150m in the ensuing 18 months. The international financial institutions' agreements were also expected to smooth the way for a debt renegotiation with the Paris Club of rich creditor nations. In return for all this, the government's promises (extracted after months of resistance) included:[66]

- *cutting a further 13,500 public-sector jobs on top of deep cuts already made since the late 1980s;*
- *freezing education and health expenditure at nominal levels despite inflation;*
- *all public investment projects to require prior World Bank approval before getting the go-ahead;*
- *reduced import tariffs;*
- *introducing fees for health and education services;*
- *raising electricity and water rates;*
- *extending sales taxes;*
- *the sale or liquidation of most remaining state companies.*

In its first years in office the government of Violeta Chamorro, which took power from the Sandinistas in the 1990 election, had faithfully and willingly followed the IMF's recipe. By 1993 the Chamorro government had fired 250,000 public employees (Nicaragua's total population is 4.5 million), unemployment had doubled to 22 per cent and industrial employment had fallen by nearly a third.[67] The UN Food and Agriculture Organization has predicted that Nicaragua's next generation will be smaller, weaker and less intelligent than today's population.[68] By 1994, the government had serious reservations about the merits of such policies, but its hands were tied; the Fund held the keys to desperately needed foreign aid, and Nicaragua had to sign after eight months of wrangling. The IMF's blinkered and self-defeating approach was demonstrated by the fate of Chamorro's previous Stand-by Arrangement – the Fund suspended disbursements in protest when the government overspent its limits on resettling rebellious former Contra guerrillas in the countryside. As a result, Chamorro was forced to renege on her promises to the rebels, who promptly took up arms again. Political instability worsened and the investment needed to rebuild the country never materialized.[69] As the economy continued its downward slide, the Fund showed itself unable to learn from over a decade of failure.

Notes

1 James Ferguson, *Dominican Republic: Beyond the Lighthouse* (London, 1992), p.93.

2 Graham Hancock, *Lords of Poverty* (London, 1991), p.38.

3 Peter Korner, Gero Maass, Thomas Siebold and Rainer Tetzlaff, *The IMF and the Debt Crisis* (London, 1986), p.44.

4 Christian Aid and the World Wildlife Fund, *The IMF and the World Bank: Facing the Next Fifty Years* (mimeo) (London, June 1994), p.1.

5 Karel Jansen, 'What are the World Bank and IMF and what do they do?', in *The World Bank and the IMF: Some Issues* (Development Education Association, London, 1994), p.4.

6 IMF, *Annual Report 1994* (Washington, DC, 1994).

7 Korner *et al.*, *op. cit.*, p.45.

8 *Ibid.*, p.43.

9 IMF, *op. cit.*

10 Overseas Development Institute, *The Inter-American Development Bank and Changing Policies for Latin America* (London, April 1991), p.3.

11 Susan George, *A Fate Worse Than Debt* (London, 1988) p.40.

12 Oxfam, *Structural Adjustment and Inequality in Latin America: How IMF and World Bank Policies Have Failed the Poor* (mimeo) (Oxford, 1994), p.20.

13 Korner *et al.*, *op. cit.*, p.42.

14 Quoted in Susan George and Fabrizio Sabelli, *Faith and Credit: The World Bank's Secular Empire* (London, 1994), p.215.

15 *Financial Times* (London), 1/2 August 1992.

16 Arthur Schlesinger, *A Thousand Days* (New York, 1965), p.158.

17 Korner *et al.*, *op. cit.*, Appendix 2.

18 Eliana Cardoso and Ann Helwege, *Latin America's Economy: Diversity, Trends and Conflicts* (Cambridge, MA, 1992), p.172.

19 Oxford Analytica, *Latin America in Perspective* (Boston, MA, 1991), p.208.

20 George and Sabelli, *op. cit.*, p.4.

21 Oxford Analytica, *op. cit.*, p.313.

22 George and Sabelli, *op. cit.*, p.130.

23 Paul Mosley, Jane Harrigan and John Toye, *Aid and Power: The World Bank and Policy-based Lending*, Vol. 1 (London, 1991), p.37.

24 World Bank, *Annual Report 1994* (Washington, DC, 1994), p.111.

25 Jackie Roddick, *The Dance of the Millions: Latin America and the Debt Crisis* (London, 1988), p.56.

26 ODI, *The Inter-American Development Bank and Changing Policies for Latin America* (London, April 1991), p.3.

27 IDB, *Annual Report 1993* (Washington, DC, 1994).

28 World Bank, *op. cit.*

29 IDB, *op. cit.*

30 J.K. Galbraith, *A History of Economics* (London, 1987), p.4.

31 CEPAL, *Balance Preliminar de la Economía de América Latina y el Caribe 1994* (Santiago, December 1994), p.39.

32 Overseas Development Institute, *Does the IMF Really Help Developing Countries?* (London, April 1993), p.3.

33 cited in *Third World Economics* (Penang, Malaysia, 16–31 March 1993).

34 Jorge Castañeda, *Utopia Unarmed: The Latin American Left after the Cold War* (New York, 1993), p.431.

35 George and Sabelli, *op. cit.*, p.5.

36 *Ibid.*, pp. 71 & 220.

37 Mosley, Harrigan and Toye, *op. cit.*, p.43.

38 George and Sabelli, *op. cit.*, p.161.

39 Patricio Meller (ed.), *The Latin American Development Debate: Neostructuralism,* *Neomonetarism and Adjustment Processes,* (Boulder, CO, 1991), p.180.

40 Talk by Hans Singer at Richmond College, (London, 28 September 1994).

41 Davison L. Budhoo, *Enough Is Enough Mr Camdessus: Open Letter of Resignation to the Managing Director of the International Monetary Fund* (New York, 1990), p.104.

42 Quoted in *Multinational Monitor,* (Washington, DC, June 1990).

43 David Woodward, *The Costs to the North of the Current Approach to Adjustment,* background paper for conference on 'The British Economy and Third World Debt' (One World Action, London, 10 June 1993).

44 'Full text of the Kirkpatrick Plan', Congressional Record, The Senate (Washington, DC, 11 May 1984).

45 George and Sabelli, *op. cit.*, p.11.

46 'Voting Policy at the IADB and IBRD: El Salvador, Guatemala, Nicaragua', memo from J.M. Watt (Mexico and Central America Desk, Foreign Office, 12 October 1984).

47 George and Sabelli, *op. cit.*, p.235.

48 Richard Jolly, 'Adjustment with a human face: A UNICEF record and perspective on the 1980s', *World Development*, Vol. 19, No. 12 (Oxford, 1991), p.1811.

49 G.A. Cornia, R. Jolly and F. Stewart, *Adjustment with a Human Face* (Oxford, 1987).

50 Frances Stewart, *Protecting the Poor during Adjustment in Latin America and the Caribbean in the Late 1980s: How Adequate Was the World Bank Response?* (mimeo) (Oxford, 1991).

51 World Bank Chief Economist for Africa, quoted in Morris Miller, *Debt and the Environment: Converging Crises* (New York, 1991), p.70.

52 Oxfam, *Embracing the Future...Avoiding the Challenge of World Poverty* (mimeo) (Oxford, September 1994), p.2.

53 Oxfam, *Structural Adjustment*, p.4.

54 Frances Stewart, 'The many faces of adjustment', *World Development*, Vol. 19, No. 12 (Oxford, 1991), p.1857.

55 Louis Emmerij, *A Critical Review of the World Bank's Approach to Social Sector Lending and Poverty Alleviation* (mimeo) (Paris, 24 June 1993).

56 Oxfam, *Embracing the Future*, and *Structural Adjustment*.

57 Oxfam, *Embracing the Future*, p.2.

58 Oxfam, *Structural Adjustment*, p.5.

59 *Ibid.*, p.5.

60 *Ibid.*, p.17.

61 *Ibid.*, p.21.

62 Oxfam, *Embracing the Future*, p.2.

63 *Ibid.*, p.1.

64 Bretton Woods Commission, *Bretton Woods: Looking to the Future* (Washington, DC, July 1994).

65 George and Sabelli, *op. cit.*, p.103.

66 Economist Intelligence Unit, *Nicaragua Country Report* (London, Third Quarter, 1994).

67 CRIES, *Towards a National Solution to the Crisis, Adjusting the Adjustment in Nicaragua* (Managua, June 1994).

68 Oxfam, *Structural Adjustment*, p.7.

69 Talk by Trevor Evans, CRIES economist, at the Catholic Institute of International Relations (London, 12 July 1994).

70 IMF Annual Report 1993 (Washington, DC, 1993).

CHAPTER 3

Silent Revolution

Latin America's Economic Transformation since 1982

The Rt Hon. Douglas Hurd MP, the quintessential patrician of the British Foreign Office, is giving a pep talk to the London Chamber of Commerce and Industry. 'The popular B movie image of a Latin America of revolution is out of date,' he drawls. Latin America is now 'a bright spot' in the global economy. His audience of British bankers, exporters and Latin American ambassadors nods in agreement, the monotony of their sea of dark suits relieved by two or three splashes of colour from power-dressing women executives. Mr Hurd is talking money, though he uses phrases like 'exciting markets', 'opportunities' and 'lower production costs', and is urging UK businesses to get in on the act. 'This needs top-level attention. It's not just sales managers. Persuade the top man to go.'[1]

Hurd's buoyant optimism shows just how far Latin America's reputation has changed since Mexico's announcement in August 1982 that it had run out of dollars and could no longer keep up payments on its foreign debt. Over the intervening years, Latin America has ridden an economic roller-coaster through recession and hyper-inflation, punctuated by a short-lived boom in the mid-1980s. Now the region seems set on the road to a partial economic recovery. Along the way, the nature of the region's economy has been dramatically overhauled in a process which, for good or ill, has touched the lives of every one of its citizens. Policy-makers have opened up the economy to foreign trade and investment, privatized innumerable state-owned companies, cut back the role of the state, got inflation under control and, in the eyes of foreign investors, turned Latin America from a basket case into an exciting investment opportunity.

The 1982 Mexican default marked the end of the era of import substitution in Latin America. The news sent Washington's financiers into panic, as they realized that the top 13 US banks were owed $16.5bn – almost half their capital – by Mexico.[2] A former president of Citibank described the state of mind at the annual IMF-World Bank meeting in

Toronto, a few weeks later: '150-odd finance ministers, 50-odd central bankers, 1,000 journalists, 1,000 commercial bankers, a large supply of whisky and a reasonably small city produced an enormous head of steam driving an engine called "the end of the world is coming".'[3] If Mexico defaulted and other major debtors joined in, a bank crash on the scale of the 1930s seemed inevitable. The debt crisis was under way, and with it Latin America's 'lost decade' of development.

Thirteen years later, the region seems to be emerging from a period of transition away from import substitution to a new, export-led neo-liberal model. The transition has entailed enormous human suffering, while the benefits for the majority of Latin Americans are not yet in sight. Besides its immediate costs, doubts also surround the new model's long-term viability. A financial crisis in Mexico in early 1995 only served to strengthen fears that Latin America's fitful recovery would prove fragile and short-lived.

Seen from on high (the human consequences will be discussed in the next chapter), Latin America's economic roller-coaster since the onset of the debt crisis can be roughly divided up into three periods:

1982–83 Deep recession caused by the immediate response to the debt crisis;

1984–87 A false dawn, led by Brazil and Argentina's 'heterodox' stabilization programmes;

1988–95 Stagnation, while structural adjustment gathers pace, followed by patchy recovery.

However, the picture differs from country to country, concealing individual booms and slumps, and the strong performance of some economies relative to others. For a country-by-country economic summary, see Appendix A. Moreover, the regional statistics are disproportionately influenced by Brazil, which accounts for over a third of Latin America's GDP. Such complications can make unravelling Latin America's economic performance since 1982 a difficult exercise, not least for the reader, but it is important to move beyond regional generalizations to get some idea of how the different countries fared during the silent revolution.

Deep recession, 1982–83

The slump in Latin America's economy which followed the Mexican collapse contributed to one war and several bloody 'IMF riots'. Argentina's military leaders invaded the Falklands to divert attention from a collapsing economy, while riots, protests and looting afflicted cities across the continent (see Table 7.1, p. 167).

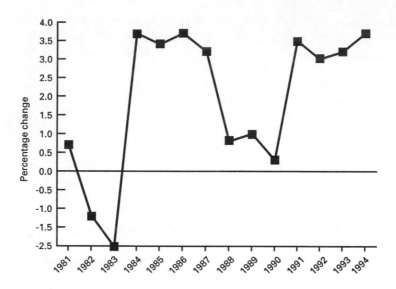

Figure 3.1: Latin America and the Caribbean: GDP growth 1981–94

Source: CEPAL, *Balance Preliminar de la Economía de América Latina y el Caribe* (Santiago, various years).

Prior to the 1980s, Latin Americans were accustomed to a growing economy. In every year between 1964 and 1980, the regional economy grew by more than 4 per cent,[4] making the recession that hit in 1982 all the more painful. In 1982 Latin America's economy shrank in real terms for the first time since the Second World War. Chile was the worst hit, with per capita GDP falling by 14.5 per cent in a single year.[5] The despair of Chile's unemployed workforce was captured in the lyrics of one of its top rock bands in the late 1980s, *Los Prisioneros*:[6]

> *They're idle, waiting for the hands*
> *that decide to make them run again*
> *The mist surrounds and rusts them...*
> *I drag myself along the damp cement,*
> *remembering a thousand laments.*
> *Of when the misery came, when they said*
> *don't come back, don't come back, don't come back*
> *The factories, all the factories have gone.*

The main cause of the recession was the sudden end to foreign capital inflows which had sustained the Latin American economy throughout

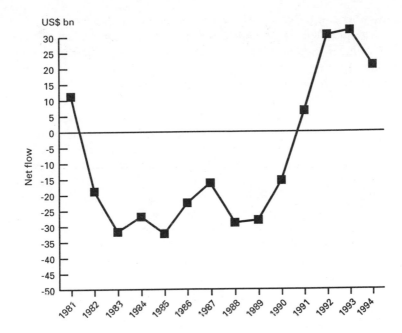

Figure 3.2: Latin America and the Caribbean: The net resource transfer, 1981–94

Source: CEPAL, *Balance Preliminar de la Economía de América Latina y el Caribe* (Santiago, various years).

the 1970s, combined with rising world oil prices after the second oil 'shock' of 1979 and a sharp rise in debt interest payments as world interest rates rose. Recession in the North also hit world commodity prices. From 1979–81 capital flowed into Latin America at an average of $13bn a year.[7] By 1983, Latin America had started to *export* capital for the first time in decades. The transfer of wealth from the poor countries of Latin America to the institutions of the rich First World went on until 1991, a net flow of $218.6bn,[8] or $534 for every man, woman and child in the continent (see Figure 3.2). Even debt service payments on this scale failed to keep up with the interest falling due, and the bizarre logic of the debt game ensured that the region's total external debt rose from $243bn in 1980 to $361bn in 1983.[9]

Yet even these figures for Latin America's capital haemorrhage may be under-estimates, since they exclude capital flight, which does not appear in the official statistics, as the nervous élites of the region used every dodge they knew to convert their wealth into dollars and spirit it to a safe haven in Zurich, New York or the Cayman Islands. By one estimate, in 1983 capital flight from the largest five Latin American economies came to a further $12.1bn.[10] As one former World Bank executive director commented at the end of the 1980s, 'Not since the conquistadores plundered Latin America has the world seen a [financial] flow in the direction we see today.'[11]

When Mexico crashed, the banks stopped lending, leaving Latin American governments to look elsewhere for the dollars with which to keep up their debt repayments. Aside from limited inflows from the international financial institutions (with all the strings attached), they had two stark choices: either declare a moratorium on their debts and become an international financial pariah, or generate a trade surplus and use the excess hard currency to pay the banks. They chose trade.

At the time of the Mexican default, Latin America's trade was roughly in balance. It therefore had either to increase exports or cut imports. Since it had neglected exports for decades under import substitution, and the world in the early 1980s was in the grip of recession, import suppression was the only realistic option. Furthermore, import suppression can usually be achieved much faster, since it is invariably easier and quicker for a government to force its citizens to stop consuming than to persuade the citizens of other countries to buy Latin American exports. Only Brazil bucked the trend, building on export promotion policies dating back to the 1960s to expand export volume by half between 1982 and 1985.[12] The IMF's recipe, accepted willingly or otherwise by 14 Latin American countries between 1982 and 1983,[13] drove country after country into devaluation (to make exporting more profitable and increase the cost of imports) and recession (to suppress domestic demand for imported goods and curb inflation). The IMF even encouraged Latin American governments to wheel out and strengthen the region's traditional barrage of import controls (supposedly anathema to the neo-liberals) in the effort to generate dollars. The results were extraordinary: Latin America's imports halved in volume between 1981 and 1983 (see Figure 3.3).[14]

Latin America's exports failed to grow significantly, due partly to the recession going on in the industrialized nations, but the import collapse turned roughly balanced trade into a mighty trade surplus, rising from $9bn in 1982 to $31.5bn a year later.[15] By the time the trade balance swung back into the red again in 1992, Latin America had generated a total trade surplus of $242.9bn.[16] Almost all of this booty promptly left the region as the $218.6bn in debt service payments.

This extraction of wealth from the region left a large hole in the economy, in the form of an investment collapse. Governments forced to adopt IMF austerity measures found it less politically costly to cut public investment than to sack employees in the middle of a recession (although many did that as well), while the private sector was deterred from investing both by the impossibility of borrowing abroad and the recession and high interest rates at home, as governments lifted interest rates to fight inflation. Foreign investors also took fright. Bank loans dried up and annual foreign direct investment fell from $8bn in 1981 to $3bn in 1983,[17] as recession and fears of instability frightened off the executives of the transnational corporations. Across the region, gross domestic investment (which includes both local and foreign investment) collapsed from $213bn in 1980 to just $136bn in 1983.[18] The level of investment is crucial to any economy's prospects; Latin America was mortgaging its people's future to pay its debts.

Falling investment and the domestic recession brought about by austerity programmes provoked an industrial collapse. By 1983, the degree of industrial development in Latin America had regressed to the levels of 1966. In Argentina and Peru it was back to 1960 levels, while in Chile and Uruguay it was more like 1950.[19]

Governments faced a further problem in turning the trade surplus into debt service payments. Except in the few countries where state enterprises earned a large slice of export income (copper in Chile, oil in Venezuela and Mexico), export dollars lay in the hands of the private sector within each economy. Yet most of the debt repayments were the government's responsibility, forcing it to find a way to buy the private sector's dollars in order then to send them abroad to the banks. At the same time, devaluation made the dollars needed for debt service more expensive in terms of local currency. Most governments were already running deficits when the debt crisis broke, and the ensuing recession and import collapse hit revenues from taxes on sales, income and imports. Despite IMF-decreed cuts in spending, few were able to generate a surplus with which to buy dollars from the private sector.

Many governments were left no option but to turn to the printing press, churning out local currency with which to buy dollars, and triggering a new bout of inflation. The largest economies (Argentina, Brazil and Mexico), managed to imitate governments in Washington and London, using exceptionally high interest rates to persuade reluctant private investors to buy government bonds. This avoided immediate recourse to the printing press, but only at the cost of running up a large domestic debt to rival the foreign debt, and at much higher interest rates. In Mexico interest payments as a percentage of central government expenditure rose from 10 per cent in 1980 to 50 per cent in 1987.[20]

The spiralling internal debt and rising cost (in local currency) of servicing the foreign debt after devaluation ensured that, despite the cuts in public investment, government expenditure went up, in Brazil reaching

51 per cent of GDP by 1985.[21] Fiscal deficits grew, forcing even the largest governments to print currency, and the inevitable upsurge in inflation ensued. In the early years of the debt crisis, the North's thirst for debt dollars took clear precedence over its neo-liberal zeal for a low-spending, non-inflationary public sector. The IMF's insistence on devaluation to generate a trade surplus further boosted inflation by triggering an immediate increase in the prices of imported goods. Between 1981 and 1983 inflation rose from 131 per cent to 434 per cent in Argentina, from 91 per cent to 179 per cent in Brazil, and from 58 per cent to 131 per cent in Latin America as a whole.[22] The debt crisis and the IMF's stabilization programmes were producing a high-inflation, recession-hit economy – the exact opposite of the Fund's stated intentions.

The false dawn, 1984–87

In the early years of the debt crisis bankers and government officials from all sides saw it as a short-term liquidity problem in which the main goal was to keep Latin America from defaulting, while the continent's economy recovered its former dynamism. In 1984 their optimism seemed about to be proved right as the region returned to positive per capita growth, and a brief and sluggish recovery began which continued until 1987. Most of the recovery was accounted for by Brazil, which in 1984 responded to a resurgent First World economy by increasing its manufactured exports by 37 per cent in a single year.[23]

Thereafter, however, Brazil's short-lived success abruptly left the neo-liberal path. In 1985 the country returned to civilian government after 21 years of military rule. The incoming president, José Sarney, promptly raised wages in pursuit of a growth-first policy which bounced the economy up to an annual growth rate of over 8 per cent. Brazil also defied the international financial community by announcing a unilateral restriction on its debt service payments. The Brazilian economy was single-handedly responsible for turning a negative per capita growth figure for the rest of Latin America into a positive figure of 1 per cent for the region as a whole.

By early 1985, doubts over the wisdom of IMF-style stabilization programmes had become widespread in the region, prompting policy-makers to look for alternative ways to end inflation without provoking a huge recession. The result was a series of so-called heterodox stabilization programmes in the mid-1980s. These used temporary government freezes on wages, prices and exchange rates and introduced a series of new currencies to symbolize a new start and to break 'inflationary expectations', whereby producers and employers constantly raise prices and wages in a self-fulfilling inflationary spiral. Heterodox programmes are designed to give the economy a cooling-off period while the government takes steps to remedy the underlying causes of inflation, such as the orthodox measure of cutting the fiscal deficit (hence the 'heterodox' nature of the formula).

Such programmes showed mixed results in achieving stabilization, registering a significant success in Mexico in 1988. But in the best-known cases, the *Austral* plan in Argentina (June 1985), the *Cruzado* plan in Brazil (February 1986) and the *Inti* plan in Peru (July 1985), the governments failed to deal with their spending deficits and merely succeeded in temporarily suppressing inflation through price controls. When the controls were finally removed, the underlying imbalances drove inflation even higher than before the programmes were introduced.

In terms of growth, the failed plans produced a short-lived boom, as stable prices without accompanying austerity led to a brief surge in consumption. In the anchor economy of Brazil, the *Cruzado* plan led to an 8.1 per cent growth rate in 1986, while the *Austral* plan produced a 1986 growth figure of 5.8 per cent in Argentina.[24] The consumption boom in Brazil diverted attention from the export drive; even though manufacturing production rose by a further 11.3 per cent in 1986, exports actually declined and the trade surplus started to fall.[25]

The domestic booms in Argentina, Brazil and Peru all petered out in 1987 as the initial growth could not be sustained, and inflation made a fierce comeback. In Brazil, inflation dropped from 228 per cent in 1985 to just 58 per cent in 1986, but was back to almost 1000 per cent by 1988. Argentina and Peru followed a similar path. The false dawn was over.

In trading terms, 1984–87 saw the beginnings of a long-term shift to the model of export-led growth and trade liberalization which was to emerge triumphant at the end of the 'lost decade' of the 1980s. In 1984, Chile and Ecuador began cutting trade tariffs and eliminating import quotas, and Mexico, Bolivia and Costa Rica followed suit a year later. However, such changes were initially masked by the impact of the heterodox programmes. After the 1984 export boom in Mexico and Brazil, the region's overall trade performance deteriorated rapidly, from the peak trade surplus of $40bn that year down to around $20bn in 1986 and 1987.[26] Heterodox booms diverted export goods to the domestic market, and the terms of trade (the price received for Latin America's exports – largely raw materials – compared to the price it had to pay for its mainly manufactured imports) continued to deteriorate. Exports fell in value and did not recover their 1984 value until 1988.[27] Moreover, trade liberalization opened the door to a rapid growth in imports which from 1986 started to bounce back from the effects of import suppression in the first days of the debt crisis.

While growth made a fleeting recovery, investment became, in the words of the Inter-American Development Bank, 'the great casualty of the debt crisis'.[28] Annual investment in the period 1984–87 never rose above $180bn, compared with $220bn in the year before the debt crisis began, and the slight rise during these years was almost entirely accounted for by investment during Brazil's heterodox experiment.[29] Foreign direct investment stayed below $6bn a year, as Latin America remained a basket case in the eyes of international investors.

Meanwhile, the debt haemorrhage continued (see Figures 3.2 and 3.3). Between 1984 and 1987, debt service payments flowed out of the region at over $30bn a year, while the total foreign debt rose past $400bn.[30] Latin America's governments continued to put debt repayments and current spending before investment, and a backlog of what became known as the 'social debt' built up – a disintegrating education and health service, and an economy dogged by crumbling infrastructure – pot-holed roads, intermittent electricity supplies and millions of

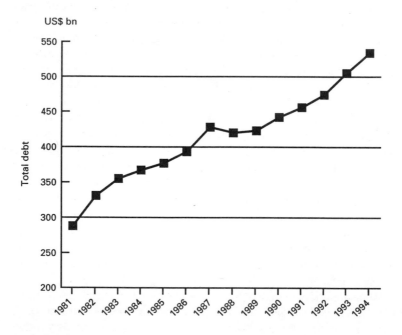

Figure 3.3: Latin America and the Caribbean: Total external debt, 1981–94

Source: CEPAL, *Balance Preliminar de la Economía de América Latina y el Caribe* (Santiago, various years).

families without access to drinking water or mains drainage. The social and economic fabric of Latin America was falling apart.

Adjustment and a return to growth, 1988-95

The collapse of heterodox programmes in Brazil, Argentina and Peru led Latin America back into slump. Per capita GDP fell steadily from 1988 to 1990, before beginning a patchy recovery. Once 'easy' heterodox solutions had been discredited, neo-liberalism spread rapidly across the region; these were the years when the longer-term structural adjustment of Latin America's economy gathered pace. Trade liberalization, government cutbacks, privatization and deregulation have since then become the norm in almost every country.

The increase in world interest rates in 1988 led to a sharp increase in the rate of Latin America's capital going overseas in 1988 and 1989. The announcement in March 1989 of the new 'Brady Plan', masterminded by US Treasury Secretary Nicholas Brady, did little to correct the outflow. The Brady Plan allows Latin American governments to reduce their debts by indulging in the kind of financial jiggery-pokery beloved of the international capital markets. Governments can exchange their debt for 'Brady bonds' at a lower face value or supposedly below-market fixed interest rate. They can also use their foreign reserves or new loans to buy back their own debt at a discount, or encourage foreign investors to swap debt for national currency with which to invest or buy up privatized companies, a practice known as 'debt-for-equity swaps'. Loans from the international financial institutions are almost always involved to finance debt buy-backs or otherwise underwrite the deals.

The direct impact of the Brady Plan on the debt burden has been limited. According to an evaluation for Oxfam by David Woodward[31] of the impact on the six countries which had Brady Plans in place by mid-1994 (Mexico, Costa Rica, Venezuela, Uruguay, Argentina and Brazil), overall effective debt reduction has been less than 6 per cent of the countries' debts. Only Costa Rica has received an effective reduction of more than 7 per cent (its debt has been reduced by 21 per cent) and Venezuela actually faces higher debt service payments over the long term, since its repayments on Brady bonds are fixed at rates higher than current global interest rates.

Debt-for-equity swaps, which have gone on outside the remit of the Brady Plan and are often linked to privatization programmes, have had a larger impact, according to Woodward, cutting about a quarter off the total debt of Argentina and Chile between 1984 and 1992. These two countries have accounted for more than half of all debt-for-equity swaps worldwide, and Mexico and Brazil for a further quarter. However this has been achieved only at the cost of the governments losing national control over large parts of the 'family silver' built up under import substitution.

Despite its limited impact on debt service payments, the Brady Plan has been a turning point in terms of investor confidence. A Brady Plan deal has come to be seen, like an IMF Stand-by Arrangement, as a bill of good economic health, opening the door to foreign investment, which has played a dominant role in the region's recovery since 1990. After squeezing nearly $220bn out of Latin America from 1982–90, the international capital markets suddenly began pouring money into the region, and by 1991 the capital tide had turned (see Figure 3.2). Debt service payments came to $31bn that year, but capital inflows more than doubled in one year to reach $38bn, leaving a net inflow of $7bn. The net inflow then rose to $31bn in 1992 and $32bn in 1993, before falling back to $21bn in 1994.[32]

Stock markets have sprung up around the continent to absorb the incoming dollars, turning extraordinary profits and becoming an essential part of international fund managers' portfolios – a titillating, high-risk/high-profit addition to their more sober investments at home. In the pages of *The Economist*, the most lucrative areas of the Third World and Eastern Europe have been renamed 'emerging markets', with an entire page devoted to weekly stock market reports from Buenos Aires to Bangkok.

The new El Dorado
Everyone smokes in the Mexican stock exchange, a beautiful new twenty-storey mirror-glass building shaped like a Stanley knife, cutting into the smog of downtown Mexico City. On a roundabout in the street below, a grimy statue of some Aztec emperor cuts a forlorn figure, marooned in the traffic. Inside, away from the glare of the sun, the disciples of the New Order rush to and fro; well-groomed men shouting orders to shoulder-padded, stiletto-wearing, peroxided women. On the trading floor, green VDUs are the only colour to break the grey and silver monochrome of business suits and stainless-steel fittings. Young men's voices shout out offers, echoing in the vast glass-domed chamber.

Efraín Caro is the Exchange's Director of International Affairs. He is 33, but looks younger. On the wall of his office a *Wall Street Journal* cartoon shows an executive being told by his boss, 'It has come to my attention that you're not under enough stress.' Next week, Efraín is hosting a world-wide conference for representatives from 60 stock markets – he has stress to spare. Chain-smoking, grabbing phones, shouting out orders to even younger subordinates, he spares ten minutes to rattle off figures in perfect English, albeit a largely unintelligible brand of investment-babble. The Mexican stock market is booming with a total of $22bn in foreign investment, 80 per cent of it raised on Wall Street. Today's papers carry vital news from the presidential campaign going on in the US, 'Clinton says yes to NAFTA'; Efraín believes that will ensure that the dollars keep coming.

Mexico has been the main beneficiary of Latin America's spectacular and sudden infusion of capital, which rose from a regional $10bn in 1989 to over six times that amount three years later.[33] The long-awaited dollars no longer come from the western banks who had lent with such abandon in the run-up to the debt crisis, but from a variety of other private sources. One is foreign direct investment, usually by transnational companies, which recovered from a low point of less than $3bn in 1986 to reach an estimated $15bn in 1994.[34]

Another new source is 'portfolio investment' of the kind courted by Efraín Caro, which began to enter the region in 1989 and by 1991 had overtaken direct investment as a source of capital, bringing in just under $12bn that year. Of that figure, $7.5bn went to Mexico and a further $3.8bn to Brazil.[35] Portfolio investment broadly consists of stocks and shares in private (and privatized) companies, government bonds and all the other financial paraphernalia which flit to and fro on the international financial markets, bought and sold by private investors and fund managers in the First World. Trading in shares in the largest Latin American companies now takes place on Wall Street, while an increasing number of specialist investment funds head south to Latin America's booming stock markets, clutching northern savings in search of lucrative investments.

One such is Singer and Friedlander's 'Aztec Fund', launched in 1994 with glossy brochures promising painless profits (along with the usual caveat that 'You may not get back the amount you originally invest'), and a free, and evidently low-budget, video in which a series of uncomfortable-looking young fund managers sing the praises of the silent revolution in capitals from Santiago to Mexico City. The language is standard marketese − franchises, market shares and profit growth; the delivery astonishingly wooden. A pot-bellied chief executive appears at the end to praise the 'all-pervading level of optimism you find at every level of society' in the new Latin America and to conclude, in a 'Greed is good' vein, by urging on the investors, 'Now is the time to buy'.[36] In naming the fund, perhaps the PR people overlooked the Aztecs' customary treatment of their victims, but the name proved unexpectedly apposite. Almost as soon as the fund was launched, Latin America's stock markets went into a nosedive, following the assassination of the favourite in Mexico's presidential campaign. Portfolio investment in Latin America fell to $5bn in 1994.[37]

One of the fastest-growing sources of capital has been government bonds, sold abroad by the larger Latin American countries. Income from bonds shot up from less than $1bn in 1989 to $24bn in 1993[38], before falling back to $17bn in 1994.[39] Again, the big countries take the lion's share; Mexico, Brazil and Argentina accounted for 85 per cent of bond sales,[40] leaving the rest of Latin America with the crumbs. One by-product of the bond boom has been a sharp rise in the total external debt, which includes bonds from both governments and private companies, but excludes stocks and shares. After staying roughly level at around $420bn from 1987 to 1989, the total debt began to rise again, reaching $534bn in 1994.[41] Despite the plaudits accorded to the impact of the Brady Plan and the shift to direct and portfolio investment as the chief source of foreign capital, debt service payments continue at around $30bn a year, although they now weigh less heavily on the expanding regional economy. Booming exports mean that the debt service ratio of debt repayments to export income has fallen steadily from a peak of 39 per cent in 1982–83 to just 19 per cent by 1994.[42]

Although the new influx of foreign investment has been greeted with fanfares in the world's financial press, it has barely taken up the slack left by the collapse of public investment caused by the debt crisis and structural adjustment. While up on previous years, gross domestic investment for 1992 came to only $209bn,[43] roughly equal to investment in 1981, the last year before the 'lost decade' began (and the population had risen by 83 million in the intervening years). Far higher investment rates than this will be needed to undo the social and physical damage left by a decade of neglect. Moreover, these will have to involve a higher proportion of local capital if they are to avoid the pitfalls of over-dependence on foreign investment.

Privatization

In the 1990s, Latin America has come to resemble a giant fire sale, as government after government sells off dozens, if not hundreds, of state-owned enterprises. As the chair of one large transnational corporation told his fellow business magnates at an IDB conference on Latin America's 'New Economic Climate', 'The race for Latin America has started and the latecomers will lose out.'[44] From 1989 to 1992 the two keenest privatizers – Argentina and Mexico – sold off 173 state companies for $32.5bn in cash and debt relief.[45] As at any fire sale, there are numerous bargains to be snapped up by the wily dealer, and the wave of privatizations has prompted a veritable feeding frenzy among foreign investors and transnational companies. The scale of the sell-off can best be judged by leafing through the pages of the *Financial Times*, where in a kind of international investors' gossip column, paid advertisements announce the value of the latest completed deals, along with the names of buyers and fixers. In just three days in July 1993, these included:

20 July
Madeco, a Chilean timber firm. Sold for 3,937,500 American Depositary Shares @ $15 each. Two-thirds of the shares sold in the US.

20 July
MASISA, another Chilean timber firm. Sold for 3,875,000 American Depositary Shares @ $14.125.

21 July
'The Republic of Argentina has sold a 59 per cent interest in Hidroeléctrica Alicurá SA to a consortium formed by Southern Electric International and the Bemberg Group for an aggregate consideration of US$315,641,771'.

22 July
The Argentine government raises $2.66bn in the form of 140 million shares in the state oil company, YPF. 'Joint Global Coordinators' for the sale were Merrill Lynch & Co and CS First Boston Group; 65 million shares were sold in the US and 35 million in Argentina, the rest elsewhere. This was a big sale, meriting a full page with all the big names: Salomon Brothers, The First Boston Corp, Credit Suisse, Deutsche Bank, Baring Brothers.

22 July
In Argentina, Hidroeléctrica Cerros Colorados SA sold to Dominion Energy Inc and SACEIF Louis Dreyfus y Cía Ltd for $146,213,232.

The pressures on governments to privatize seems irresistible. The growing fiscal crisis of the state sector, provoked by both foreign and domestic debt payments, has forced governments to increase revenue or cut expenditure; privatization achieves both, shedding loss-making companies while raising substantial amounts of cash. In Argentina, President Carlos Menem's selling spree raised $9.8bn in cash, and enabled the government to lop a further $15.6bn off its foreign debt between 1989 and 1993 as transnational corporations bought up debt paper and swapped it for a stake in the newly privatized companies.[46] In Mexico, the family silver raised a total of $13.7bn in 1990–91, during which time privatization receipts provided just under a tenth of government revenues.[47]

Privatization is also part of the broader ideological shift, since neo-liberals believe in cutting back the state and passing ever-larger chunks of the economy over to the private sector. Once privatized, they argue, management will be able to take decisions based on economic efficiency rather than politics and a company's performance is bound to improve.

The rhetoric employed is the same as in Mrs Thatcher's Britain, the only country to surpass the large Latin American economies in its privatizing zeal. In Latin America, privatization also provides a juicy carrot with which to attract foreign investment back into the region after the capital famine of the debt crisis. Transnational corporations are expected to introduce capital and new technology into a region starved of both. Overshadowing the internal debate over privatization lies the brooding presence of the international financial institutions, especially the World Bank, which increasingly makes such sell-offs a condition for its loans.

Although Chile pioneered privatization during the Pinochet years in the 1970s, its efforts were dwarfed by Mexico's programme in the early 1990s. The greatest prizes were Telmex, the state telecommunications company, which raised $4bn, and the 12 state banks, which jointly brought in a further $10bn. The Telmex sale and subsequent large privatizations included flotations on the New York Stock Exchange, and became Mexico's 'ticket to the world capital markets' according to the head of Mexico's privatization unit.[48] Following Mexico's example, Argentina's Carlos Menem sought to privatize just about every state company between 1990 and 1993. In the first two years, privatization revenues covered a fifth of government spending.[49]

State airlines and telecommunications companies have gone on the block throughout the region, but so far only Argentina has allowed its rush to market to sweep away the state oil company, YPF. Elsewhere, governments have been reluctant to hand over such strategic or highly profitable companies, preferring instead to encourage joint ventures with transnational corporations to attract technology and investment while retaining some degree of overall control.

The track record of privatizations has varied enormously. One analysis of the telecommunications sector[50] concluded that while there has been a significant improvement in the quality of services, 'in virtually all cases' there has been much less progress in bringing down extortionate charges for installing new lines and international calls. In Argentina call charges rose 60 per cent after privatization, leading to accusations that privatization was merely turning a shoddy public service into an improved but exclusive service for the better-off. The improvements have failed to convince everyone of the merits of privatization; one opinion poll revealed that 25 per cent of the Mexican public feel that the directors of the Telmex company, privatized in 1991, should be thrown in jail, and one in five Mexicans believe that it should be re-nationalized.[51]

The telecommunications sector, however, is unusually suited to privatization in that it requires constant injections of rapidly-advancing technology. Moreover, the state companies had long since given up the chase, partly due to the freezing of public investment in the early years of the debt crisis. In Argentina in the early 1980s, houses and flats were advertised for sale or rent 'with telephone' – a major selling point, since the waiting time for a new telephone line to be installed could be several years. In Venezuela's pre-privatization system, 80 per cent of international calls and 70 per cent of domestic calls simply failed to get through.[52]

Other areas of the economy seem to benefit far less from privatization than the high-tech telecoms sector. In 1990 the Argentine government awarded contracts to resurface and repair nearly 10,000 km of roads. 'Nine months later', reported the *Miami Herald*, 'most concessionaires have done little more than erect tollbooths'. The paper continued:

> *Other routes have seen even more startling abuses. Contractors in control of a road leading to a popular beach resort sparked protests by building earthen barriers across alternative routes in order to force motorists to pass through their pay booths. And after travelers complained about the rip-off along another highway, contractors parked a fleet of phony squad cars at tollbooths to give the appearance of police backing.*[53]

In many sell-offs, governments desperate for cash merely transform public monopolies into virtually unregulated private monopolies, which promptly raise prices to consumers and make enormous profits. Telmex's profits shot up 77 per cent to $2.3bn in the year after privatization.[54] If all this sounds familiar to British readers, it is hardly surprising. British consultants fresh from the experience of *Thatcherismo* back home have been highly sought after as advisers to privatizing Latin American governments.

One of the most criticized sell-offs has been that of the Argentine airline, Aerolíneas Argentinas, to Spain's Iberia. The new-look airline got off to a bad start when it tried to sack a third of its employees, provoking weeks of strikes and demonstrations. At the height of the unrest less than half of its aircraft flew on time.[55] But customers risked more than an irritating delay; shortly after its privatization Aerolíneas scored an international public relations disaster when 65 passengers reported symptoms of cholera (one died) after taking one of its flights to California.[56] The privatized airline ran up losses of $500m in its first three years in the private sector.[57]

Critics of the privatization process argue that governments have missed the chance to divide up giant companies and introduce competition, and have been lax in regulating the newly-privatized companies. Privatization programmes are, however, extremely good news for the local business class with the capital (often through joint ventures with foreign companies) to snap up the bargains. Mexico's stock of billionaires rose from 2 to 24 during the privatizing presidency of Carlos Salinas de Gortari (1988–94), all of them with close ties to the ruling Institutional Revolutionary Party (PRI).[58] In another echo of the British experience, Chile's pioneering privatizers in the 1970s operated a highly questionable revolving door system, moving from government posts in which they oversaw the privatizations to top jobs in the big conglomerates who cashed in on the sell-offs.[59]

Inflation

By disposing of loss-making companies and pulling in one-off windfalls, the privatization bonanza has played a crucial part in curbing governments' spending deficits and getting inflation down in many Latin American countries in the early 1990s. Inflation in the region as a whole peaked at around 1200 per cent in 1989 and 1990,[60] largely as a result of the collapse of the heterodox programmes in Argentina, Brazil and Peru. Since then, privatizations, further government cut-backs in spending and investment and improved tax collection have all helped to get fiscal deficits down. Furthermore, privatization and the Brady Plan deals have contributed to the general rehabilitation of Latin America in the eyes of the world's investors. The capital inflow took off in 1991, allowing governments to cover their deficits in a non-inflationary manner by borrowing abroad, rather than printing money. Excluding Brazil, which continued its hyper-inflationary ways until late 1994, average regional inflation fell to 49 per cent in 1991, then declined steadily to an estimated 1994 figure of 16 per cent.[61] By 1993 no country apart from Brazil had inflation over 55 per cent;[62] this may be still high by northern standards, but it represents a massive improvement on the late 1980s.

For some countries, the renewed capital influx has also helped to ease the pain (and political costs) of economic stabilization. In the first years of the 1980s, stabilizing countries had both to reduce inflation and generate a massive trade surplus with which to keep up their debt service. The only means to achieve this double objective was to inflict a huge recession at home.

Since the late 1980s, there has been another option, as foreign capital has come to provide a cushion against the worst effects of adjustment. Latecomers to stabilization, such as Argentina's Carlos Menem have found themselves able to get inflation under control without the same degree of austerity, by using capital inflows to keep up debt repayments. Large capital inflows have also led to overvalued currencies, which help suppress inflation by holding down import prices. The cost of this strategy is a loss of export competitiveness and ensuing trade deficit, but this too can be covered by capital inflows, as long as they last.

The effects have been spectacular: Argentina's inflation fell from 4923 per cent in 1989 to 18 per cent three years later,[63] and within months of the adjustment package, the economy moved smoothly into four years of record-breaking growth – over 6 per cent in every year from 1991 to 1994.[64] Nevertheless, the Mexican crash of early 1995 (see p. 85) seemed to mark the end of this 'easy option' of foreign investment-driven stabilization, heralding a return to the more painful, recessionary methods of the early 1980s.

Latin American governments desperate for foreign capital and technology go to enormous lengths to outbid their rivals. David Mulford, George Bush's Undersecretary of the Treasury for International Affairs chose a questionable metaphor to describe their lot: 'The countries that do not make themselves more attractive will not get investors' attention. This is like a girl trying to get a boyfriend. She has to go out, have her hair done up, wear make-up.'[65] Besides the privatization programme, Latin America's 'make-up' includes perks such as tax exemptions for incoming investors, easing restrictions on profit remittances, reducing all kinds of red tape and establishing special export processing zones along the lines of Mexico's *maquiladoras*. Governments have also watered down labour legislation and gone out of their way to ensure a compliant labour force for foreign companies.

Can the private sector adapt?

For Latin America's private sector, adjustment has been like a hurricane, sweeping away the old certainties of import substitution, when local companies could rely on the state for protection from outside competition, allowing them to fix prices and skimp on investment. Since 1982, privatization has greatly expanded the size and importance of the private sector while trade liberalization has bankrupted thousands of companies. The survivors have been forced to play by the new rules of the game, investing in new technology and improving productivity to remain competitive. One of the most ferocious industrial shake-outs has been in Mexico, where trade liberalization had a seismic impact even before NAFTA came into force:

> *Only birdsong disturbs the silence inside the La Josefina textile factory in the village of Panzacola in the central Mexican state of Tlaxcala. Yards of white cotton cloth still hang from its lines of looms, stopped in mid-weave when the factory shut a year ago and its 100 workers were laid off. The nameplates on the machines explain what happened. They are from a bygone Lancashire: the cast iron looms were made more than a century ago by John M. Summer of Manchester, J. Dugdale & Sons of Blackburn and*

*G. Keighly of Burnley. The spinning machines came from Dobson &
Barlow Ltd, Bolton, in 1912, and the carding equipment from Platt Bros
of Oldham in 1920.*

*Since 1881, La Josefina had made yarn and cotton cloth for the Mexican
market. It closed because its machines, though still in perfect working
order, could not compete with modern, electronically controlled rivals. In
the past five years, Mexico has become one of the world's most open
economies, scrapping import licences and slashing its maximum external
tariff from 100 per cent to 20 per cent. Consumers have benefited from
low priced imports, but many businesses are struggling. 'Yarn came in
from India, Korea and Taiwan at half the price we sold at,' Valentín
Rangel, La Josefina's administrator, says. 'We were caught out, technologically backward and without the capital to renew our machinery.' La
Josefina is one of thousands of Mexican companies that have fallen victim
to a savagely swift process of economic change.*[66]

Bankruptcy is commonest among small and medium-sized firms who
cannot afford to invest in the necessary improvements when local interest rates are sky high as part of the adjustment process. Larger companies
and transnational subsidiaries can borrow abroad at lower interest rates
and find it easier to compete.

Companies which can adapt to the new environment stand to benefit
from pro-business government policies, improved access to foreign
investment and technology and more opportunities to export their products. Sometimes the benefits outweigh the costs; in Monterrey, Mexico's
industrial heartland, the manufacturers' association lost 3730 members
from 1987 to 1992, but 4976 new firms joined. The impact on jobs was
roughly neutral. Some of the biggest Monterrey companies, such as the
glass manufacturer Vitro and the cement producer Cemex, are well on
the way to becoming Latin America's first genuine transnationals, buying
up US companies to ensure they have a commanding position within the
North American market under NAFTA.[67]

In Mexico, many of the success stories have been in services, rather
than manufacturing. The largest national retailer, Cifra, has seen profits
boom since it went into a joint venture with the US chain, Wal-Mart,
and other large Mexican chain stores have rapidly followed suit.[68]

Almost without exception, successful companies have had to sack large
parts of their workforce in the drive for greater productivity, but such
'rationalization' is not sufficient to ensure competitivity. Labour costs in
Colombia's textile industry are about four times those of Pakistan and
China, so firms have to compete on the basis of quality. The Coltejer
company is one of the survivors from a shake-out which in 1993 saw 5000

jobs go in Medellín's cloth mills. It kept its position as industry leader by cutting its workforce from 8900 to 7200 over a few months, investing $32m in new machinery and cutting its range of 4000 product lines in half. It has now won a contract to supply Wal-Mart jeans for the US market.[69]

Some of the most successful companies have also adopted more modern management methods. At the Brazilian company of Acesita, privatized in 1992, management sacked a quarter of the workforce, then turned years of heavy losses into growing turnover and profits by abolishing time clocks, improving training and cutting three out of seven management layers as well as looking for a more specialist, high-profit market niche and investing heavily in new technology. Those who kept their jobs have seen real wages rise by 11 per cent.[70]

The silent revolution has introduced many broad policy changes which have helped business back into profit. Peru's largest private company is the US-owned Southern Peru Copper Corporation, producing two-thirds of the country's copper output. Prior to adjustment, according to its president, Charles Preble, the mining industry was used as a 'milch-cow' to fund the state; SPCC calculates that almost half of its total sales went in taxes. In 1990 Alberto Fujimori took office and introduced a shock adjustment programme, with immediate benefits to SPCC. Import tariffs and taxes were reduced and tighter restrictions on the right to strike introduced. By mid-1993 about 95 per cent of company employees had signed individual 'labour peace' agreements with the company, giving them bonuses in return for rejecting strike action. SPCC has also been snapping up companies under Fujimori's privatization programme.[71]

In many cases, however, the hype which surrounds the best-known success stories conceals a widespread failure by the private sector to cope with the speed and depth of change. Five years after Carlos Menem began his adjustment programme in Argentina, according to the *Financial Times*, 'There has been no great burst of entrepreneurial energy, no investment boom, no management revolution, no aggressive pursuit of exports.' Most Argentine businesses continue to huddle behind dwindling protectionist barriers, investing in sectors that are still sheltered from import competition such as services, privatized utilities or industry's few remaining protected sectors such as cars.[72]

Trade

As the end of the 1980s approached, Latin America's exports finally started to respond to trade liberalization. In Brazil and Argentina, the collapse of heterodox reflation freed up goods for export, while in Chile and Mexico, the new export-or-die philosophy has started to pay off.

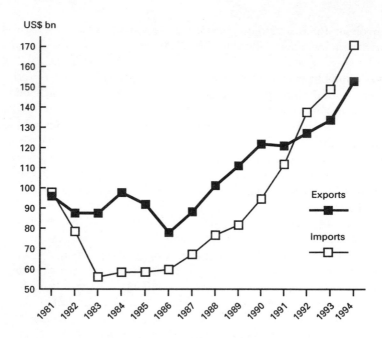

Figure 3.4: Latin America and the Caribbean: Merchandise trade, 1981–94

Source: CEPAL, *Balance Preliminar de la Economía de América Latina y el Caribe* (Santiago, various years).

Yet although Latin America's exports doubled from $78bn in 1986 to $153bn in 1994,[73] they have failed to keep pace with the explosion in imports which has followed trade liberalization and the reappearance of overvalued exchange rates. Imports almost trebled from $60bn to $171bn over the same period, turning a large trade surplus into a $18bn deficit,[74] financed by the renewed influx of capital. The main culprit was Mexico, which in 1994 ran a huge trade deficit of $24bn.[75] The main beneficiary has been the US, which in seven years managed to double its exports to the region to a 1993 figure of $80bn.[76]

As the free trade orthodoxy has spread, countries have scrambled to sign free trade agreements as guarantees, however flimsy, against resurgent First World protectionism. Mexico joined GATT in 1986 and went on in 1992 to sign a North American Free Trade Agreement with the US and Canada. Bolivia, Costa Rica, El Salvador, Guatemala, Paraguay and Venezuela all joined GATT in the early 1990s.[77] Regional free trade agreements have also sprung up, such as Mercosur in the southern cone, involving Brazil, Argentina, Uruguay and Paraguay. The spread of such free trade agreements is described in Chapter 6.

Variations between countries

The blanket term 'neo-liberalism' conceals numerous differences between the different countries in the region, in terms of both policy and macro-economic performance. These are spelt out in more detail in Appendix A. No one country has implemented the full neo-liberal recipe. Several supposedly exemplary neo-liberal regimes have clung on to lucrative and strategically important state enterprises in copper (Chile) and oil (Mexico, Venezuela).

Elsewhere, political opposition has forced governments to abandon or water down their privatization programmes (Uruguay, Colombia, Brazil, Bolivia, Nicaragua, Ecuador). Several of the most successful countries have mixed orthodox neo-liberal adjustment with heterodox government controls; Mexico set wages and prices in its successful adjustment programme, while both Mexico and Argentina have deliberately kept the exchange rate overvalued in order to bring down inflation.

Up until mid-1994 Brazil appeared to be bucking the regional trend, opting for an apparently haphazard blend of cautious trade liberalization with minimal internal adjustment to the role of the state or the other domestic elements of the usual neo-liberal recipe. The *Real* plan of July 1994 and the subsequent election of Fernando Henrique Cardoso appeared to promise some kind of domestic stabilization and adjustment programme, but the incoming president faced powerful political obstacles in his bid to rewrite the constitution, an essential step in reducing the role of the Brazilian state and centralizing power in central government.

One of the region's economic success stories, Colombia, has been notably more cautious over trade liberalization than the more zealous free marketeers in Argentina, Peru, Chile or Costa Rica. Revealing comparisons can be made between Chile and Colombia – the region's two most successful economies from 1982 to 1994. Under both General Pinochet and President Aylwin, Chile implemented almost the full neo-liberal programme, while the Colombian government pursued a far more cautious form of deregulation, eschewing the latest economic fashions just as it had in refusing to become over-indebted during the 1970s. Chile's abrupt changes of policy under General Pinochet produced the region's wildest booms and busts, while Colombia experienced a decade of sustained, if unspectacular, growth as its Latin American neighbours were disintegrating around it. The benefits to the poor of economic stability showed as Colombia became one of the few countries where inequality (as well as the number of people below the poverty line) fell over the course of the decade. This little-known side of Colombia contrasts with its international notoriety as the country of drug barons, civil war, routine human rights abuses and the world's highest murder rate.

In some countries, stabilization laid the basis for several years of strong growth (Chile, Argentina, Costa Rica, Uruguay), while in others reform got inflation under control, but left the economy struggling to recover (Nicaragua, Dominican Republic, Guatemala). In most cases, however, the record is distinctly mixed, as countries veer between good and bad years, with no clear long-term growth pattern emerging (Mexico, Bolivia, Jamaica, Venezuela, Peru, Honduras).

At the outset of the whole adjustment experience, reducing inflation was one of the IMF's declared aims in the region. By 1995, the Fund could point to success, after 13 years of drawn-out adjustment. Brazil was the last country to grapple with inflation, which in May 1994 was running at close to the hyper-inflation watershed of 50 per cent a month. In July, then Finance Minister Fernando Henrique Cardoso launched the *Real* plan, named after a new currency, the fifth since 1986. The plan got inflation down to 1.5 per cent a month by the time of the presidential elections, which Cardoso duly won by a landslide. Supporters hoped that his political skills would enable President Cardoso to make the stabilization stick, unlike previous 'shock programmes' which have temporarily curbed inflation only for it to rebound to higher levels than before.

By 1995 countries which had gone through hyper-inflationary bouts in the 1980s such as Argentina, Bolivia and Nicaragua had all got inflation down into single figures, while Peru's ferocious 'Fujishock' adjustment programme (named after its president, Alberto Fujimori) had reduced inflation down to around 18 per cent in 1994 from its 7600 per cent peak of 1990.[78] While never having matched such inflation horror-stories as Nicaragua's 33,547.6 per cent (at that level the '.6' corresponds to just 9 hours of inflation) in 1988, Mexico had also got its figure down from 160 per cent in 1987 to just 7 per cent in 1994.[79] Other countries, including Colombia, Ecuador, Jamaica, Uruguay and Venezuela, have preferred to tolerate double-digit inflation levels, rather than risk using over-valued exchange rates or a recession to get them down.

Export performance, one of the key long-term aims of neo-liberal adjustment, has also varied enormously (see Chapter 6). By the end of 1994, Chile, Colombia, Costa Rica, Brazil, Mexico and Panama had all more than doubled their 1980 export income, (Paraguay had tripled it), but several countries, notably Venezuela and Bolivia, were still exporting less than before the debt crisis.

The two largest economies, Brazil and Mexico, have been the most successful in reducing the burden of their enormous foreign debts. As a percentage of their exports, Mexico's debt service fell from 32 per cent in 1979–81 to 24 per cent in 1994, while Brazil's ratio fell from 36 per cent to 22 per cent over the same period.[80] Chile, Paraguay and Costa Rica have also reduced their debt service ratios to single figures. However the ratio in several countries actually increased over the same period, notably in Peru, Venezuela and several Central American countries.

By 1993 Latin America's gross domestic investment, the greatest casualty of the debt crisis, had still not regained its 1980 value. Even the countries with the highest rates of investment, Peru, Chile and Colombia, were still well short of the levels achieved by newly-emerging Asian economies such as Indonesia or Thailand.[81] Brazil was the most seriously affected country, with total investment falling from $81bn in 1980 to $68bn in 1992.[82] Peru, Argentina, Mexico, Venezuela and Bolivia were some of the worst hit in the 1980s, but have showed the strongest recovery in investment in the early years of the 1990s. In terms of foreign investment, Mexico has emerged from the 1980s as the star performer, with a share of the regional total rising from 36 per cent in 1980 to 65 per cent in 1991, before falling back to 46 per cent in 1992.[83] The economic Darwinism of the market has ensured that the larger economies absorb a disproportionate amount of the incoming capital, with the top six (Mexico, Brazil, Venezuela, Argentina, Colombia and Chile) taking up 95 per cent of the inflow.[84] Little is left for the smaller (and poorer) countries of the region, which still go through the motions. In 1994, even Nicaragua hopefully announced it was opening a stock market, but its chances of competing with São Paulo or Mexico City seem minimal.

Latin America in 1995

Neo-liberalism prefers to think and act in terms of macro-economic variables like growth and inflation, paying little attention to other issues such as income distribution, quality of life, or job security. It is therefore to be expected that the silent revolution is more likely to register success at the macro-economic level than in the lives of the poor. Even so, the macro-economic record of 13 years of stabilization and adjustment is decidedly mixed.

The one single, unmitigated success has probably been getting the region's inflation under control, albeit after IMF-style measures had *increased* inflation in the early 1980s. Low inflation is good for business and good for the poor, and conquering it is, by any standards, a triumph.

While the region's gross domestic product has grown by some 25 per cent since 1981, in per capita terms this has been cancelled out by population growth. Latin Americans have gone through a recession and a recovery which has got them back to where they started. The record on investment is even more discouraging, for gross domestic investment in real terms has barely recovered its pre-crisis levels, and must now cope with a larger population and the accumulated decay of the region's infrastructure after a decade-long investment slump.

The record on the region's foreign debt is also mixed. Despite 13 years of debt rescheduling and other measures, the region's total debt has now surpassed half a trillion dollars ($500bn), more than double its level at the start of the debt crisis, while the burden of the debt on the region's economy, measured by the level of debt service payments relative to export earnings, is now only a few percentage points lower than in the late 1970s.[85] Furthermore the debt is more diverse than in the 1970s, both in terms of the kind of debt, and the type of creditor, which should make the region less vulnerable to a re-run of the debt crisis.

While exports have risen by half compared to 1980, Latin America can hardly claim to be showing the dynamic, export-led growth which is the long-term goal of the reforms of the last 13 years. The region is still falling behind in the world league, and is now saddled with a growing trade deficit, in large part the result of the neo-liberals' insistence on import liberalization.

Reform has rehabilitated the region in the eyes of foreign investors, but Latin America's extreme dependence on foreign capital has always been a mixed blessing and the current availability of easy money on the world's capital markets could well divert governments from trying to chart a path of long-term development based on the region's own resources.

In the end, however, the only just way to judge neo-liberalism's impact on the region is through its impact on the lives of ordinary Latin Americans, a topic largely ignored by most coverage of the issue. It is to these 'silences of the revolution' that we now turn.

Postscript: fragile miracle – the Mexican economic crisis of early 1995

At the end of 1994, the Mexican economy went into crisis, marking the end of a disastrous first year for the new, post-NAFTA Mexico of *los perfumados*, the perfumed boys, as the stars of Mexico's technocratic élite are known.

The immediate origins of the crisis lay more in political hubris than economics. When US interest rates started to rise in early 1994, investors rapidly lost their appetite for Mexican bonds, preferring to invest at home. Mexico, with its mighty $23bn trade deficit, was faced with a foreign exchange shortage, which should have forced a devaluation.

But devaluation is anathema to any politician's machismo, especially in an election year. Moreover, in his last year in office, President Salinas wanted to go down in history as the hero of NAFTA and structural adjustment, not as a devaluer. He needed such credentials if he was to become the first head of the new World Trade Organisation, as both he and the US government planned.

Rather than devalue, Salinas chose to use Mexico's reserves to prop up the peso. By December, he had squandered $22bn, leaving only $7bn in the kitty for his successor, Ernesto Zedillo.[86] Prior to taking office, Zedillo had twice begged Salinas to devalue, but had been rebuffed.[87] Zedillo bit the bullet and attempted a controlled devaluation, but investor panic broke out and a run on the peso ensued. The speed with which the money men fled the Mexican economy was startling, prompting IMF Managing Director Michel Camdessus to describe it as 'the first major crisis of our new world of globalised financial markets'.[88] With the state coffers all but empty, the new president was powerless to prevent the peso's exchange rate falling by 40 per cent.

As foreign investors rushed to off-load Mexican stocks and bonds, a far greater menace threatened; another Mexican default on a par with the 1982 crash. More than in any other economy, the Mexican government had become dependent for its financing on selling short-term bonds, known as *tesobonos*. $7bn of these bonds were set to fall due for repayment in the first two months of 1995, more than Mexico's remaining international reserves.[89] A default was possible, raising the spectre of huge losses among *tesobono* buyers on Wall Street.

The impending collapse of its NAFTA partner and its likely impact on US investors forced Washington to put together an unprecedented $50bn international rescue package, including $20bn from President Clinton's discretionary funds, and $17.8bn from the IMF (more than three times larger than any previous IMF loan).

Behind Washington's immediate concerns lay a more long-term fear, according to US Treasury Secretary Robert Rubin. 'The effect [of a Mexican default] would be considerable both on immediate capital flows and, perhaps more important, on the mindset of politicians considering whether to reform.'[90] If the neo-liberal flagship sank with all hands in Mexico, the silent revolution's unquestioned dominance would be likely to crumble.

The crisis exposed the fragility of the neo-liberal model, based on indiscriminate trade and investment liberalization, yet instead of prompting a search for alternatives, the immediate effect of the Mexican crisis was to force Mexico to swallow more of the same, reverting to the painful brand of adjustment of the 1980s. In return for its bail-out, Mexico was forced to promise renewed recession and austerity; holding down wages well below inflation, increasing taxes, cutting back on investment plans, and raising interest rates ever-higher to lure back wary foreign investment. The impact was immediate, a rash of bankruptcies, a threatened banking crash, and an abrupt plunge into recession. By March 1995, the labour minister was forecasting half a million job losses over the next three months.[91]

The crisis also increased pressure on Zedillo to privatize the remaining state companies running the railways, ports, electricity generation and above all, the last great prize to escape privatisation – the oil industry.

Like the devaluation of 1982, the 1995 crash will, however, be good news for US companies in the *maquiladora* belt, who saw their dollar wage bill cut in half overnight. President Zedillo immediately went touting for new customers, telling *Newsweek* magazine, 'With the new exchange rate, investment profitability, especially in exports – has increased significantly.'[92] By February 1995, booming exports and a sharp fall in imports had produced Mexico's first monthly trade surplus since 1990.

The impact on the Latin American economy stretches well beyond Mexico. Stock markets in Buenos Aires and Sao Paulo tumbled (as did those in Bangkok and Budapest). Now that much of the glitter has gone from 'emerging markets', Latin American governments will have to pay higher rates of interest on their bonds to lure in foreign capital which has suddenly rediscovered that investing in the South can be a risky business. Interest rate hikes immediately made themselves felt in Argentina and Brazil, with a rash of company bankruptcies and signs of a serious banking collapse as banks saw their number of bad loans rise.

The Mexican crisis spelt the end of the relatively painless form of adjustment practised in Mexico, Argentina and Cardoso's Brazil, using an overvalued exchange rate to hold down inflation. Such programmes have little future if foreign investment cannot be found to plug the resulting trade deficit.

The shock waves spread well beyond Latin America, as investors' fears over US involvement in bailing out Mexico prompted a run on the dollar and a period of worldwide currency turmoil which strengthened calls for some kind of global regulation of international financial markets.

The Mexican crisis is, in essence, a repeat of the debt crisis of the early 1980s. A return to the kind of frenetic and indiscriminate borrowing last seen in the 1970s 'dance of the millions' has ended abruptly in another crash. This time, however, the population had already suffered 13 years of adjustment. The $50bn will go to keep capital markets and investors happy, and in return the Mexican people will be put through another round of austerity. Furthermore, should other economies go the way of Mexico's, the US is highly unlikely to go as far in preventing a collapse. After 13 years of neo-liberal adjustment, the prospects for Latin America's economy look far from healthy.

Notes

1 Speech by British Foreign Minister Douglas Hurd MP (London Chamber of Commerce, 26 May 1993).

2 Alan Riding, *Mexico: Inside the Volcano* (London, 1985), p.156.

3 Walter Wriston, cited in Joseph Kraft, *The Mexican Rescue* (New York, 1984), p.40.

4 IDB, *Economic and Social Progress in Latin America 1983 Report* (Washington, DC, 1983), p.115.

5 CEPAL, *Balance Preliminar de la Economía de América Latina y el Caribe 1989* (Santiago, December 1989), p.19.

6 *Latinamerica Press* (Lima), 2 July 1987, p.3.

7 Victor Bulmer-Thomas, *The Economic History of Latin America Since Independence* (Cambridge, 1994), p.373.

8 CEPAL, *Balance Preliminar de la Economía de América Latina y el Caribe 1993* (Santiago, December 1993), p.47.

9 IDB, *Economic and Social Progress in Latin America 1990 Report* (Washington, DC, 1990), p.303.

10 Bulmer-Thomas, *op. cit.*, p.373.

11 Quoted in Morris Miller, *Debt and the Environment: Converging Crises* (New York, 1991).

12 Bulmer-Thomas, *op. cit.*, p.382.

13 Jackie Roddick, *The Dance of the Millions: Latin America and the Debt Crisis* (London, 1988), p.45.

14 IDB, *Economic and Social Progress in Latin America 1984 Report* (Washington, DC, 1984), p.188.

15 CEPAL, *Balance Preliminar de la Economía de América Latina y el Caribe 1988* (Santiago, December 1988), p.17.

16 CEPAL, *Balance Preliminar de la Economía de América Latina y el Caribe 1987 & 1993* (Santiago).

17 IDB, *Economic and Social Progress in Latin America 1990 Report* (Washington, DC, 1990), p.297.

18 *Ibid.*, p.267.

19 Patricio Meller (ed.), *The Latin American Development Debate: Neostructuralism, Neomonetarism and Adjustment Processes* (Boulder, CO, 1991), p.80.

20 Bulmer-Thomas, *op. cit.*, p.394.

21 *Ibid.*

22 CEPAL, *Balance Preliminar de la Economía de América Latina y el Caribe 1989* (Santiago, December 1989), p.20.

23 IDB, *Economic and Social Progress in Latin America 1985 Report* (Washington, DC, 1985), p.211.

24 CEPAL, *Balance Preliminar de la Economía de América Latina y el Caribe 1988* (Santiago, December 1988), p.17.

25 IDB, *Economic and Social Progress in Latin America 1987 Report* (Washington, DC, 1987), p.247.

26 CEPAL, *Balance Preliminar de la Economía de América Latina y el Caribe 1991* (Santiago, December 1991), p.38.

27 *Ibid.*

28 IDB, *Economic and Social Progress in Latin America 1988 Report* (Washington, DC, 1988), p.29.

29 IDB, *Economic and Social Progress in Latin America 1991 Report* (Washington, DC, 1991) p.275.

30 CEPAL, *Balance Preliminar de la Economía de América Latina y el Caribe 1991* (Santiago, December 1991), p.38.

31 David Woodward, *Latin American Debt: An Assessment of Recent Developments and Prospects* (mimeo) (Study for Oxfam, Oxford, 18 July 1994).

32 CEPAL, *Balance Preliminar de la Economía de América Latina y el Caribe 1994* (Santiago, December 1994), p.54.

33 *Ibid.*, p.47.

34 ECLAC, *Economic Survey of Latin America and the Caribbean 1992, Vol. I* (Santiago, 1994), p.261. and *Financial Times* (London), 21 December 1994.

35 IDB, *Economic and Social Progress in Latin America 1993 Report* (Washington, DC, 1993), p.294.

36 Aztec Fund brochure and video, Singer and Friedlander Investment Funds (London, 1994).

37 *Financial Times* (London), 21 December 1994.

38 Stephanie Griffith-Jones, *European Private Flows to Latin America: The Facts and Issues* (mimeo) (London, 1994), p.4.

39 *Financial Times* (London), 21 December 1994.

40 CEPAL, *Balance Preliminar de la Economía de América Latina y el Caribe 1993* (Santiago, December 1993), p.25.

41 CEPAL, *Panorama Económico de América Latina 1994* (Santiago, September 1994), p.10. and *Financial Times* (London), 21 December 1994.

42 CEPAL, *Balance Preliminar de la Economía de América Latina y el Caribe 1994* (Santiago, December 1994), p.58.

43 IDB, *Economic and Social Progress in Latin America 1993 Report* (Washington, DC, 1993), p.265.

44 David de Pury, Co-Chairman of Asia Brown Boveri Group, in IDB, *Latin America: The New Economic Climate* (Washington, DC, 1992), p.68.

45 ECLAC, *Economic Survey 1992, op. cit.*, p.285.

46 West Merchant Bank, *Investment Review* (London, August 1994).

47 Robert Devlin, 'Privatisations and Social welfare', in *Cepal Review* No. 49 (Santiago, 1993), p.159.

48 Latin American Finance supplement, *Financial Times* (London), 6 April 1992, p.5.

49 Devlin, *op. cit.*, p.160.

50 Latin American Newsletters, *Special Report*, (London, October 1993).

51 *Ibid.*

52 *Ibid.*

53 *Miami Herald*, 3 March 1991, quoted in David Martin, *In the Public Interest? Privatisation and Public Sector Reform* (London, 1993), p.121.

54 *Financial Times* (London), 6 April 1992.

55 *Financial Times* (London), 7 December 1993.

56 *Independent on Sunday* (London), 23 February 1992.

57 Latin America Monitor, *Southern Cone* (London, March 1994), p.4.

58 *Newsweek* (New York), 8 August 1994, p.34.

59 Pamela Constable and Arturo Valenzuela, *A Nation of Enemies: Chile Under Pinochet* (New York, 1991), p.191.

60 CEPAL, *Balance Preliminar de la Economía de América Latina y el Caribe 1993* (Santiago, December 1993), p.33.

61 CEPAL, *Panorama Económico de América Latina 1994* (Santiago, September 1994), p.5.

62 *Ibid.*, p.12.

63 CEPAL, *Balance Preliminar de la Economía de América Latina y el Caribe 1993* (Santiago, December 1993), p.35.

64 CEPAL, *Panorama Económico de América Latina 1994, op. cit.*, p.18.

65 Quoted in John Cavanagh and John Gershman, 'Free Trade Fiasco', in *The Progressive* (Madison, WI, February 1992), p.32.

66 Michael Reid, *The Guardian* (London), 3 July 1992.

67 *The Economist* (London), 27 June 1992.

68 *Financial Times* (London), 19 January 1993).

69 *The Economist* (London), 12 March 1994.

70 *The Economist* (London), 5 November 1994.

71 *Financial Times* (London), 29 September 1993.

72 *Financial Times* (London), 13 July 1994.

73 CEPAL, *Balance Preliminar de la Economía de América Latina y el Caribe 1994* (Santiago, December 1994), p.39.

74 *Ibid.* p.39.

75 *Ibid.*, p.52.

76 *Financial Times* (London), 11 April 1994, p.5.

77 *Understanding Global Issues* (Cheltenham, February 1994), p.11.

78 CEPAL, *Balance Preliminar de la Economía de América Latina y el Caribe 1994* (Santiago, December 1994), p.43.

79 *Ibid.*, p.43.

80 *Ibid.*, p.50.

81 *The Economist* (London), 12 November 1994.

82 IDB, *Economic and Social Progress in Latin America 1993 Report* (Washington, DC, 1993), p.265. and *1990 Report*, p.267.

83 IDB, *Economic and Social Progress in Latin America 1993 Report* (Washington, DC, 1993), p.293. and *1990 Report*, p.296.

84 IDB, *Economic and Social Progress in Latin America 1993 Report* (Washington, DC, 1993), p.293.

85 CEPAL, *Balance Preliminar de la Economía de América Latina y el Caribe 1994* (Santiago, December 1994), p.58.

86 *The Economist* (London), 7 January 1995, p.43.

87 *Financial Times* (London), 27 January 1995.

88 *Financial Times* (London), 16 February 1995.

89 Latin America Monitor, *Mexico* (London), February 1995, p.4.

90 *Financial Times* (London), 16 February 1995.

91 *Financial Times* (London), 14 March 1995.

92 *Newsweek* (New York), 10 April 1995.

CHAPTER 4

Silences of the Revolution

The Human and Environmental Costs of Adjustment

The tiny adobe house is crammed with gnarled *pailliris* (mining women) in patched shawls and battered felt hats, whose calloused hands work breaking up rocks on the surface in search of scraps of tin ore. Outside, the scene is one of high-altitude poverty, all greys and browns in the thin air. The paths between the miners' huts are strewn with plastic bags and human excrement, dried black in the unforgiving *altiplano* sun. Rising beyond the squalid settlement, the barren hills and grey slag-heaps of the tin mines complete the bleak panorama. The litany of poor women's woes begins, gathering momentum as it goes:

Before, it was not too bad, but now we never have a good month. We're mainly widows or abandoned. My husband left to look for work and never came back. Now I have to look after four kids — I can't pay for their schoolbooks and clothes. I've been doing this work for seven years now and my lungs are finished. I've vomited blood for weeks at a time and still had to keep working.

In the old days, women used to stay at home because the men had work. Now, with the recession, we've had to go out to work. Many of our children have been abandoned. Their fathers have left and there's no love left in us when we get home late from work. We leave food for them, they play in the streets — there are always accidents, and no doctors. I feel like a slave in my own country — we get up at 4am and at 11 at night we are still mending and patching.

The speaker, Josefina Muruchi, breaks down in a coughing fit. Suddenly, in a mixture of Spanish and Quechua, all the other women burst into speech, unleashing a torrent of pain and suffering. In the gloom, most of the women are sobbing.

This is doloroso for us. We have nothing. Nothing. Only coca [a stimulant leaf chewed to suppress hunger] to keep us going. It's the children, we want them to study, but they're so malnourished and the price of tin is so

low. Our kids say, 'Mami, I want to help' and don't do their homework,
but then they fail their exams and have to repeat the year and the teachers
are always asking for money and we haven't got it and because our chil-
dren are so ashamed they drop out of school. If I start vomiting blood
again, what's going to happen to my children?

This is life below the poverty line, a daily round of pain and exhaustion which seems far removed from the dry exchange of statistics which
dominates debate outside the continent on the social cost of the silent
revolution. Although the desolation in the women's faces can be seen in
shanty towns and rural villages up and down the continent, it is especially
prevalent in Bolivia, where according to the government, over 80 per
cent of households lived below the poverty line by 1991 (defined as the
income below which a family cannot satisfy a number of basic needs such
as food, clothing, adequate housing, health services and education).[1] The
same survey showed that half Bolivia's households were 'indigent', with
an income that could not even feed the family, let alone meet its other
needs. In dollar terms, the Latin American poverty line stands at an
income per individual of roughly $60 a month, while indigence occurs at
half that figure.[2]

Throughout the region, after decades in which the percentage of Latin
Americans living in poverty had been falling (though not their actual
number), poverty is once again on the rise. By 1993, CEPAL reported
that the 1980s had seen 60 million new names join the grim roll call
of the poor, leaving 46 per cent of the population, nearly 200 million
people,[3] living in poverty. Almost half of them were indigent, barely
existing on an income of less than a dollar a day.

Shrinking wages, rising prices for food and other essentials, increased
unemployment or 'under-employment' and collapsing government services. The human cost has mounted inexorably throughout the silent
revolution, exacting a toll of hunger, disease and despair. According to
the director of the UN's International Fund for Agricultural
Development, 'chronic and persistent hunger' weakens and kills 40,000
people a day. Some 55 million people suffer from undernourishment in
the region, while the mortality rate due to 'chronic non-infectious dis-
eases' typical of malnutrition, has doubled in the past few years.[4]
Neglected sewage and water systems, victims of the investment collapse
of the 1980s, played an important role in allowing cholera to return to
the continent in 1991 after a gap of over 60 years. By the end of 1993,
nearly a million people had been infected, of whom 8793 had died.[5]
Malaria and tuberculosis are also making a comeback in the new,
structurally-adjusted Latin America.

While Latin America is not as poor as Africa or parts of Asia, it leads the world in inequality, and since 1982, inequality has got worse. The World Bank concludes that in the 1980s, 'The wealthy were better able to protect themselves from the impact of the recession than were the poor.'[6] *The Economist* puts it more bluntly, commenting that 'Stabilisation and structural adjustment have brought magnificent returns to the rich.'[7] One study of a group of countries for the period from 1980 to 1986 shows that the top 5 per cent of the population actually got richer, even during the worst years of the debt crisis, while the bottom 75 per cent lost income.[8] The poor got poorer, and the rich really did get richer, especially the very rich: according to *Forbes* magazine, the number of Latin American billionaires rose from six in 1987 to 42 in 1994.[9]

Since the mid-1980s, the picture has become more mixed, as the level of inequality has fallen in the urban areas of Chile, Colombia, and Costa Rica, while continuing to worsen in Argentina, Mexico, Guatemala and Panama. Even in the cases where inequality has fallen in recent years, income distribution in the early 1990s remained considerably more skewed than in the years preceding the debt crisis.[10] Colombia is one of the few countries where inequality fell throughout the 1980s. It is probably no coincidence that Colombia is also one of the few countries which has not had to turn to the IMF. Even there, however, a belated adjustment has increased both urban poverty and inequality since the start of the 1990s.[11]

Some of the more zealous neo-liberals argue that inequality is a necessary evil, providing workers and managers alike with the incentive to work hard and generate economic growth. One, Samuel Morley, concludes: 'Rising inequality is the short-run cost that society must pay for the long-run improvement in the well being of the poor.'[12] Such arguments conveniently ignore the extraordinary track record of the South East Asian economies, where Taiwan, for example, has one of the most impressive growth records in the world over the last 30 years, yet also enjoys the world's fairest distribution of income.[13] Most observers agree that the extreme levels of inequality occurring in Latin America are an obstacle to development, depressing the domestic market and generating political instability and repression in the continuing war between the haves and the have-nots.

And there *is* enough money to go round. Latin American inequality is on such a scale that a comparatively minor move towards a fairer distribution of income could eradicate poverty overnight, according to the World Bank's 1990 *World Development Report*: 'Raising all the poor in the continent to just above the poverty line would cost only 0.7 per cent of regional GDP – the approximate equivalent of a 2 per cent income tax on the wealthiest fifth of the population.'[14]

Top of Latin America's inequality league table comes Brazil, the second most unequal nation on earth, where the richest 20 per cent of the population earn more than 32 times the income of the poorest 20 per cent (by comparison, the figures for the US and Britain are 8.9 and 6.8 respectively).[15] Brazil has been scathingly re-christened 'Belindia' – a hybrid where the middle class enjoy the European lifestyle of a Belgium, surrounded by the impoverished masses of an India. Mexico has also gained ground rapidly in the inequality stakes since structural adjustment accelerated in the late 1980s.

Poverty and inequality may have blighted millions of lives since 1982, but if you believe the World Bank, structural adjustment bears no trace of blame. On the contrary, 'Without adjustment, the condition of the poor would undoubtedly have been worse,' the Bank claims.[16] Other voices within the world of the international financial institutions are far less gung-ho. Most notable is the InterAmerican Development Bank, which in 1993 concluded:

> There is growing doubt as to whether macro-economic policy can move from adjustment to growth, whether reforming the trade regime can move from removing distortions to stimulating dynamic export growth, and whether private sector reforms will increase output and employment sufficiently to meet the wider social goals of social equity, political participation and environmental balance.[17]

Unfortunately, there is no scientifically watertight means of proving whether the World Bank is right or not. Economists are faced with several unsatisfactory options: they can compare a country's economy after adjustment with its condition before adjustment began, but that ignores changes in the world economy in the meantime. They can compare a country's performance with that of countries that have not adjusted, but factors other than adjustment can cloud the issue. They can compare a country's performance with its own or the international financial institutions' stated targets, but the targets may well have been unrealistic in the first place.

The World Bank's response has been to spend a good deal of time and effort on the largely futile exercise of exploring counterfactuals, otherwise known as the 'what if' question. If Latin America had not adjusted, would things be better or worse? The problem with this approach is that one must first come up with a model of what Latin America would have done instead of adjusting, then compare the likely outcomes with and without adjustment. The discussion rapidly becomes so hypothetical that it sheds little light, and various counterfactual studies have come to diametrically opposed conclusions.[18] In any case, given that the continent was in a state of economic collapse in 1982, continuing the *status quo ante* was not an option. Moreover, as the chief purveyor of structural adjustment policies to the Third World, the World Bank is hardly a disinterested party and is highly unlikely to conclude that things would have been *better* without adjustment.

Back in real life, the link between neo-liberalism and Latin America's increased poverty and inequality can be all too obvious. In Bolivia the redundancy notices issued to thousands of factory workers since the government began its structural adjustment with the infamous 'Decree 21060' make their neo-liberal origins brutally clear: 'The Company has found it necessary to rationalise the workforce,' goes the notice to Richard Ardaya, a trade union activist, from his employers at the La Modelo textile plant, 'Therefore with recourse to Article 55 of Decree 21060 of 1985, I regret to inform you that your services are no longer required.' The headed notepaper is bordered with the logos of La Modelo's fashionable customers: Pierre Cardin, Playboy and Van Heusen.

In other cases, however, the connection is less direct and harder to prove or disentangle from all the other influences on Latin America's economy – international commodity prices, the end of commercial bank lending to the region after 1982, world recession, international interest rates and domestic influences such as political instability and the effectiveness (or otherwise) of government. The suffering in Bolivia's tin mines is a good example; critics blame it on structural adjustment, yet the government's supporters point out, with considerable justification, that it would be unfair to blame adjustment for the collapse in world tin prices that occurred just two months after decree 21060 was issued.

Organizations such as the British development agencies Christian Aid and Oxfam, which work on a daily basis with Latin America's poor, are in no doubt about the connection. Christian Aid believes that 'Throughout the third world … Structural Adjustment Programmes spell hardship for people in every aspect of their lives – health, education, work, culture.'[19]

One way to try and reach some firmer ground beyond the war of words is to look at adjustment's impact on each of the main elements which determine the daily fate of poor Latin Americans. There are many ways that economic changes can affect people's quality of life: incomes, taxes, working conditions, prices, state services, the impact on home life and the family, and the broader impact on the environment. Adjustment and stabilization measures have a profound influence on all of them.

A living wage

The rural poor sometimes have a plot of land on which to grow food, but the urban poor have few assets beyond their labour, so their well-being depends to a large extent on what they can earn. According to the UN's CEPAL, the main causes of increasing poverty and inequality have been the 'massive decline in real wages ... the rise in unemployment and ... the number of people employed in very low-productivity jobs.'[20]

Structural adjustment affects wages in numerous ways. There is an undeniable link between macro-economic performance and wages. If the economy is shrinking, people lose their jobs and wages fall. The recession unleashed by stabilization programmes in the early 1980s led to a sudden deterioration in living standards. From the mid-1980s open unemployment began to fall in most countries and growth resumed in some, but wages have only risen in a few cases, as the changes to the labour market wrought by structural adjustment have taken a further toll on wage levels. From 1980 to 1990 real wages fell in Venezuela and Argentina by 53 per cent and 26 per cent respectively.[21]

Government cutbacks have led to numerous redundancies, but their main impact has been a sharp fall in wages among remaining public employees, the sector worst hit by adjustment. Public-sector pay packets shrank by 24 per cent in Costa Rica (1981–88)[22] and 56 per cent in Venezuela (1981–90).[23] Many of those worst affected are middle-class, thousands of whom end up joining the ranks of the 'new poor' created by adjustment policies. Johny López is a gentle, middle-aged Bolivian. He and his wife are professional teachers, but their prestigious occupation became a torment under structural adjustment.

> *Things got bad with the hyper-inflation in the 1980s, then decree 21060 came and it got worse. The price of food went up, wages did not. By 1986 we were each earning about £30 a month, and half of that would go in fares to get into town once a week to buy supplies. I gave up teaching in 1986 and have worked as a street vendor ever since.*[24]

At a regional level, from 1980 to 1986, wages fell faster for those with more than nine years of schooling than for any other sector of the work-force,[25] and many professionals were forced to take second or even third jobs to make ends meet.

Adjustment policies have sought to 'flexibilize' labour. In practice, this has meant cracking down on trade unions and making it easier for managers to hire and fire employees, shift to part-time work and to cut costs by subcontracting work to smaller companies, often little more than sweatshops. The proportion of the workforce employed by large companies fell from 44 per cent to 32 per cent between 1980 and 1990,[26] the slack being taken up by a boom in small companies and the informal sector, where wages are generally lower. In Chile, the neo-liberal tiger, a labour force once accustomed to secure, unionised jobs has been turned into a nation of anxious individualists. According to a recent World Health Organisation survey, over half of all visits to Chile's public health system involve psychological ailments, mainly depression.[27] 'The repression isn't physical any more, it's economic – feeding your family, educating your child,' says María Peña, who works in a fishmeal factory in Concepción. 'I feel real anxiety about the future', she adds, 'They can chuck us out at any time. You can't think five years ahead. If you've got money you can get an education and health care; money is everything here now.'[28] In Argentina such changes mean that having a job is no longer enough to stave off hunger. By the early 1990s, 23 per cent of wage-earners in the manufacturing sector were living below the poverty line, whereas before the debt crisis a job in a factory virtually guaranteed a pay packet big enough to keep a family out of poverty.[29]

Stronger growth since 1990 has led to a faltering recovery in countries like Chile and Mexico (at least until the return to recession and austerity in Mexico in 1995), but wages have continued to fall in Argentina and Brazil. By 1994, average real wages in Peru, a late entry to the neo-liberal game, were down to just 47 per cent of their 1980 value, while they had still not recovered their 1980 value in Argentina, Mexico, or Costa Rica[30] – the very countries whose adjustments were being lauded by the international financial community as neo-liberal triumphs. Furthermore, Argentina's unemployment had risen from 6 per cent in late 1991 to 10.8 per cent by mid-1994.[31] Like Britain, much of Latin America is experiencing the phenomenon of jobless growth. According to delegates at a meeting in 1994 of the Latin American Economic System (SELA), unemployment grew by 3 per cent a year in Latin America during the 1990–93 period of renewed growth.[32] The recovery in the Latin American economy is in danger of bypassing its citizens.

Despite the evidence of the human costs of its push for labour 'flexibilization', the World Bank has made it one of the lynchpins of its poverty relief programme since 1990. The Bank believes that labour must be made more flexible to increase productivity and attract investment for the kind of labour-intensive industry that import substitution never managed to create. Since jobs are the main source of income for the poor, the argument goes, labour deregulation will relieve poverty, at least in the long term. It seems a particularly twisted form of economic logic to argue that the poor's pay packet must be forced down and their working conditions deteriorate in order to reduce their poverty.

The Bank's view is whole-heartedly shared by some of Latin

America's leading neo-liberals. By 1995, from Argentina to Mexico, the new generation of technocrats were banking on further labour market deregulation to generate growth and jobs. In Argentina the economy minister Domingo Cavallo, architect of the country's adjustment, told the *Financial Times* that he put the country's rising unemployment rate down to 'the complexity ... and high costs associated with labour norms'. He went on to promise reforms to make hiring and firing easier, to reduce the role of collective bargaining and to amend legislation on compensation for accidents at work.[33]

Incomes for non wage-earners have also taken a battering at the hands of adjustment. Government cutbacks have whittled away at Latin America's already paltry welfare system, as the elderly in particular have seen state pensions dwindle in value. In 1991 Argentina's president, Carlos Menem, decided to stop indexing pension payments to inflation, which reached 84 per cent that year. By late 1994, 70 per cent of Argentina's pensioners, some 2.2 million elderly people, were stuck on the poverty line earning the minimum pension of $150 a month.[34] As the real value of pensions fell, protests erupted. 'OAPs riot' ran one headline, as a dozen people were wounded in clashes between pensioners and riot police.[35] Pensioners also took to the courts, filing an astonishing 350,000 individual cases by late 1994. Of these, 100,000 had already been settled in the pensioners' favour, pending appeals, throwing the future of the government's austerity policies into doubt.[36]

Taxes

The tax system is important in determining what portion of income actually reaches the home as well as how much the government has to spend on social services. Since the late 1980s, tax reform has also gained increasing importance as a means of balancing government budgets and curbing inflation. However, some of the resulting changes in the tax regime have penalized the poor.

On the positive side, as part of their adjustment programme, several countries have improved their level of income tax collection either by closing loopholes (Mexico, Argentina) or in some instances (Chile 1990, Colombia 1992) by increasing taxation rates.[37] Most countries, however, have switched away from income taxes (already among the lowest in the world, since the Latin American élite has always been violently averse to parting with its wealth) towards greater emphasis on sales taxes. Governments argue that this is easier to collect, especially where in some cases over half the workforce are in the informal sector and therefore are not registered to pay taxes.

In the 1980s, the average top rate of personal income tax in Latin

America fell from 48 per cent to 35 per cent, and the average rate of corporate tax from 43 per cent to 36 per cent. Bolivia, darling of the neo-liberals, has effectively abolished both.[38] Sales taxes, on the other hand, have boomed. In Argentina revenues from value-added tax (VAT) rose from 0.6 per cent of GDP in 1989 to over 9 per cent by the end of 1992.[39] However, sales taxes are usually regressive, costing the poor more than the rich, since they spend a larger proportion of their income on buying goods and services.

Credit

Since the neo-liberal understanding of the economy is essentially monetarist, it believes that cutting the amount of money circulating in the economy is the best means of curbing inflation. Removing money from the economy means reducing credit, which has largely been achieved by imposing high interest rates to make borrowing more expensive. The result has been a collapse in demand for credit and a deep recession in many countries, as local industry has suddenly found it impossibly expensive to take out loans for investment.

When many economies returned to growth in the late 1980s, they often relied for their success on continued inflows of foreign capital, which had to be lured in by offering appetisingly high interest rates. The squeeze on borrowers has continued, as only the largest firms have been able to borrow abroad at lower interest rates. Since the late 1980s, privatization has also done away with numerous state banks, some of which targeted at least some of their credit to small and medium-sized farmers and small businesses in the towns. Experience shows that, left to their own instincts, Latin America's private banks prefer to lend to big business. Just as millions of people have been joining the informal sector, they have seen their attempt at self-help crippled by the scarcity of credit.

As inflows of capital fell away in 1995, in the wake of the Mexico crisis, governments in Argentina, Brazil and Mexico were forced to raise interest rates ever higher in a desperate attempt to reverse the trend. The result was a rash of bankruptcies, as firms were unable to repay their loans, and the growing danger of a banking crash, obliging the governments in all three countries to intervene to bail out endangered banks. A survey in Mexico revealed that over half the country's small and medium businesses believed they could be forced into bankruptcy by the end of 1995, largely due to the rocketing interest burden.[40]

Prices

Inflation has been aptly described as 'a tax on the poor'. In a high inflation economy, the better-off usually find ways to defend their incomes from its erosive effects by investing their money in index-linked bank accounts or turning it into dollars. The poor have no such options, and for them, the fall in inflation in the early 1990s was neo-liberalism's single greatest achievement.

However, they had to wait nearly a decade to reap the reward, for under adjustment Latin America first saw its inflation levels rise until the end of the 1980s (barring a short fall caused by the heterodox experiments of 1984-87), before they fell back again after 1990.

Adjustment has also seen the end of government subsidies and price controls on many basic foods and fuel. This has created both winners and losers, since peasant farmers can now charge higher prices for their food crops, but the urban poor have been especially hard-hit. The sudden removal of fuel subsidies, and the subsequent increase in public transport fares, has been one of the commonest causes of anti-IMF rioting in the region, notably in Venezuela in 1989 (see Table 7.1, p. 167). Most governments have replaced general subsidies with attempts to 'target' subsidies at the poorest. Although the neo-liberal argument (that general subsidies are a waste of money and often end up subsidizing the wealthy middle-class consumer) is at first sight convincing, talk of targeting is in practice often little more than a smokescreen for government cuts, while the logistical difficulties of identifying the poor and getting subsidies to them often mean that many slip through the extremely tattered safety net. When Jamaica replaced a general subsidy with a targeted subsidy, it managed to reach only 49 per cent of those identified as the target group. Those it reached were much better off than under the general subsidy, but the remainder were faced with a jump in food prices and no help from the state.[41]

Trade liberalization has been one positive development for the urban poor, bringing cheaper food imports. Removing protective tariffs on imports often means lower prices and higher quality for the consumer. Often, however, the main beneficiaries of this kind of economic integration are the middleclass, from buyers of computers to those in need of a Big Mac or state-of-the-art disposable nappies.

The combined impact of changes to prices and the labour market under adjustment has shifted poverty away from the rural to urban areas. From 1980 to 1990 the number of poor Latin Americans in rural areas increased from 73 million to 80 million, but was overtaken for the first time by the battalions of the urban poor, which jumped from 63 million people to 116 million.[42]

State services
The health centre in Argentina's Ciudad Oculta is in a sorry state.

Occupying the ground floor of an abandoned 14-floor hospital, the walls are running with damp. In the dark corridors ragged men and women, many of them with the Indian features of migrant workers from Paraguay or Bolivia, hold their snot-nosed babies and wait in a depressed silence, punctuated by the coughing of the children. On the walls a hand-written sign says, 'The social workers have stopped working because there are no wages. We won't work until it's been sorted out.' The notice is dated March 1990; the newly elected president Carlos Menem's 'economic miracle' is in its first flush.

Despite the pressures on public spending in the wake of the debt crisis, over the region as a whole, health indicators such as infant mortality have continued to improve, though at a slower rate than in previous years. According to CEPAL, however, the overall improvement conceals numerous 'situations where the tragedy of poverty continues to be felt with extraordinary force'.[43] Such cases include the spread of malaria and cholera in recent years. CEPAL puts continued improvements down to the spread of low-cost, effective technology such as vaccinations. These helped counteract the fall in wages and rising poverty which took place under adjustment.

Decent education and health care are two of the most effective ways of lifting people out of poverty, and from the late 1980s onwards, the World Bank and other institutions began to urge Latin American governments to increase spending on health and education, the areas of social spending which most affect the poor.

The World Bank's conversion to the cause of increased social spending looks like a remarkable U-turn. Figures for the share of government spending devoted to education and health between 1981 and 1989 show that the heaviest cuts fell precisely in those countries defined by the World Bank as 'intensively adjusting'. All of them cut health expenditure, and only one failed to cut spending on education. In part, this was because the intensively adjusting countries also saw the sharpest rise in interest payments on the governments' domestic debts, which doubled to an average of 40 per cent of total government spending over the period. As one analyst concluded, 'The evidence bears out the view of the international financial institutions as efficient debt collectors.'[44]

An extreme example occurred in Peru, where in August 1990 the newly-elected President Alberto Fujimori unleashed a particularly radical adjustment programme which became known as 'Fujishock'. Educational spending which in 1980 had averaged $62.50 per student fell to just $19.80, according to Ministry of Education figures. Teachers' wages fell to a quarter of their former value, leading to a mass exodus from the profession,[45] while 30 per cent of registered students dropped out, as children left school to supplement dwindling family incomes.[46]

Across the region, spending per child fell by 28 per cent during the 1980s, while lack of resources, family pressures and inadequate teaching gave Latin America the highest repetition rates in the world.[47]

Since 1990, the pressure from the Bank, coupled with the growing realization that cutting social spending undermines the region's prospects for growth, has begun to lead to policy changes. After the cuts of the 1980s, all the intensively adjusting countries have increased spending on health, and all but Brazil have increased their education budgets.[48] However, by 1992 the improvements had still to make up the lost ground. In the period 1981–92, taken as a percentage of Gross National Product (GNP, equivalent to GDP corrected for the net flow of capital into or out of the country), spending on health and education fell in seven countries and rose in only five.[49] Since per capita GNP was also falling, the net effect was a substantial decline in real per capita expenditure on health and education.

But total spending is only part of the story. The impact of public spending on the lives of the poor also depends on how the money is spent. Primary education is far more effective in improving their prospects than universities which they hardly ever attend. The evidence here is that the poor have benefited from changes in education spending which have placed more priority on primary education, but that there has been a deterioration in their slice of health sector expenditure in all the intensively adjusting countries.[50] Cuts in health spending are all the more painful since the social impact of adjustment has simultaneously undermined people's health. In Lima, the 1990 Fujishock programme led to a 30 per cent fall in the average protein intake between July and November.[51]

Many governments have followed in the footsteps of Mrs Thatcher and General Pinochet, encouraging the middle classes to 'opt out' of the crumbling state system and put their money into the burgeoning private education and health care sectors. The shiniest new buildings in Santiago's current construction boom are invariably banks or private hospitals. The World Bank concluded that, 'By targeting the richest segments of Chilean society, the [new health insurance funds] impoverished the rest of the social insurance system ... They have "skimmed" the population for good risks, leaving the public sector to care for the sick and the elderly.'[52] Chile's move to a two-tier health care system has exacerbated Pinochet's legacy of social inequality. A study for Chile's Ministry of Health in 1993 showed that infant mortality is 7 per 1000 births for the richest fifth of the population, and 40 per 1000 for the poorest 20 per cent, the Chilean underclass.[53]

Although the Bank is pushing for increased government spending, it has also pressed governments to improve 'cost recovery', its euphemism for introducing charges for what used to be free health and education services. Carmen, a sad-faced grandmother from a poor quarter of Mexico City, has seen the collapse of the public health system from close up. 'They operated on my husband six months ago. He'd paid social security all his life, but they told him he had to buy his medicine privately and provide two litres of blood – my son had to give it. All they give you is penicillin for everything – it's the magic ingredient!'[54] In Nicaragua the adjustment programme introduced by Violeta Chamorro in 1990–91 has hit the health budget so severely that individual health centres have only been able to stay open by introducing charges, even though it has not yet become official government policy. The volume of drugs bought by the health service has fallen to just an eighth of its 1989 figure, forcing patients to buy their own medicines.[55] The inevitable effect is to make health care impossibly expensive for large numbers of poor Nicaraguans. In return for agreeing a three-year loan in April 1994, the IMF turned the screw, forcing the government to promise to freeze health spending at nominal levels, allowing it to be further eroded by inflation.[56]

Studies of educational attainment in the region point to a number of alarming developments since the early 1980s. Although educational standards across the population have continued to rise, partly due to the expansion of educational provision in the two previous decades, signs began to emerge in the late 1980s of a growing number of children falling behind in their studies or dropping out altogether.[57] The likely causes are the dilapidated state of the educational system and low teacher morale, combined with the growing crisis in the family and pressure on children to go out to work. Inequality in educational achievement has also increased, partly as a result of the boom in private schools. In 1990, one out of every two poor children in Brazil's cities was behind in their education, compared to only one out of every ten of the richest 25 per cent of society.[58] The lack of a decent education system is ensuring that the region's inequalities will be passed on from generation to generation.

Young people who have acquired a full education leave school to find that the only jobs available are worse paid and more insecure than in their parents' time. As an exhausted mother in a Chilean shanty town commented, 'Why should kids read Neruda or go to the theatre if they're just going to end up picking oranges?'[59] One CEPAL study concluded that in the 1990s, 'For the young people of Latin America ... expectations are being increasingly thwarted.'[60]

Safety nets

Another element in the international financial institutions' growing attention to poverty alleviation since the late 1980s has been the use of special compensatory programmes, aimed at softening the impact of adjustment by extending the new vogue of 'targeting' to job creation, community improvements and other areas. The most prominent examples to date have been in Mexico, Bolivia and Chile. A study by the International Labour Organisation of the Bolivian and Chilean cases concluded that 'although social funds have been able to take the sting out of the hardships of adjustment', they have mostly benefited 'only a small number of people', and that, like targeted food subsidies, such programmes often provide a public relations smokescreen for wider cuts in government spending.[61]

Home and family

At the eye of the social and economic storm unleashed by the silent revolution lies the family. Home is where future generations are born, grow up and become citizens; it can be a sanctuary in troubled times, or a torment, or sometimes both. The central figure in the Latin American family is the mother. Traditionally, her main role may have been childbearing, childrearing and housework, but economic and social change has added new tasks to her workload. Women form an increasing percentage of the workforce, rising from 22 per cent in 1980 to 38 per cent by 1990.[62] Many of the new, low-waged or part-time jobs generated by adjustment go to women, while many men have lost their role as family breadwinner as full-time waged jobs disappear, or wages fall so far that a single income becomes insufficient to feed a family.

On top of this 'double day' of work and running the home, the deterioration of social services, especially in urban areas, has forced women into a third role, taking responsibility for running their communities, fighting or substituting for inadequate state services in schools, health, drainage, water supply, or roads.

Adjustment has made all these tasks more vital to the family's survival and more exhausting: 'flexibilization' often means lower wages, longer hours and greater insecurity, just as cuts in state subsidies have brought steep price rises in basics like food and public transport. Television has become accessible to most poor homes in the region's shanty towns. In a cruel widening of the 'frustration gap', the number of TVs per thousand homes rose by 40 per cent in the 1980s and real wages fell by the same amount.[63] Teenagers, out of work or out of school, or fed up with dead-end jobs, are taunted by the racy lifestyles they see on the daily diet of imported US TV shows or local soap operas. They want Reeboks and Ray-Bans and on a good day they get rice and beans. Losing their jobs and status as breadwinners, men turn to alcohol and rage, while grown-up children have neither the money nor the opportunity to leave home. Houses have filled with frustrated, hungry people and the results are predictable: family breakdown, alcoholism, domestic violence, drug abuse and crime spread through the region, creating a state of near panic and social disintegration. In the slums of Brazil the fear of street crime is such that most people support the 'social cleansing' of the death squads who make their nightly cull of street children.

A study by Caroline Moser offers a unique glimpse of how adjustment and the debt crisis affected the women of one poor community in Guayaquil, Ecuador's largest city.[64] From 1978 to 1988, Moser regularly visited and studied the community of Indio Guayas, an area of swamp-land shanty town which in 1978 had about 3000 residents. She was therefore able to take a series of socio-economic snapshots of the community as the Ecuadorean government adopted eight different stabiliza-tion/adjustment packages between 1982 and 1988. Her findings are a microcosm of the human cost of adjustment, above all on women.

Women's jobs

The proportion of women in work rose from 40 per cent to 52 per cent over the period, most of the increase being in the informal sector or domestic work. Women identified rising prices and the increased cost of sending their children to school as the main reasons for going out to work. Wages for domestic workers fell by a third over the period. Whereas women had cleaned or laundered for one or sometimes two families in 1978, ten years later they were forced to work for at least two families, working as long as 60 hours a week, just to keep earning at the same level. Many of those interviewed had to leave the house at 6 am to travel across the city to their jobs, only returning home at 8 or 9 pm. Women were also forced to go out to work when their children were younger than before, often having no choice but to leave small children locked up in the home while they were away.

Men's jobs

The number of men with fixed-term contracts fell, as more and more were forced to find work on a day-by-day basis. Many men were also forced to leave home to find work on the shrimp farms which became one of Ecuador's prime export sectors during the 1980s.

Households

The number of homes with only one wage-earner fell from 49 per cent to 34 per cent over the period, while the number with three or more members in work rose from 19 per cent to 32 per cent. The number of households headed by women rose from 12 per cent to 19 per cent, often as a result of men leaving to work on the shrimp farms and never coming back. There was an increase in the number of married sons and daughters still living with their parents despite starting families of their own.

Consumption

Successive adjustment packages led to large price rises and falling real incomes. By July 1988, those families who could still afford milk had cut their consumption from 4.6 litres a week to 1.4. People ate fish less than two times a week instead of three and drank powdered fruit drink instead of fresh fruit juice. At first, families ate smaller meals, then cut out supper, then cut out breakfast. By 1988, a quarter of households ate only one meal a day, and 79 per cent of the children attending the local health centre showed some degree of malnutrition. Women fed themselves last and least, and many were suffering from anaemia.

Self-help

Women had taken the lead in organizing schemes such as a savings club to help pay for school fees and new clothes at Christmas. They had also set up a scheme whereby forty families paid weekly quotas into a rotating fund used exclusively for buying housing materials.

Education

Although state schools were technically 'free', a number of fees were imposed on parents during the course of the decade. By 1988, the cost of keeping a child at school, including a uniform, books and bus fares, came to between one and two minimum salaries.

Housework

Despite women's growing role outside the home, men took on no new housework. Instead, as mothers were forced to leave home for longer and longer periods to earn a living, they got up at 4 am or 5 am to cook food for the family to eat during the day. As eldest daughters reached 10 or 11 years old, they were expected to take over cooking and housework, neglecting their school homework and falling behind the boys in their studies. Instead of getting more rest, women simply worked longer hours once their daughters had freed them from some of the housework.

Children

With mothers out all day, the rate of truancy among children increased. Mothers were also not present to ensure a fair distribution of food, so the smallest children often lost out to their hungry elder brothers and sisters.

One of the greatest concerns expressed by women forced out to work was that they could no longer keep an eye on their sons, who were increasingly prone to drop out of school, get involved in street gangs, and start taking drugs. During the research, the community's first-ever suicide occurred; a young male cocaine addict killed himself in despair after an argument with his wife about using their money to pay for his habit instead of feeding their three small children.

Domestic violence

Almost half the women said that there had been an increase in domestic violence. Trouble nearly always started when the women had to ask the men for more money – men either grew angry and ashamed at not earning enough to feed the family, or wanted to spend what they had on themselves. However, adjustment also worked in the other direction. One in five women reported an improvement, putting it down to their increased independence once they had been forced to go out to work.

Moser found that women reacted in three different ways to the impact of adjustment on their lives. About 30 per cent of the women were coping, juggling the competing demands of their three roles in the workplace, home and community. They were more likely to be in stable relationships with partners who had steady jobs. Another group, about 15 per cent of the women, were simply 'burnt out', no longer able to be superwomen 24 hours a day. They were most likely to be single mothers or the main breadwinners and were often older women, physically and mentally exhausted after the effort of bringing up a family against such heavy odds. They tried to hand over all household responsibilities to their oldest daughter, while their younger children frequently dropped out of school and roamed the streets. The remaining group, about 55 per cent, Moser described as simply 'hanging on', sacrificing their families by sending sons out to work or keeping daughters home from school to help with the housework. If nothing is done to change the impact of adjustment policies, Moser believes that many of these women will burn out, swelling the number of families broken by the impact of Latin America's silent revolution.

Working the streets

At first sight the Guatemala city dump looks like a scene from Dante, an infernal pit in which smoke from burning piles of rubbish obscures the bottom of the ravine, adding an acrid edge to the sweet stench of rotting garbage. Through the smoke and morning mist, the denizens of the dump sift through the piles in search of bounty: plump pigs root about, dogs fight and snarl over scraps of meat, vultures flop from mound to mound, stretching out their wings to the morning sun.

At the top of the dump's pecking order are the people – garbage pickers working through each fresh consignment, filling sacks with anything that can be recycled: cardboard, glass, food. It may look like hell, but there is a queue to work here. A large jolly woman with big teeth sees life on the dump as just another job. 'I've got five kids, three are in school. I've been here since I was seven, had all my kids here. The 15-year-old wants to be a nurse – we're going to have to pay for her.'[65]

SELA believes that over 80 per cent of new jobs in recent years have been in the so-called 'informal sector' of the self-employed, spanning everything from garbage recyclers to street vendors, with a sprinkling of high-powered business consultants.[66] The informal sector has become the last and only resort for millions of Latin Americans entering the job market for the first time, as well as those sacked during recession and 'rationalization'. The thousands of new arrivals have ended up in a self-defeating scramble for survival. Here, at least, the laws of supply and demand work all too well; as the streets of Latin America's cities have become clogged with street vendors desperately seeking customers, income has fallen. By 1989 the income of the average Latin American working in the informal sector had shrunk to just 58 per cent of its 1980 figure, harder hit than even the public sector.[67]

Adjusting the countryside

Although structural adjustment's greatest impact has been in the cities, it has also exacted a high human price in the countryside. The half-hearted agrarian reform programmes of the 1960s and 1970s have been swept aside by the cut and thrust of the 'export or die' mentality. Public spending cuts and the determination to leave everything to the market have meant the end for a range of institutions which at least gave some limited support to peasant farmers: state development banks, state marketing boards and guaranteed prices for their crops have all been curtailed (although in some cases this has allowed farmers to charge higher prices). Import liberalization has produced floods of cheap imports, undercutting peasant crops like potatoes and maize. NAFTA opens the door to cheap US maize for Mexico's urban masses, but spells disaster for nearly two million peasant farmers whose livelihood will be ruined by the competition,[68] while Peru, the country where potatoes were first cultivated, now eats imported potatoes from France.

As elsewhere, in rural areas the deregulated market has increased inequality. Banks lend to big landowners and transnationals with collateral, and ignore small peasants with nothing to pledge. Peasants get squeezed off the land by bankruptcy or offers which they cannot refuse, and end up becoming paid workers on their former lands. In Chile, just six large firms control 52 per cent of fresh fruit exports,[69] and the richest 10 per cent of the rural population saw their income rise by 90 per cent between 1987 and 1990. The share of the poorest 25 per cent fell from 11 per cent to 7 per cent.[70] In Costa Rica, another pioneer of non-traditional exports, agricultural credit to small farmers halved between 1984 and 1988, while the value of government bonds to exporters (effectively a state subsidy) rose by 1900 per cent, with 80 to 90 per cent of the benefits from the bonds going to five transnational corporations.[71]

Adjusting the environment

According to a World Wide Fund for Nature study of the environmental impact of adjustment lending by organizations like the World Bank, such loans 'have had, at best, a random impact on the environment and, without qualification [have] failed in placing adjusting countries on a sustainable development path'.[72] Such conclusions are hardly surprising since, when drawing up a structural adjustment programme, the Bank's economists prefer to ignore its impact on a country's 'natural capital'. Like women's work in the home, environmental damage is one of those 'externalities' which is missing from the indicators such as GDP used to measure progress, neo-liberal style. Former top Bank economist Larry Summers best summarized the astonishingly blinkered views of the people branded by Susan George as 'techno-cultists'[73]:

> There are no ... limits to the carrying capacity of the earth that are likely to bind any time in the foreseeable future. There isn't a risk of an apocalypse due to global warming or anything else. The idea that we should put limits to growth, because of some natural limit, is a profound error.[74]

On the ground, the WWF study concluded that adjustment programmes can have a positive impact on the environment by reducing the use of high-energy inputs such as fertilizers (devaluation makes them more expensive) and improved access to technology can reduce waste. Unfortunately, the negative side of the balance sheet is a good deal longer.

'Twelve years ago we came to live here,' says Maurilio Sánchez Pachuca, the stout president of the local residents' committee in a dingy *colonia* just outside Tijuana, Mexico. 'We thought we'd be in glory because it was an ecological reserve – lots of vegetation, animals, birds. Two years later the *maquiladoras* started to arrive up there.' A fat thumb gestures up at the plateau overlooking the *colonia*, with its clean blue and white *maquiladora* assembly plants. 'Now many of us have skin problems – rashes, hair falling out, we get eye pains, fevers. My kids' legs are really bad – all the kids have nervous problems and on the way to school the dust and streams are all polluted. We've tried to stop them playing in the streams, but kids are kids.'[75] He flicks despairingly through a treasured folder full of blurred photocopies of the hand-typed letters he has written to the authorities and their replies, a nine-year Kafkaesque exercise in futility. 'The first thing [the *maquiladoras*] do is buy the local officials. There are too many vested interests – dark interests, dollars. I have so many lovely letters from the government – but they aren't real.'

Up on the plateau, huge container trucks are at the loading bays, gorging themselves on the products of the 189 factories – Maxell cassettes, a crisp new Sanyo plant, Tabuchi Electric de México. A security guard ushers unwelcome visitors from the site. A black and pink slag-heap of battery casings is piled up by the fence surrounding the factories, where truckloads of old batteries from the US are broken up to recycle the lead and acid. By law, the remnants should be returned to the US, but they are just dumped here on the edge of the plateau.

Beyond the world of home and workplace, school and hospital, adjustment is leaving its mark on the earth, air and water of Latin America. Since the days of the *conquistadores*, Latin America has seemed condemned to a development model based on plunder, but neo-liberalism has greatly increased the pressure on an already fragile eco-system. In the rush to export, the region turned to its natural resources, sacrificing long-term sustainability for short-term gains.

One of adjustment's most immediate impacts has been on Latin America's rainforests – the largest remaining reserve of trees in the world. In Costa Rica, the World Bank's push for increased beef exports drives the 'hamburger connection', whereby forests are felled to make way for cattle which are subsequently sold to the US fast food industry. By one calculation, Costa Rica loses 2.5 tonnes of topsoil for every kilogramme of beef it exports.[76] Governments have also encouraged logging as a further export earner. The leader of Brazil's Workers Party (PT), Luís Inácio da Silva (Lula) put it better than most: 'If the Amazon is the lungs of the world, then debt is its pneumonia.'[77] Brazil is both the Third World's top debtor and the globe's top deforester.

The soyabean agribusiness boom in southern Brazil has driven vast numbers of peasant farmers from their land, forcing them to head for the 'agricultural frontier' of the Amazon in search of farmland, cutting down forest in slash-and-burn agriculture. They make the trek along the new roads built with World Bank and international bank loans in the 1970s and 1980s, the very loans which drove up Brazil's debt and created the hunger for export dollars in the first place. By 1987, 'Satellite photographs showed 6000 forest fires burning across the entire Amazon Basin – every one of them deliberately started by land clearers. Many of the fires were burning close to the [World Bank funded] Highway BR-364.'[78] Thousands of the hungry migrants also find work turning mile upon mile of rainforest into charcoal to feed the smelters of the Amazon's giant Carajas development. Carajas turns huge deposits of iron ore and bauxite (the raw material for aluminium) into export dollars (which then promptly leave the country as debt service).

In neighbouring Guyana, largely untouched forests have come under the hammer as part of an adjustment programme agreed with the IMF in the late 1980s. Guyana has duly parcelled out its forests and rivers to an unholy alliance of Brazilian and Asian mining and logging companies. In return for a 50-year licence on a 4.13 million acre concession, the notorious Sarawak-based logger, Samling Timbers, promised to export 1.2 million cubic feet of Guyanese timber a year (compared to national exports of just 94,000 cubic feet in 1989). Meanwhile, Brazilian miners are attacking the rivers with powerful dredges like vast hoovers, sucking up the banks and silting the waterways[79], while poisoning the water with the mercury they use to extract the gold.

The human and environmental costs of deforestation are enormous.[80] Deforested land is quickly eroded, and tons of topsoil are washed into the watercourses, silting up streams and rivers, clogging hydro-electric installations and disrupting marine eco-systems along the coast. Deforestation disrupts the local climate, since the trees regulate the storage and release of rain water. By returning water vapour to the atmosphere, trees also encourage further rainfall. The loss of forests therefore makes both drought and flooding, as well as mudslides, more likely. In Panama, deforestation has reduced the rainfall needed to replenish the Panama Canal's lock system, endangering the Canal's future as a major trade route. Many of Latin America's poor rely on firewood for fuel. As the forests become depleted, they must travel farther afield to scavenge for supplies, and in the towns the price rises to reflect wood's increasing scarcity.

A number of investigations show that the commercial potential of the forest is far greater than that of the pasture which replaces it. In addition, the forest can be farmed in a sustainable way, yielding rubber, brazil nuts and many kinds of fruit. The rainforest is a repository of plant and animal species which, besides their intrinsic value, are a vital source of new genetic material; a quarter of all pharmaceutical products are derived from rainforest products, even though only 1 per cent of all Amazon plants have been intensively investigated for their medicinal properties. Tropical forest plants have provided treatments for leukaemia, Hodgkin's disease, breast, cervical and testicular cancer and are currently being used in AIDS research. Costa Rica may have more species of plants and animals per square foot than any other country on earth, but it also has one of the world's highest per capita debts, forcing it into a series of structural adjustment agreements in the 1980s which helped turn it into one of the world's fastest deforesters.[81]

Elsewhere, the growth of non-traditional agricultural exports has also had some disastrous side effects. In targeting the luxury fruit and vegetable market, Latin American farmers have to ensure unblemished products to satisfy finicky western consumers, while the trend towards monocultures like soyabean in Brazil offers ideal breeding grounds for pests. In both cases farmers have responded with massive doses of pesticides and fungicides, poisoning workers and local communities. In a 1990 survey in Costa Rica of farmers growing melons (one of its most successful non-traditional exports), 70 per cent of the farmers using such agro-chemicals as Tamaron, Paraquat and Lannate (metomil) reported seeing animals die after spraying and 58 per cent of them knew of water supplies poisoned by the sprays.[82] In Jacona, Mexico, farmworkers pay a high price for getting 4.5 million kg of strawberries a year to US tables in the middle of winter. According to his death certificate, Blas López Vásquez, 36, died in December 1992 from a 'respiratory insufficiency' caused by 'intoxication from organophosphates' after backpack spraying a strawberry field.[83] Three other workers died that year in Jacona, and 14 others were hospitalized.

A painful wait

By 1995, after 13 years of debt crisis, adjustment and undoubted pain, most Latin Americans are still waiting for the long-promised benefits of structural adjustment to 'trickle down' to their neighbourhoods. The further round of belt-tightening and austerity which followed the Mexican crash of 1995 will push the promised revival still further off. Although the rich have had a vintage decade, most of the region's people are poorer and more insecure; their homes, communities, schools and hospitals are collapsing around them, while their cities, towns and villages are increasingly polluted. Latin America is left trying to find its way in a cut-throat global economy, saddled with a population weakened by poverty and ignorance. Neo-liberals have moderated their tone and now talk more about social cost and public spending, but their basic recipe remains unchanged as they insist that the pay-off lies just around the corner. Small wonder that so many doubt their good faith, and that disillusion with politicians of all hues grows daily.

Notes

1 CEDLA, based on INE, *Encuesta de Hogares* (La Paz).

2 CEPAL, *Panorama Social de América Latina 1993* (Santiago, 1993), p.100.

3 *Ibid.*, p.100.

4 Latin American Newsletters Special Report, *Poverty: An Issue Making a Comeback* (London, October 1992), p.3.

5 Centers for Disease Control and Prevention, *The Spread of Epidemic Cholera in Latin America 1991-93* (Atlanta, GA, 1994).

6 George Psacharopoulos *et al.*, *Poverty and Income Distribution in Latin America: The Story of the 1980s* (Washington, DC, December 1992), p.ix.

7 *The Economist* (London), 'A survey of Latin America', 13 November 1993.

8 CEPAL, *Social Equity and Changing Production Patterns: An Integrated Approach* (Santiago, 1992), p.39.

9 Latin American Newsletters, *Weekly Report* (London, 14 July 1994).

10 CEPAL, *Panorama Social 1993*, p.22.

11 CEPAL, *Panorama Social de América Latina 1994* (Santiago, 1994), p.19.

12 Samuel Morley, *Labour Markets and Inequitable Growth* (Cambridge, 1982).

13 *The Economist* (London), 17 April 1990.

14 *Financial Times* (London), 26 March 1993.

15 United Nations Development Programme, *Human Development Report 1994* (New York, 1994), pp.164 and 196.

16 Psacharopoulos *et al.*, *op. cit.*, preface.

17 IDB, *Socio-economic Reform in Latin America, the Social Agenda Study* (Washington, DC, 28 April 1993).

18 See Frances Stewart, 'The many faces of adjustment', in *World Development*, Vol. 19, No.12 (Oxford, 1991), p.1849.

19 John Madeley, Dee Sullivan, and Jessica Woodroffe, *Who Runs the World?* (Christian Aid, London, 1994), p.26.

20 CEPAL, *The Social Summit: A View from Latin America and the Caribbean* (Santiago, 1994), p.16.

21 CEPAL, *Panorama Social 1993*, p.9.

22 CEPAL, *Social Equity*, p.37.

23 CEPAL, *Panorama Social 1993*, p.16.

24 Interview by Sara Burns (Christian Aid, London, August 1993).

25 CEPAL, *Social Equity*, p.38.

26 Rolph van der Hoeven and Frances Stewart, *Social Development during Periods of Structural Adjustment in Latin America* (ILO, Geneva, 1994), p.5.

27 *El Mercurio* (Santiago), 30 September 1993.

28 Author interview (Concepción), September 1993.

29 CEPAL, *Panorama Social 1993*, p.8.

30 CEPAL, *Balance Preliminar de la Economía de América Latina y el Caribe 1994* (Santiago, December 1994), p.44.

31 West Merchant Bank, *Investment Review* (London), August 1994.

32 *Latinamerica Press* (Lima), 24 November 1994, p.7.

33 *Financial Times* (London), 13 December 1994.

34 *Buenos Aires Herald*, 2 October 1994.

35 *Guardian* (London), 28 October 1993.

36 Latin America Monitor, *Southern Cone* (London), December 1994.

37 Eliana Cardoso and Ann Helwege, *Latin America's Economy: Diversity, Trends and Conflicts* (Cambridge, MA, 1992), p.178.

38 *Ibid.*, p.173.

39 *Ibid.*, p.175.

40 Latin America Monitor, *Mexico* (London, March 1995).

41 Stewart, *op. cit.*, p.24.

42 CEPAL, *Panorama Social 1993*, p.100.

43 CEPAL, *Social Equity*, p.42.

44 Stewart, *op. cit.*, p.18.

45 *Latinamerica Press* (Lima), 18 June 1992, p.5.

46 Deborah Poole and Gerardo Rénique, *Peru: Time of Fear* (London, 1992), p.152.

47 *Financial Times* (London), 30 June 1994.

48 World Bank, *World Development Report* (New York, various years).

49 *Ibid.*

50 Stewart, *op. cit.*, p.20.

51 International Save the Children Alliance, *El impacto de la crisis económica, el ajuste y la deuda externa sobre la niñez en América Latina* (Lima, April 1992), p.45.

52 World Bank, *World Development Report 1993* (New York, 1993), p.162.

53 Oxfam, *Structural Adjustment and Inequality in Latin America: How IMF and World Bank Policies Have Failed the Poor* (mimeo) (Oxford, 1994), p.16.

54 Author interview (Mexico City), September 1992.

55 Talk by Trevor Evans, CRIES, at the Catholic Institute of International Relations (London) 12 July 1994.

56 Economist Intelligence Unit, *Nicaragua Country Report* (London, 3rd quarter 1994).

57 CEPAL, *Panorama Social*, p.44.

58 *Ibid.*, p.45.

59 Author interview (Santiago), September 1993.

60 CEPAL, *Social Panorama of Latin America 1993* (Santiago, 1993), p.11.

61 Van der Hoeven and Stewart, *op. cit.*, p.20.

62 International Labour Organisation, *World Labour Report* (Geneva), 1993.

63 *Comercio Exterior* (Mexico City, December 1992).

64 Caroline Moser, 'Adjustment from below: Low-income women, time and the triple role in Guayaquil, Ecuador', in Sarah Radcliffe and Sallie Westwood (eds), *Viva: Women and Popular Protest in Latin America* (London, 1993).

65 Author interview (Guatemala City), January 1992.

66 *Latinamerica Press* (Lima), 24 November 1994, p.7.

67 Stewart, *op. cit.*, p.14c.

68 Harry Browne, *For Richer for Poorer: Shaping US-Mexican Integration* (Albuquerque, NM, 1994), p.24.

69 Estrella Díaz, *Impact of the Export Model on Workers and the Environment: Analysis of the Fruit and Fishing Sectors*, (Santiago, June 1994).

70 CEPAL, *Social Panorama 1993*, p.22.

71 Karen Hansen-Kuhn, *Structural Adjustment in Central America: The Case of Costa Rica*, The Development Gap (Washington, DC, June 1993), p.12.

72 David Reed, *Structural Adjustment and the Environment* (London, 1992), p.161.

73 Susan George and Fabrizio Sabelli, *Faith and Credit: The World Bank's Secular Empire* (London, 1994), p.175.

74 Larry Summers interview with Kirsten Garrett, 'Background briefing', on ABC, 10 November 1991.

75 Author interview (Tijuana), September 1992.

76 Duncan Green, *Faces of Latin America* (London, 1991), p.39.

77 Quoted in Susan George, *The Debt Boomerang* (London, 1992), p.1.

78 Graham Hancock, *Lords of Poverty* (London, 1989), p.132.

79 Dominic Hogg, Sapping the forest: Structural adjustment in Guyana, *The Ecologist* (Newton, 1993).

80 Green, *op. cit.*, p.39.

81 George, *op. cit.*, p.23.

82 The Development Gap, *The Other Side of the Story: The Real Impact of World Bank and IMF Structural Adjustment Programs* (Washington, DC, 1992), p.20.

83 *Latinamerica Press* (Lima), 28 October 1993, p.6.

CHAPTER 5

Trading Places

Latin America in a Changing World Economy

The neo-liberal plan for Latin America's return to growth relies on exports based on a country's 'comparative advantage', usually a combination of agricultural products and manufactured goods based on cheap labour. The supporters of the silent revolution argue that no country can afford to opt out of a world economy where both production and investment are ever more globalized, integrated and beyond regulation or control by even the most powerful governments.

In this New World Order, the ownership and control of technology increasingly determines power and influence. The growing importance of free trade agreements such as NAFTA, GATT and its successor body, the World Trade Organisation, is partly explained by the need of large transnational corporations to ensure continued technological leadership, as well as their practical need to prevent politics getting in the way of globalization. The North's support for free trade agreements such as these is often both hypocritical and self-serving, locking Latin America into a development model based on cheap labour and dependence on foreign investment and technology, and preventing it from achieving the independent technological capacity which has underpinned the spectacular rise of Asian economies such as Japan, South Korea and Malaysia.

Europe's lust for commodities was the driving force behind its colonial crusade, and shaped the pattern of Latin American development from the Conquest to the present day. In a series of commodity booms which subsequently ended in collapse, Latin America's natural resources were pillaged to provide the rich countries of the North with cheap supplies of everything from sugar to coffee to copper. When one product stopped being profitable, producers merely shifted to the next dream export. In return, the region imported manufactured goods from the factories of Manchester and Chicago. This neo-colonial form of free trade lasted from independence to the onset of the great depression and the switch to import substitution in the 1930s. Gandhi once remarked that, 'Free trade for India has proved her curse and held her in bondage.'[1] Much the same can be said of Latin America.

Comparative advantage

The great thinkers of liberal economics believed that free trade would benefit all parties through the mechanism of what they termed 'comparative advantage'. The Scottish economist David Ricardo established comparative advantage as the logical basis for free trade as long ago as 1817. He showed that everyone would enjoy higher incomes and a better standard of living if every producer, be they country, company, or individual, concentrated their activity in areas where they had the greatest cost advantage (or the smallest cost disadvantage) over their competitors. To illustrate his theory, he took the example of two countries, Britain and Portugal and two products, wine and cloth. In the early nineteenth century Britain was the most technologically advanced economy in the world, but Portugal has a much better climate for grapes, so Ricardo argued that the welfare of both would be maximized if Britain stuck to making cloth, and imported Portuguese wine. Any other arrangement would be a waste of time and money.

There are numerous objections to the modern application of this theory[2] (George Bernard Shaw once described free trade as 'heartbreaking nonsense'[3]), and its application to Latin America. It ignores the key question of how Britain came to be technologically advanced in the first place. To frame the discussion in terms of a comparative advantage which is static and, by implication, permanent, ignores the way a government or other agents can change the nature of a country's strengths. In Ricardo's example, Portugal could decide to compete with Britain by sending some engineers to learn the secrets of the British textile industry, then set up its own textile sector by importing some British looms or learning how to make them in Portugal. At that point the lower wages in Portugal would make its cloth cheaper than the British variety and it could export cloth *and* wine.

In that situation, the British textile industry could survive if the government imposed tariffs against Portuguese cloth or drove down wages to Portuguese levels, but a more positive solution would be for British companies to pursue a *dynamic* comparative advantage in textile production, seeking to maintain a sufficient technological edge over their Portuguese competitors to compensate for the difference in wages. This requires a commitment to invest in research and development (R&D). In recent years, rapidly industrializing Asian economies such as Japan or South Korea have built their success on the basis of this kind of dynamic comparative advantage. If they had followed the World Bank's current advice, they would still be exporting rice.

Moreover, experience has shown that the economies which rely on exporting raw materials fare worse than those which have managed to industrialize. The 'terms of trade' – the amount of raw materials a Third World country must export to pay for a particular range of manufactured goods – have historically tended to deteriorate, obliging the commodity producer to 'run just to stand still', exporting ever greater quantities of primary products to buy the same amount of industrial goods. One reason is that technological advance has reduced the amount of raw materials required by the advanced economies; in 1984, for instance, Japan used only 60 per cent of the raw materials it needed in 1973 to manufacture an equivalent industrial product.[4] Tin cans use less and less tin as production processes improve, bad news for Bolivia; fibre optic cables replace copper wire in telecommunications, hitting Chile's main export; biotechnology allows US companies to use corn syrup in soft drinks, and prices plummet for the cane sugar grown in the Caribbean.

Raw material exports also suffer from abrupt price swings and are subject to substitution by other products. World trade in manufactured goods in the 1980s grew eight times faster than that in commodities.[5] Commodity exports are becoming a less and less important part of world trade, so, argue the critics, why back a loser?

Changes in the world economy in recent years challenge some of Ricardo's underlying assumptions. The whole idea that trade takes place between independent nations is looking increasingly outdated. So-called 'intra-firm' trade, where different subsidiaries of the same transnational company trade with each other, accounted for around 40 per cent of global trade by the early 1980s[6] and has risen considerably since then. The spectacular rise in size and power of the transnational companies is increasingly making national borders irrelevant, and provides the driving force behind the world-wide spread of free trade agreements.

Ricardo believed that British technology and capital would always prefer to stay in Britain. In a passage which sounds wonderfully innocent in the age of the footloose transnational investor, he wrote of the 'natural disinclination which every man has to quit the country of his birth and connections' and argued that 'most men of property' would 'be satisfied with a low rate of profits in their own country, rather than seek a more advantageous employment for their wealth in foreign nations.'[7] Today's Lancashire mill-owner would be far more likely to relocate his factory in Lisbon to cut his costs and boost his profits.

Yet despite the arguments against applying the concept of static comparative advantage in the late twentieth century, it remains central to the neo-liberal gospel. The apostles of the silent revolution are convinced that everyone will benefit if each country sticks to what it is 'naturally' good at, and removes trade barriers to unleash the efficiency of open markets. Chilean citizens will be best off if their country exports kiwi fruit and imports computers. If Chile tries to develop a computer industry, it will mean trade barriers, higher prices for computers, and second-rate products. Although the arguments are usually carried on in technical, abstract terms, self-interest is never far from the surface. First World industries clearly stand to gain from keeping Third World countries in their place as suppliers of raw materials and cheap labour. Instead of allowing local firms to become industrial competitors, transnational corporations build local factories in Third World countries, enabling them to take advantage of their low local wage levels and to use the threat of such relocation to hold down wages in their remaining plants in the North.

Besides the pressure exerted via the international financial institutions, the major economies use import tariffs to discourage developing countries from trying to process their own primary products. In a phenomenon known as 'tariff escalation', the EU's tariff on instant coffee is twice that on unroasted coffee beans, while the US levies import taxes on fruit juice three times higher than those on fresh fruit.[8]

In historical terms, the US is a relatively recent convert to the merits of free trade. In a prophetic speech the US President Ulysses S. Grant (1869–77) once said:

> *For centuries England has relied on protection, has carried it to extremes and has obtained satisfactory results from it. There is no doubt that it is to this system that it owes its present strength. After two centuries, England has found it convenient to adopt free trade because it thinks that protection can no longer offer it anything. Very well then, Gentlemen, my knowledge of our country leads me to believe that within 200 years, when America has gotten out of protection all that it can offer, it too will adopt free trade.*[9]

President Grant apparently underestimated the speed of history – the US became the world's foremost economic power and its most determined advocate of free trade within 70 years of his death.

From Fords to Toyotas

Within Latin America free trade has won the day as a reaction to import substitution's poor trading record and the consequent crippling shortage of foreign exchange. The continent's share of world exports fell inexorably from 12.4 per cent in 1950 to 5.5 per cent in 1980, on the eve of the debt crisis, as Latin America became a neglected backwater of world trade.[10] Import substitution's critics claimed that Latin America could only lay the basis for sustained, export-led growth, by opening itself to the world economy on the basis of its comparative advantage in two broad categories – natural resources and cheap labour. Yet the region had already tried this path once, and it ended in disaster with the Great Depression of the 1930s. The continent then turned its back on exports, choosing instead the path of import substitution to lead it to development. Now it is again consigning its fate to the 'invisible hand' of the global marketplace. Neo-liberals argue that this is not just the result of short historical memories, but a response to changes in the world economy which have left export-led growth the only feasible road to development.

Many of these changes stem from the breakneck pace of technological innovation, which has changed the structure of the world's industry in the last thirty years, bringing sweeping social and political change in its wake. In the years immediately after the Second World War, the United States became the world's economic juggernaut. Washington's heyday was also the golden era of Fordism, captured (and vilified) in the unforgettable Charlie Chaplin film, *Modern Times*. Named after Henry Ford, the father of the modern car assembly line, Fordism involved the mass production of identical objects in which every part and process was rigidly standardized. Mass production brought economies of scale, making a plethora of goods such as cars and TVs accessible to new generations of consumers. Fordism lay at the heart of US economic might and placed a growing chunk of the world economy in the hands of a small number of huge transnational corporations, the majority of them US owned.

Fordism's political backdrop was the New Deal, an alliance between business, labour and government, with the government committed to an interventionist role to ensure political and social stability and low rates of unemployment. The arrangement worked superbly from its origins in the Great Depression until the late 1960s, by which time Fordism, like Keynesianism, was showing its age. Transnational corporations were finding that the high wages at their factories in the US were making them unable to compete with new competitors in Asia and elsewhere, while technological and managerial changes were freeing the transnational corporations from their remaining links to their countries of origin. In the US, these changes prompted the crumbling of the New Deal contract, and prompted the rise of the neo-liberal right, led by Ronald Reagan.

At the same time, Japanese companies were revolutionizing working practices, led by the Toyota car company, and making better and cheaper products than the lumbering US giants. Whereas General Motors or Ford made every part themselves, Toyota created an efficient network of subcontractors tied to the parent company; in order to cut costs they kept their stocks at close to zero, relying on a nimble 'Just in Time' (JIT) ordering system to keep themselves supplied; they placed greater emphasis on quality control, rotated and trained their workforce, promised them jobs for life and avoided the rigid hierarchies of western companies, insisting that managers share the canteen with their workers.

Japanese practices suited perfectly the technological revolution just getting under way. From the late 1960s the advent of the microelectronic age rapidly transformed the way goods were produced. Computerization allowed managers to perfect JIT techniques; computer-aided design and programmable machine tools allowed the same factory painlessly to adapt its products to changing consumer demand. The new systems required a smaller, more adaptable, enterprising and highly trained workforce; Charlie Chaplin would not have survived five minutes in a Toyota factory.

Technology, politics and power

Beyond the factory, the information revolution has transformed the global economy and provided the driving force behind the spread of free trade areas such as NAFTA, the European Union and the General Agreement on Tariffs and Trade (GATT). From his office in Santiago, at the heart of Chile's brave new neo-liberal world, CEPAL's dapper Executive Secretary, Gert Rosenthal, surveys the changing world economy and concludes that the days of protectionism and state planning are gone forever.

'The pendulum can't go back to the 1950s because of the way the international economy now functions', he explains. 'The single most important change has been the explosion of information – the possibility of controlling a very decentralised production and marketing structure makes the workings of the international economy very different. Not even Albania can afford to isolate itself.'[11]

A range of new technologies such as satellite transmission, fibre-optic cables, faxes and electronic mail have made telecommunication systems into 'the electronic highways of the informational age, equivalent to the role played by the railway systems in the process of industrialisation'.[12] The analogy is especially apt for Latin America: like the railways in the last century, the new electronic highways largely belong to outsiders, in this case the transnational corporations, and are used primarily for their benefit. Latin Americans can only hope for the crumbs left by the technological revolution.

In the global village created by improved telecommunications, transnational corporations can shop around before deciding where to locate their factories. A century ago, when pioneering transnationals such as United Fruit sited production in far-flung outposts, they could only communicate haphazardly with head office by mail or telegraph. These days a world-wide network linking the head office, affiliates and subcontractors can be in constant, on-line contact 24 hours a day (if the local phone lines are up to it). A company can safely divide up the different stages of the old Fordist assembly line between factories spread across the globe, according to the relative strengths of each country, be they a skilled labour force, proximity to markets, low wage levels or local government tax breaks. Cut-throat competition between transnational corporations means that no company can stay aloof from this global chess match and remain competitive:

> The production of Hitachi televisions by the Japanese electronics giant illustrates the process of globalization. First, Hitachi marketers in the US estimate how many of which models their distributors will need in six weeks. Based on this information, orders go out to a Singaporean subcontractor, who manufactures the specified transistors and ships them to a Malaysian circuit board assembler. From Malaysia the circuit boards travel to Taiwan, where workers assemble controller chassis, again following Hitachi's product mix instructions. With two weeks to go other components are ordered from Hitachi affiliates in Japan. A week later the chassis and other parts arrive in Tijuana, where they are joined by picture tubes and deflection yokes made by a Dutch company in the US. Mexican workers assemble wood and plastic panels shipped from the US, attach the electronic innards, and run the televisions through a battery of quality control tests. Workers then package the TVs and ship them to the US with two or three days to spare.[13]

Political and economic stability is vital to any transnational corporation in the new global system; companies operating JIT systems are extremely vulnerable to any disruption in supply, whether from strikes, civil unrest or government interference. The answer has been to lock-in the key countries in the production chain through a two stage process. First (via the international financial institutions) encourage unilateral liberalization as part of structural adjustment, then lock the new rules permanently in place with free trade agreements such as NAFTA and GATT. Lock-in guarantees security for a transnational corporation's investments and makes it harder for tariff barriers to be reimposed at the whim of a future president, slicing an elaborate globalized production chain in half.

The pressure on Third World governments to accept being locked into the global system on these terms comes both from political decisions and the blind mechanisms of the market. Foreign investors seeking to minimize risk may not have a conscious political agenda, but they prefer to invest in countries where the government has ensured long-term investment stability by signing free trade agreements and otherwise deregulating trade and investment. Overall, this ensures that foreign investment and technology pour into countries that toe the line, such as Mexico.

On the political front, transnationals are active lobbyists for free trade agreements and some even see themselves as the central players in the whole process. According to Roberto Goizueta, Chief Executive Officer and Chairman of the Board of Coca-Cola, 'Private investment is overtaking government regulation as the most influential element in economic change, pushing the world towards regional trade agreements.'[14]

The new technological revolution is permanent. The only certainty left is that everything will change; adaptability is all. Successful companies are engaged in a breakneck cycle of R&D: conception, design, testing, manufacture, marketing and rapid obsolescence follow each other at an increasingly hectic pace as the 'product cycle' grows ever shorter. Records are replaced by cassettes, which are swiftly supplanted by compact discs; at the technological cutting edge, the processing power of an integrated circuit doubles every 18 months while the transmission capacity of fibre optic systems doubles each year.[15]

Along the way, much R&D has moved out of the genteel world of the universities and been taken over by transnational corporations. The rewards and risks for the companies involved are huge, as are the investments required in the scramble for new products and markets. A company must develop a new product, get it into the world market, and sell in huge quantities to recoup its investment before the product is in turn superseded by the next generation of technology. Speed and scale are essential if a company is to reach the ever-receding technological frontier, and even the largest transnational corporations increasingly spread the risk by forging strategic alliances to share R&D costs and maximize sales. In 1992, for example, rival micro-electronics transnationals IBM (US), Toshiba (Japan) and Siemens (Germany) agreed to pool resources to develop a new generation of 256 megabyte computer chips by the end of the century. The estimated cost of the project is $1bn, and if another company beats them to it, most of it could be lost.[16]

The rise of the transnational corporations seems unstoppable. By 1990, total sales by the foreign affiliates of the estimated 37,000 transnational corporations came to $5500bn, equivalent to over a quarter of the world's entire economic output, and, thanks to transnationals' sales in domestic markets, considerably more than total world trade.[17] By 1989, only 19 countries had a GDP larger than the global sales of General

Motors.[18] Since the mid-1980s world-wide foreign direct investment –
bricks, mortar, wages and machinery – has grown twice as fast as domestic investment and at three times the rate of the world economy. In the
developing world, inflows of foreign direct investment tripled between
1988 and 1993, reaching $80bn a year[19] and supplanting bank loans as the
main source of long-term inflows of private capital.[20]

In a world divided into technological haves and have-nots, the have-
nots are left to jostle for foreign investment and technology, desperately
undercutting their neighbours to offer the transnationals cheaper wages,
bigger tax breaks, fewer restrictions on profit repatriations. The corporations have the whip hand in negotiations with local governments, and
the resulting foreign investment brings fewer and fewer benefits to the
host country, exacerbating global inequality. In 1950 the people of the
rich nations could, on average, buy about 10 times more than the people
of the poor nations; by 1988 it was 30 times as much.[21]

The growing divisions are as much within countries as between them,
widening inequality within the old industrialized countries. In the words
of Lee Kuan Yew, the Prime Minister who has overseen Singapore's economic miracle in recent decades, 'America's top ten per cent will still
enjoy the highest standard of living in the world. But the wages of the
less educated citizens will drop to those of the workers in developing
countries with equal or higher education.'[22]

Transnational companies have a positive dislike of 'technology transfer'
to potential competitors. This is the case, even though *maquiladoras* have
in many cases developed from being low-tech 'screwdriver industries' to
state-of-the-art auto plants. The transnational corporations do their
utmost to ensure that ownership and control of technology remain firmly
north of the border. The US-based Pharmaceutical Manufacturers'
Association (PMA) has 100 members with combined global sales of over
$75bn in 1991.[23] One of its main purposes is to strengthen international
codes on 'Intellectual Property Rights' (IPR), including patent protection
to avoid other countries copying its members' technology. The PMA
works closely with the US government to use the 'Special 301' trade law
which allows Washington to launch investigations and retaliatory action
against countries whose IPR codes do not live up to US expectations. In
February 1992 the PMA asked the government to consider actions against
Argentina, Brazil, Colombia and Venezuela under this rule.

Under PMA pressure, US trade negotiators have also entrenched
intellectual property rights in free trade agreements like the NAFTA and
GATT, and local transnational corporation subsidiaries have even managed to include IPR chapters in regional trade agreements within Latin
America such as the Andean Pact. As a precondition for the US agreeing

to sign NAFTA, Mexico passed a patent law in 1991, giving drug companies 20 years' patent protection and placing severe restrictions on cheaper 'generic' drugs.

Global money

Computerization has also transformed world capital markets, creating a 'vast, integrated global money and capital system, almost totally outside all government regulation, that can send billions of ... "stateless" currencies hurtling round the world 24 hours a day'.[24] Some authors blame the new system for the conservative revival world-wide, claiming it has so reduced the state's room for manoeuvre in economic policy that governments have little choice but to fall in with the market consensus, or have their currency destroyed by the global money managers. Neo-liberals may preach that the state should withdraw from managing the economy, but in practice the workings of the global economy have increasingly withdrawn beyond the reach of the state.

The heart of the global money markets is the Eurodollar, a peculiar stateless relative of the US currency, held in dollar deposit accounts outside the US. Free of government regulation, reporting requirements or any other limitations on their movements, Eurodollars can flow untrammelled round the world. The US government has given up even trying to count them, but it is estimated that the world Eurodollar market went up from $100bn in 1973 to $1000bn ten years later, largely due to the vast amount of dollars generated by the oil price hike of 1973, which were subsequently recycled into the Eurodollar market.[25]

Eurodollars have become the universal world currency, financing trade and transnational corporations, which borrow them to invest abroad. In the New World Order, money never sleeps:

> As evening comes to America, US bank deposits are in a sense released from duty ... Therefore, the out-of-service deposits are loaned overnight by ... the big banks to financial centres such as Hong Kong or Singapore, where the business day has just begun. There the deposits play their formal role of backing credit transactions until the sun sets in the Orient and the time comes for funds, like Cinderellas, to return to work in America.[26]

The fund managers who control these flows have acquired enormous economic influence. At the end of 1991, 200 funds in Europe and the US managed $8.2 trillion[27] (a trillion is 1000 billion) between them, and they kept the money moving; in four days, $4 trillion changes hands just on global foreign exchange markets – more than world trade is worth in a whole year.[28] Of these flows, a mere 18 per cent was involved in supporting international trade or investment – the ostensible reason for a foreign exchange market. The rest was purely speculative, buying and selling in order to generate profits from minor changes in exchange rates.[29]

The fund managers command such vast resources that their clashes with governments in the global marketplace usually end in humiliating defeat for the politicians. One former chairman of the giant Citicorp bank described the New Order as 'an attack on the very nature of sovereign power.'[30] In 1992, US financier George Soros single-handedly destroyed the British government's attempts to keep the pound in the European Exchange Rate Mechanism (ERM). Soros effectively bet, and won, that he could force the British government to devalue. Using his huge resources, he engineered a run on the pound, overwhelming the Bank of England's attempts to use its reserves to keep sterling within its ERM band. The British government capitulated by suspending sterling's membership of the ERM (an effective devaluation) and Soros came away from his victory some $1bn the richer. Fund managers then picked off other currencies one by one, derailing the drive for European monetary union, which would, incidentally, have cut their profits by making them unable to buy and sell between the different European currencies.

Any government defying the neo-liberal orthodoxy now faces a two-pronged attack. Computerization makes it possible for foreign and local investors to transfer capital out of the country at the push of a button, while on the international money markets, fund managers like Soros can punish the dissident government by selling huge amounts of the country's currency, forcing it either to devalue or change its policies. All those incomprehensible newspaper articles which begin with variants on 'The pound/dollar/mark came under strong pressure on the foreign exchanges today' are signs that money managers are snapping at the heels of the politicians. Governments are reluctant to devalue because of the inflationary consequences and impact on confidence, as foreign investors will be reluctant to convert their wealth into local currency if the government has acquired a reputation as a devaluer. Resisting devaluation has also become the test of a politician's nationalist machismo, as governments stress the virtues of a 'strong currency', even if it means no one wants to buy their over-valued exports.

Critics argue that without an international agreement to regulate capital flows and the Eurodollar market, any government defying the neo-liberal tide will be rapidly isolated and defeated by the money markets. Some see this as a more constructive role for the IMF than its current position as chief enforcer of structural adjustment on the South. So far however, there is little sign of the political will required for governments to defy the money markets and agree such regulation.

Can Latin America industrialize?

Industrialization requires the successful combination of a number of factors: capital, technology, a good workforce, the right wage levels, access to markets, infrastructure such as electricity, water supplies and transport networks, and the laws and political conditions which encourage investment and trade.

Driven by the relentless pace of technological change, the relative weight of these different factors is changing fast. Cheap, unskilled labour is becoming less and less important compared to factors such as technological know-how, a well-educated and motivated workforce, political and economic stability and infrastructure. Increasingly, the international division of knowledge is replacing the international division of labour in determining which countries sink, and which swim.

To succeed, a country therefore has to invest in its people, its R&D, and its infrastructure. It can then either develop its own industries and technology, or bargain with transnational corporations from a position of strength. Yet Latin America's record in these areas is poor. The number of scientists and engineers per 10,000 population is a fair guide to the technological level of a society: in Japan it is 50, in Germany 27, and in South Korea it is 13. Latin America languishes far behind with 4 in Brazil and just 2 in Mexico.[31] In the neo-liberal showcase of Chile:

> *Enrique D'Etigny, President of the National Commission for Scientific Research and Technology, lamented recently that the university science faculties were virtually empty. He noted that each year only three students graduated in maths and four in physics from the University of Chile. The reason: there's no living to be made out of science in Chile these days.*[32]

In the silent revolution's rush to cut state spending, chopping public investment in infrastructure and R&D (largely state-financed in Latin America) has been one of the politically easiest options, but has only served to widen the technology gap at a time when the successful economies of Europe and Asia are increasing their outlays on both. The poor R&D spending record of both the US and Britain is one of the chief causes of their relative industrial decline. In the 1990s the World Bank's renewed emphasis on 'human capital' has led to some recovery in education spending, but only at primary level as a means of poverty reduction. The Bank even argues for switching resources from university level to primary education, often increasing the costs to students of acquiring a university education. There is as yet little sign of priority being given to training future generations of scientists and engineers to try to give the region a technological future.

From the early 1980s, parts of Latin America's existing technological base deteriorated rapidly as structural adjustment forced governments to cut public spending.[33] In some countries, the shift from state to informal sector that has taken place under adjustment has been a technological catastrophe. Next to the rusting hulk of the abandoned mineral-processing plant in Siglo XX, Bolivia's remaining tin miners are now reduced to crushing the ore by hand, rocking giant half-moons filled with concrete and rubble to and fro over the ore. The evening air is filled with the sounds of grinding, shovelling and a cacophony of radios. Just one of the derelict ore-crushers in the dead factory, which was closed when the state withdrew from the tin sector as part of its adjustment programme, could do the job better than this whole grinding, rocking hillside.

GATT and the World Trade Organisation[34]

Neo-liberalism's crusade to make free trade the guiding principle of world commerce recorded a victory in December 1993 with the signature of the Uruguay Round of the General Agreement on Tariffs and Trade (GATT), following seven years of haggling. The event was described by GATT's understandably overwrought director-general, Peter Sutherland, as 'a defining moment in modern history'. Overall, the main beneficiaries of the GATT agreement are Europe and the US, with a few crumbs passing to large exporters within Latin America. Within Latin America, each country will have its winners and losers, largely along the same lines as for NAFTA.

GATT was born in the 1940s as the poor relation of the other Bretton Woods institutions, the IMF and World Bank. The original intention had been to set up a third powerful institution, the International Trade Organisation, but the suggestion was blocked by the US Congress. Instead, GATT was created, an amorphous entity comprised of a series of periodic negotiations rather than a regulatory authority.[35] One of the main fruits of the Uruguay Round was the agreement to set up, 50 years after the Bretton Woods conference, a World Trade Organisation with much greater powers than GATT.

Much of the hard-bargaining during the seven years of the Uruguay Round was an unsightly squabble between the three economic super-powers – the US, EU and Japan – over each others' use of subsidies and other 'non-tariff barriers' to trade. The main obstacle to an agreement was the abyss which separates the superpowers' free trade rhetoric from their protectionist practice, especially over agriculture.

For the developing world in general, and Latin America in particular, the GATT agreement is expected to bring some minor benefits, as protected northern markets are opened up to southern crops. Mostly, GATT reduces barriers to trade in temperate crops such as wheat and dairy products, since the rich northern nations have historically had little reason to protect themselves against tropical crops such as coffee and bananas which they could not grow themselves. Overall the reduction in subsidies to northern producers will mean that world agricultural prices will rise, and the main beneficiaries in Latin America will be the temperate climate agricultural producers such as Argentina and Chile.

However, the new GATT agreement leaves the rich governments with 'considerable leeway to treat imports unfairly'[36] via anti-dumping and anti-subsidy measures. These measures are frequently an exercise in protectionist double-speak, used by the US and EU to justify punishing imports from other countries on the often debatable grounds that those countries are 'dumping' goods on the US or EU at below cost price or unfairly subsidizing their producers. The powerful countries can thus impose protectionist barriers in the name of free trade.

The GATT agreement extends free trade rules to almost all sectors of world trade, including agriculture and services such as banking, insurance and retail which now constitute a fifth of world trade. Two of the main ways in which the agreement will influence Latin America's future development are by extending 'national treatment' of foreign investors, whereby governments are banned from discriminating between national and foreign investors, and ruling against so-called 'Trade Related Investment Measures' (TRIMs), which are any attempts by a national government to place conditions on investors, whether foreign or domestic, engaged in producing tradeable goods. These include positive TRIMs such as tax incentives to corporations to invest in a certain location, or negative measures such as obliging a corporation to use a certain percentage of locally produced goods in its production.

As in other areas of the GATT agreement, the final compromise resulted from prolonged horse-trading between the most powerful participants, who largely ignored the Third World. The Economist Intelligence Unit concluded that the agreement on TRIMs 'reflects a compromise between the EU and the USA, with the developing world being shut out. TRIMs commonly used by developed countries, such as subsidies and grants, are excluded from the remit of the agreement, whereas the most common TRIMs used by developing countries are included.'[37]

The GATT agreement also extends the new World Trade Organisation's remit to overseeing international respect for 'Intellectual Property Rights', such as patents and copyrights. The vast majority of such patents are in the hands of First World companies and institutions, and the Third World sees US insistence on including property rights as a deliberate attempt to inhibit technology transfer from North to South, thereby undermining the South's efforts to acquire its own industrial base.

The new, more powerful policing of world trade achieved in the Uruguay Round will make it harder for developing countries to follow in the footsteps of the industrialized economies. At the turn of the century, the US refused to enforce British patents as part of its drive to acquire its own technological base for development, while if the GATT agreement had been in place in the 1950s, it would have been far harder for countries such as Japan, South Korea and Taiwan to develop their industries, since their early success was based on protecting and nurturing local industry, and successfully copying US technology. It is probably no coincidence that two of today's most successfully industrializing economies, Taiwan and China, are not GATT members, although both are now fearful of being left out in the cold and are eager to join.

In such circumstances it is hardly surprising if many in the Third World tend towards conspiracy theories which see the free trade crusade as part of a deliberate policy of 'global rollback' by the US and other industrialized powers, using the power of the IMF, World Bank, GATT, free trade agreements and US trade legislation to *prevent* industrialization in the South and to force the Asian economies to open up to US investment and trade. Each tightens the straitjacket which has been placed around Latin America's economic future, forcing it along the neo-liberal road, while increasingly depriving its people of the right to choose a different destiny, should neo-liberalism turn out not to be the nirvana promised from Washington and Geneva. One prominent Filipino critic of adjustment claims that the 'imposition of a state of permanent stagnation' in the South was 'precisely the idea' behind the North's handling of the debt crisis and ensuing adjustment.[38] This view could hardly be further from the World Bank's self-image as an aid provider and friend of the poor.

Notes

1 Quoted in Tim Lang and Colin Hines, *The New Protectionism: Protecting the Future against Free Trade* (London, 1993), p.28.

2 See Joan Robinson, 'The new mercantilism', in *Contributions to Modern Economics* (Oxford, 1978), pp. 201-2.

3 Quoted in Lang and Hines, *op. cit.*, p.1.

4 Fernando Fajnzylber, *Unavoidable Industrial Restructuring in Latin America* (Durham, NC, 1990), p.47.

5 IDB, *Economic and Social Progress in Latin America 1992 Report* (Washington, DC, 1992).

6 Doug Henwood, 'Impeccable logic: Trade, development and free markets in the Clinton era', *NACLA Report on the Americas* (New York, May 1993).

7 David Ricardo, *The Principles of Political Economy and Taxation* (London, 1992).

8 Belinda Coote, *The Trade Trap* (Oxford, 1992), p.94.

9 Quoted in Andre Gunder Frank, *Capitalism and Underdevelopment in Latin America* (New York, 1967), p.164.

10 *Comercio Exterior* (Mexico City, December 1992), p.1105.

11 Author interview (Santiago), September 1993.

12 United Nations Transnational Corporations and Management Division, *World Investment Report 1992* (New York, 1992), p.101.

13 Harry Browne, *For Richer for Poorer: Shaping US-Mexican Integration* (London, 1994), p.2.

14 Speech by Roberto Goizueta at conference on *Integración Económica en el Hemisferio: Perspectivas para América Latina*, 18–19 April 1993, at The Helen Kellogg Institute for International Studies, University of Notre Dame, Notre Dame, p.36 (author's translation).

15 UN Transnational Corporations and Management Division, *World Investment Report 1992*, p.102.

16 United Nations Transnational Corporations and Management Division, *World Investment Report 1993* (New York, 1993), p.143.

17 *Ibid.*, p.15.

18 *Guardian* (London), 11 February 1994, p.16.

19 *Financial Times* (London), 31 August 1994.

20 UN Transnational Corporations and Management Division, *World Investment Report 1992*, p.1.

21 Paul Ekins, *Wealth Beyond Measure: An Atlas of New Economics* (London, 1992), p.32.

22 Quoted in John Cavanagh, Daphne Wysham and Marcos Arruda, *Beyond Bretton Woods: Alternatives to the Global Economic Order* (London, 1994), p.175.

23 Latin American and Caribbean Trade Alert, *Free or Fair Trade?* (Bogotá, March 1993), p.6.

24 'Stateless money, a new force in world economics', *Business Week* (New York, 21 August 1978), p.76.

25 Howard M. Wachtel, *The Politics of Supranational Money* (Amsterdam, 1987), p.19.

26 Robert Heilbroner, quoted in Wachtel, *op. cit.*, p.25.

27 IMF, *International Capital Markets, World Economic and Financial Surveys* (Washington, DC, April 1993), p.3.

28 IMF, *International Capital Markets*, p.4 and IMF, *International Financial Statistics Yearbook 1993* (Washington, DC, 1993), p.109.

29 Howard M. Wachtel, 'Taming global money', in Cavanagh *et al.*, *op. cit.*, p.74.

30 Walter Wriston, quoted in Cavanagh *et al.*, *op. cit.*, p.74.

31 IDB, *Economic and Social Progress in Latin America 1992 Report* (Washington, DC, 1992), p.215.

32 Sebastian Brett, 'Let a hundred flowers bloom', *Guardian* (London), 21 September 1993.

33 Fajnzylber, *op. cit.*, p.30.

34 This section is based on Phillip Evans and James Walsh, *The EIU Guide to the New GATT* (Economist Intelligence Unit, London, 1994).

35 'NAFTA and GATT: The impact of free trade', *Understanding Global Issues* (Cheltenham), February 1994.

36 Evans and Walsh, *op. cit.*, p.2.

37 *Ibid.*, p.36.

38 Walden Bello, *Dark Victory: The United States, Structural Adjustment and Global Poverty* (London, 1994), p.69.

CHAPTER 6

Export or Die

Export-led Growth and Regional Trade

It hits you from hundreds of yards away, the rich sweet smell of fermenting wood floating through the crisp air of a Chilean night. The scent emanates from several huge mounds of wood chip, silhouetted against the dockside floodlights. Dwarfing the wooden houses and shops of the southern port of Puerto Montt, the mounds steam gently as they await loading onto the Japanese ship which rides at anchor in the bay. Each pile contains the remnants of a different species of Chilean tree, hauled from the country's dwindling native forest.

Along the southern coast, the wire-mesh tanks of innumerable salmon farms dot the picturesque fjords and inlets. On the beaches, the black strings of *pelillo* seaweed lie drying, before being sent to Japan for processing into food preservative. In the ports, the fishmeal factories grind mackerel into animal fodder. All these products will be shipped overseas as part of the Chilean export boom, a vast enterprise which has turned the country into the fastest-growing economy in Latin America and the flagship of the neo-liberal model.

The phenomenon is being repeated across the region. On the runway at Guatemala City airport, a forklift truck loads boxes of leaves into a cargo plane. Within hours the lush tropical foliage will arrive in Miami, for use in the next day's flower arrangements throughout Florida. In Colombia thousands of women toil, drenched in pesticides and fertilizers, among extraordinary swathes of colour. They are growing carnations for sale by the florists of Europe. Other, less-palatable entrepreneurs have also got in on the act; one drug kingpin of Colombia's Cali cartel was convicted after 22 tons of cocaine was found hidden in consignments of frozen broccoli bound for the US.[1]

These burgeoning 'non-traditional exports' are part of Latin America's new thrust for export-led growth, cashing in on improved transport and packing technologies to diversify the kind of primary products which have traditionally dominated Latin American exports. The other side of the export drive is an attempt to increase the exports of manufactured goods, usually low-tech products such as shoes or textiles, or the output of assembly plants, such as the *maquiladoras* strung along the US-Mexican border, where imported components are assembled by cheap Latin American labour.

Diversification lowers a country's vulnerability to sudden swings in world prices for a single, all-important export product. By moving into fruit, timber and fisheries, Chile reduced the preponderance of copper in its exports from 79 per cent in 1970 to 41 per cent in 1991.[2] The more exotic 'non-traditional exports', such as fresh salmon or strawberries (or cocaine) also carry a higher profit margin than tanker loads of copper ore or soyabeans. In Chile, Costa Rica and Guatemala, three leading exponents of the new trend, export income from non-traditional agricultural exports rose by 100 per cent, 200 per cent and 70 per cent respectively between 1984 and 1989.[3]

However, Latin America's attempt to get in on the ground floor of the global economy as a purveyor of raw materials risks confining it to one of the most sluggish areas of world trade, continuing its traditional reliance on the fickle prices of the commodity markets. The recovery in its exports since 1982 has been swamped by a flood of imports, following blanket trade liberalization, bankrupting potentially competitive local producers and raising fears that the 'opening' has undermined the region's industrial future. Furthermore, the boom in non-traditional exports has been achieved at a high social cost, exacerbating inequality and undermining the region's food security, while both assembly plants and pesticide-intensive agriculture have damaged the environment.

Statistics, as always, only tell half the story. Orchards fill the Aconcagua valley north-east of Santiago de Chile. Parallel rows of peach trees stretch off to infinity, playing tricks with the eye. The monotony is punctuated by the occasional fat-trunked palm tree or weeping willow, shining with new leaf on a cold and dusty spring day.

Carlos Vidal is a union leader, president of the local *temporeros*, the temporary farm labourers who plant, pick and pack the peaches, kiwi fruit and grapes for the tables of Europe, Asia and North America. A shock of black curls streaked with grey fringes his round, gap-toothed face. A freezing wind off the nearby Andes blows across the vineyards as Carlos tells his story.

> On this land there were 48 families who got land under [former President] Allende. We grew vegetables, maize and beans together, as an asentamiento [farming cooperative]. There were a few fruit farms then, but we planned them. After the coup the land was divided up between 38 families – the others had to leave. Then it started to get

difficult, we got the land but nothing else – the military auctioned off the machinery.

Then the empresarios started to arrive, especially an Argentine guy called Melitón Moreno. The bank started taking people's land – foreclosing on loans – and Moreno bought it up. Three compañeros committed suicide here because they lost their farms. Melitón got bank loans and bought yet more land and machinery. He planted nothing but fruit – grapes at first, then others.

My father was a leader of the asentamiento. The first year after the coup we were hungry, lunch was a sad time. We began to sell everything in the house, then we looked for a patrón to sell us seeds and plough our land for us, and we paid him with part of the harvest. Next year we got a bank loan and managed to pay it off, but the following year they sold us bad seed. We lost all the maize and the whole thing collapsed. We had to sell the land and Melitón Moreno bought it.

Of the 38 families, most are now temporeros. We all sold our land but kept our houses and a small garden to grow food. Trouble is, even the gardens are no good, the water's full of pesticides from the fruit. This area used to be famous for watermelons and now they don't grow properly any more. They chuck fertilizer and pesticide everywhere, it doesn't matter that the earth is dead because the fruit trees live artificially. No one grows potatoes or maize any more – it's cheaper to buy the imported ones from Argentina.

Life is hard for the *temporeros*, most of them women. 'They work you like a slave here, squeeze you dry then throw you out,' says Roxana, a smartly dressed 30-year-old. She can only find work during the harvest and packing seasons, seven months in the year. The few permanent jobs all go to men, she complains. Roxana's house is a wooden hut with a tin roof, a few sticks of furniture, no heating and no glass in the windows. The family bakes in summer and freezes in winter. Cold poverty is not as blatant or exotic as the tropical poverty of Haiti or Nicaragua, but the runny-nosed children are pale and bronchitic and the cold cuts to the bone.

Carlos' allegations about pesticides have been confirmed by a series of horrific birth defects. In the regional hospital at Rancagua, investigations showed that every one of 90 babies born with a range of neural tube defects in the first nine months of 1993 was the child of a *temporera* working on the fruit farms. The Rancagua figure is three times the national average. Pesticide poisoning is a feature of non-traditional agriculture throughout the region. Women in the Colombian flower industry report

miscarriages, premature births and respiratory and neurological problems,[4] while in Ecuador 62 per cent of workers in one survey said they
had suffered health disorders from exposure to pesticides at work.[5]

The ownership of farms producing non-traditional exports varies
widely. In Chile or Colombia, many are in the hands of wealthy local
growers, while foreign ownership is widespread in Costa Rica. Of the 14
largest flower growers there, only two are Costa Rican. The degree of
foreign control also varies according to the crop; Del Monte in Costa
Rica and Dole in Honduras produce the majority of pineapples and
bananas respectively, and control virtually all the transport and marketing
(often the most lucrative parts of the production chain).

Ownership tends to be in the hands of rich farmers, whether local or
foreign. Peasant farmers rarely have the access to technology or capital
required; flower plantations, for example, require a capital investment of
$80,000 per acre and few banks are prepared to lend such sums to poor
farmers.[6] When small farmers try to climb aboard the export bandwagon, they run serious risks. Costa Rica's countryside is littered with
failures like Norberto Fernández, a small farmer in the north. Norberto
received a loan in 1990 to switch from growing corn for the domestic
market to red peppers for export. He says that a non-traditional promoter
passed through his village, 'promising riches, a new car, a better house,
education for my children,' if he switched crops. When his crop of red
peppers came in, Norberto was told they did not meet export quality
control standards. He had to sell his 30 cows to repay the loans.[7]

Elsewhere in Central America, small farmers have overcome some of
the obstacles by forming cooperatives. In Guatemala, some 20,000 mainly
Indian peasant farmers produce non-traditionals including broccoli and
mange-tout, often on plots of less than two acres. But such cooperatives
are usually unable to export their crops themselves, forcing them to sell at
lower prices to exporters.

There are other drawbacks to the non-traditional craze. As more and
more developing countries leap aboard the bandwagon, the increased
competition floods the market. As one author asked, 'How many
macadamia nuts or mangoes can North Americans be expected to eat,
even at lower prices?'[8] In the Aconcagua valley, growers are hacking
down hectares of kiwi fruit trees because of a world glut. Chile's apple
growers have suffered a different kind of setback, by competing with EU
producers they have triggered off a bout of First World protectionism; in
1993 the EU responded to a bumper apple crop at home by virtually
closing its doors to Chilean apples.

This is little more than a new twist to Latin America's historical travails
with the terms of trade. The silent revolution has done little to reduce the

region's traditional reliance on the commodity trade; two-thirds of Latin America's exports still stem from agriculture or mining.[9] With each passing year the region has had to export more and more raw materials to import the same amount of manufactured goods. One study showed that some $75bn out of the $179bn of debt accumulated by Latin America between 1980 and 1988, or 42 per cent of the total, was accounted for by the deteriorating terms of trade.[10] As the region struggled out of recession in the early 1990s, commodity prices fell again, depriving the region of a further $12bn in income in 1991–92[11], although prices then recovered in 1994. The neo-liberal response to falling prices resembles a hamster on a treadmill, churning out ever greater quantities of raw materials to compensate. Consumers in the northern countries reap the benefits of cheaper broccoli, fresh strawberries at Christmas or exotic tropical leaves for their winter flower arrangements, but in developmental terms, it is a strategy with no future.

In Chile, government economists acknowledge these limitations, and argue for a new kind of industrialization, based on natural resources and destined for export rather than import substitution. Chile should export wine, not grapes, and furniture instead of wood chip. By processing natural resources before selling them, Chile would capture more of the final selling price of the finished product, made up of the price of the original commodity, plus the 'value added' in turning it into something fit to stock on a supermarket shelf. In the longer term, it should try and mimic Finland, which successfully found a niche in the world market when it developed timber processing and paper machinery on the foundations of its forestry sector.[12]

To date, however, the Chilean government has failed to shake off its neo-liberal inferiority complex, believing that the state can only harm the economy by stepping in to protect and nurture this process. There has been sharp growth in a few areas (wine exports have grown at over 50 per cent a year for the last five years), but without a concerted government industrial policy, the leap to a broader resource-based industrialization will never happen, even in a country as uniquely endowed with natural riches as Chile.

Across Latin America, governments have neglected food crops in the rush for exports. In the early 1980s, about 90 per cent of the money spent in Latin America on agricultural research went on food crops, especially beans, which contribute about 30 per cent of the protein consumed by the region's 200 million low-income families. Now only about 20 per cent of research money goes on food crops, as scientists and spending have been redirected into the export drive. Every Latin American country apart from Argentina, Chile and Ecuador has become a net importer of beans.[13]

At first sight, this is not necessarily a bad thing; if Chinese-grown beans are cheaper than the domestic variety, consumers should benefit from switching to cheap imports. In 1988, the then President of Costa Rica's Central Bank, Eduardo Lizano, confided that he saw no reason why his country should grow *any* food if it could all be imported more cheaply.[14] But what is at stake is known as 'food security'. When it is lost, market forces acquire control over the very stomachs of the poor.

If a country switches from growing to importing its food, access to food becomes dependent on income; poor peasants with a piece of land can grow maize or beans to survive, but once they have been ousted by export-oriented agribusiness growing fruit, vegetables or acres of carnations, they are far more likely to go hungry. More generally, reliance on food imports make a country more vulnerable to sanctions and trade disputes, while a sudden devaluation or removal of subsidies can raise prices overnight beyond the reach of the poor.

Cheap labour

It's 36 minutes after midnight when the factory bell rings, and José González emerges from the air-conditioned world of the Zenith television assembly plant in Reynosa, Mexico. Gonzalez' pay for eight hours of work comes to $8.50. He counts off 50 cents for the bus and heads home to the shantytown known as Voluntad y Trabajo – Will and Work – *and his one-room, scrap-board shack that lacks running water, electricity and sewer lines.*

Up north, in the Chicago suburb of Melrose Park, Pedro Camacho's eight hours of work at the Zenith picture-tube plant earn him $60 in take-home pay. When his shift ends at 3 pm, he hops in his car and drives home to a recently purchased, three-bedroom, wood-frame house nearby. Dinner is pizza, heated in his microwave.

Both men are Mexican by birth, about the same age and quit school in Mexico in sixth grade [end of primary]. Both are married, both have two children.[15]

A step across the 2000-mile US–Mexican border takes US companies into a corporate paradise of cheap labour, compliant unions, and lax environmental, health and safety regulations. Hundreds of factories have moved there from the US since the border strip was turned into a long snaking free trade zone in 1965.

The Border Industrialization Program allowed export-oriented assembly plants to set up within 12.5 miles of the border. The plants paid no duties on imported parts, which they then assembled into the finished product, packaged and sold back to the US. The result by 1994 was a chain of 2056 factories employing around 580,000 people,[16] and a massive boost in 'Mexican' manufactured exports. In terms of the net value added (i.e. the difference in value between the imported parts and the exported final product), *maquila* exports rose from $454m in 1975 to a projected $7bn in 1994.[17] The 1982 debt crisis was a watershed for the *maquila* industry. When Mexico was forced to devalue the peso in 1982, the dollar value of wages fell from $1.69 an hour in 1982 to just 60 cents by 1986. This was one-third of Taiwanese wage levels, and foreign investment flooded in.[18] The 40 per cent devaluation of the Mexican peso in early 1995 promised another boom for the *maquiladoras*.

The arguments over who wins and loses from the *maquiladoras* are heated, and central to the debate over the North American Free Trade Agreement (NAFTA) and the rapid spread of free trade zones (also known as export processing zones) throughout Central America and the Caribbean. 'New duty-free trading zones are emerging from North America to the Southern Cone, creating opportunities for both established and emerging transnational corporations to lower production costs', gushes a brochure from the Economist Intelligence Unit, advertising its *Seizing Free Trade Opportunities in the Americas* publication, a snip at just £210 ($300) a copy.[19] Jobs in the zones, which usually resemble industrial parks, include everything from making clothes and assembling TVs and computers to data input; doing the electronic drudgery for US supermarket chains and credit card companies. In return for setting up there, companies are allowed to import goods for final assembly and then re-export them free of taxes or restrictions on profit repatriation. The only value that accrues to the host country is that of the jobs generated in the zone and the usually low level of 'linkage' with the local economy in the form of local materials or services.

For their employees and local people in the border zone, the experience of the *maquiladoras* and other free trade zones offers pointers to what can be expected under NAFTA. Local residents have complained at the pollution created by *maquiladoras*, which are often run by 'dirty industries' fleeing the US to avoid its expensive environmental protection legislation. Individual workers complain at the low wages, ailments stemming from overwork and poor health and safety standards, minimal job security and frequent industrial injuries. Some of the injuries have been particularly horrific.

> *The director of the Matamoros School for Special Education, Isabel de la O Alonso, first began to notice them in 1982. Dr de la O worked with about 200 youngsters with physical and mental handicaps, the majority of*

them children of working class parents. But one small group stood out. Their disabilities ranged from severe retardation to slow learning. Physically they bore similar characteristics, such as broad noses, thin lips, bushy eyebrows, and webbed hands and feet. A few were deaf. Yet the children did not fit any of the categories of birth defects that she had previously studied or observed. Dr de la O decided to compile a clinical history and soon found that all the children had one thing in common – their mothers, while pregnant, had worked in the same Matamoros maquiladora. It had been called Mallory Capacitors, and the children became known as the Mallory Children.

The Mallory workers had to handle a range of toxic chemicals in the plant, but one in particular seemed the most likely cause for such severe birth defects. The capacitors – small devices for television sets which store an electrical charge – were washed in a product the workers only knew as 'electrolito'. Dr de la O believes that this liquid might well have contained PCBs, as her research indicated some similarities in the women's descriptions of the effects of the fluid and studies already carried out in the United States. PCBs, or polychlorinated biphenyls, have been banned in the US because of their links to cancer. They are also believed to affect the body's chromosomes. The women recalled that working with 'electrolito' caused their finger nails to turn black, a classic reaction to PCB exposure.

They are growing up now, leaving their teenage years and entering young adulthood, but they will always be the Mallory Children. Together they represent the most obvious legacy of the perilous conditions under which thousands of Mexicans toil for their minimum wage.[20]

But protests over such abuses have been largely ineffective, since most trade unions are in the pocket of the Mexican government, which is determined to avoid rocking the *maquiladora* boat by enforcing environmental legislation or antagonizing employers. In any case, most unemployed Mexicans would jump at a job in a *maquiladora*, where conditions, although bad by First World standards, are often better than those in nationally-owned factories.

In the US, the *maquiladoras* have been used by US business to depress wages and cut costs, either by relocating to Mexico, or threatening to do so during negotiations with US employees.[21] In the mid-1980s, General Motors' Packard Electric Division gave its employees in Cleveland, Ohio, a taste of things to come, when it threatened to move their jobs to Mexico unless they accepted a 62 per cent pay cut for all future employees. Since GM already had tens of thousands of workers in Mexico, it was no idle threat. Negotiations eventually reduced the cut to 43 per cent. In Centralia, Ontario, Fleck Manufacturing's employees refused to be bullied by similar threats and went on strike; hours later the plant shut down and moved to Ciudad Juárez, Mexico.[22]

Wages in free trade zones elsewhere in the region are even lower. In Nicaragua's Las Mercedes Industrial Free Zone, Korean and US textile companies were paying 58 cents an hour in 1993, including vacations and social security.[23] In the Dominican Republic, hourly wages in 1990 were a mere 35 cents.[24]

Changes in Latin American trade since 1982

Since the onset of the debt crisis in 1982, new primary products and *maquiladora*-produced manufactured goods have led the drive for the neo-liberal goal of export-led growth, yet results to date have been patchy. The regional ratio of exports to GDP, often used as a guide to the importance of trade to an economy, rose from 14 per cent to 22 per cent between 1980 and 1992,[25] but this was partly because GDP performed so badly. Exports which had shot up seven-fold in value between 1970 and 1980 rose by just 32 per cent from 1980 to 1993. Yet over the same period, world trade almost doubled, and Asian exports quadrupled. Latin America has continued to slide down the global pecking order as its share of world trade slipped further from 5.7 per cent to 4.0 per cent.[26] Export-led growth is barely getting off the ground.

In the early years of the debt crisis, the IMF's standard recipe of severe devaluation and import controls in Mexico and Brazil (hardly part of the neo-liberal panacea, but sins to which the IMF turned a blind eye[27]) not only made Latin American goods more competitive on the world market, but also made imports from abroad prohibitively expensive. The result was a slump in imports and a large trade surplus, used to pay off vast sums in debt service rather than in productive investment. The results can be seen in Figure 6.1.

From the late 1980s, under pressure from the international financial institutions, Latin America began to liberalize imports at a breakneck rate, despite the lack of any reciprocal opening from US or European governments. In all the major economies, maximum import tariffs which had typically exceeded 100 per cent were reduced to 35 per cent or less. Between 1989 and the end of 1992, Argentina's average tariff fell from 39 per cent to 15 per cent, Colombia's from 44 per cent to 12 per cent and Peru's from 66 per cent to 18 per cent.[28]

Neo-liberals argue that liberalizing imports improves economic efficiency and benefits everyone. Local factories can import the best available machinery and other inputs to improve their productivity,

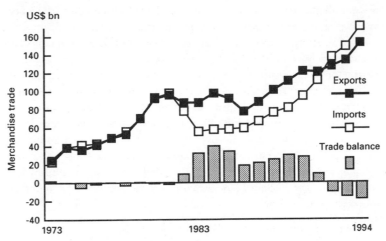

Figure 6.1: Latin American trade, 1973–94

Source: IMF, *Direction of Trade Statistics Yearbook*, Washington, DC, 1990 and 1994.

while consumers can shop around, rather than be forced to buy shoddy home-produced goods. Competition from abroad will force local factories either to close, or to improve their products until they become competitive with other countries' goods, paving the way for increased manufactured exports.

In practice, import liberalization has unleashed a consumer boom, as Latin Americans have flocked to snap up imported goods at bargain prices, with a drastic impact on the region's trade balance. Mexico and later Argentina have run up huge trade deficits as import bills have rocketed – in Argentina imports quintupled between 1990 and 1994. Latin America's regional trade balance swung back into the red in 1992 and by 1994 was heading for a $18bn trade deficit. By 1994, Brazil alone maintained a large trade surplus, while only Chile and Venezuela were even slightly in the black.[29]

As in many other areas, the neo-liberal revolution has increased inequality between countries, as the largest economies have strengthened their position and the weaker ones have fallen behind. Between 1982 and 1992 the largest economies, Brazil, Mexico and Argentina (a distant third), increased their share of Latin America's exports from 49 per cent to 61 per cent, with a similar rise in their share of imports.[30] All countries increased their exports of low-tech manufactured goods such as furniture or footwear, but only the largest economies moved into high-tech exports such as cars, steel or electronics.[31] For full details of individual countries' trade performance, see Appendix A.

Two respected Latin American economists, Ricardo Ffrench-Davis and Manuel Agosín,[32] have laid out some clear conditions for a successful trade reform: the value created by new activities must exceed that lost due to the number of factories destroyed by competition from cheap imports; export industries must be sufficiently linked to the rest of the national economy to spread the benefits of improved exports throughout the country, and increased competitivity must be achieved by continuous gains in productivity rather than through low wages or ever-greater subsidies or tax breaks. The authors do not believe these conditions have been met in the recent Latin American trade reforms and point out numerous serious failings:

- *countries have unilaterally opened up their economies in a protectionist and stagnant world economy, allowing other regions to increase their imports to Latin America without having to reciprocate by buying the region's exports;*
- *countries have liberalized far too rapidly, not allowing local firms sufficient time to make the necessary changes and investments to adapt to the new rules and improve their productivity before the import floodgates open. This has wiped out numerous potentially competitive companies in a wholly avoidable manner;*
- *Latin America has fallen back into relying on its static comparative advantage, which has led it to concentrate its efforts in the least dynamic areas of the world economy, such as commodity exports;*
- *the deregulation of Latin America's financial markets and influx of foreign capital, which has coincided with trade liberalization, has led to overvalued exchange rates and high interest rates (set by governments to attract foreign currency). Overvalued currencies have made the region's exports less competitive, while high interest rates have discouraged exporters from borrowing to invest in increasing production.*

Trade patterns

Table 6.1 shows the wide variations between different Latin American countries' trading patterns and the changes that took place over the course of the 'lost decade'. Some of the most outstanding points are:

- *the southernmost economies such as Argentina and Brazil have a much more even spread of trade between Latin America, the US, Europe and Japan, whereas Mexico, Central America and the Caribbean are highly dependent on the US economy;*

- *over the course of the 1980s, these differences became more pronounced as the* maquila *boom brought growing de facto integration between Mexico and the US. Trade with the US accounted for about 70 per cent of Mexican trade by 1992;*
- *with the exception of Mexico, the late 1980s brought a boom in trade between Latin American countries, especially in the Southern Cone, where trade between Argentina and Brazil took off following the Mercosur agreement [see p. 144];*
- *the US increased its dominance over Latin American trade as a whole, although a large part of this was due to the US-Mexican trade boom. US exports to the region came to $78bn by 1993, and if they continue to grow at the current rate will surpass exports to Western Europe by the year 2000. According to Clinton administration officials, exports to Latin America now account for three million US jobs.*[33]

Agreeing to trade

Everybody's doing it. Since the late 1980s, Latin America's economists have been spending a large slice of their waking hours negotiating a bewildering variety of bilateral, trilateral and multilateral regional trade agreements (RTAs) with each other. By mid-1994, Latin America could boast 22 bilateral accords and several sub-regional pacts.[34] However, the best known (and most controversial) is the only RTA between First and Third Worlds. The North American Free Trade Agreement, between the US, Canada and Mexico, came into force in 1994 despite fierce opposition within the US from an unlikely opposition movement including Ross Perot, the US trade union establishment and grassroots environmentalists.

RTAs enshrine comparative advantage at the heart of the economic relationship between nations. If each country sticks to what it does best, goes the argument, and imports everything else it needs, everyone will be better off. In the case of NAFTA, Mexican and US exporters and investors will obtain guaranteed access to each other's economies; Mexican consumers can enjoy the benefits of cheap food imports, the latest computer technology and even experience the joy of an invasion of US fast food chains. According to the comparative advantage school of thought, the best option would be a free trade world, but an RTA can be a step towards it.

When signing RTAs, governments typically agree to phase out, or drastically reduce, tariff barriers between RTA members and eliminate non-tariff barriers such as import quotas. Over time, RTAs may lead to deeper forms of integration such as a customs union, which charges a common external tariff on imports from outside the RTA, a common market which allows free movement of labour and capital between members, or even a monetary union as agreed by the European Union in the Maastricht Treaty.[35]

Within Latin America, the upsurge in RTAs has involved reviving and strengthening moribund agreements from the previous round of free trade areas in the 1960s and 1970s. These include the Andean Pact (originally made up of Bolivia, Chile, Colombia, Ecuador, Peru and Venezuela); the Central American Common Market (Nicaragua, El Salvador, Honduras, Guatemala, Costa Rica) and the Caribbean Common Market, (Caricom), which covers the English-speaking Caribbean. The most ambitious of them all was the Latin American Free Trade Association (LAFTA), set up in 1960 and comprising Argentina, Bolivia, Brazil, Chile, Colombia, Ecuador, Mexico, Paraguay, Peru, Uruguay and Venezuela. LAFTA proposed the establishment of a Latin American Common Market by 1980.

The first generation of agreements sprang up in the 1960s in response to the difficulties experienced under import substitution, principally the limited size of domestic markets for locally-produced goods. The aim was to nurture import substitution's 'fledgling industries' by providing a large captive market for their goods (in essence an extension of import substitution's protectionism to a wider geographical area). The early RTAs floundered and eventually collapsed at the onset of the debt crisis. In 1980, LAFTA's grand design was watered down and its name changed to the Latin American Integration Association. Such organizations never solved import substitution's basic problem of the shortage of hard currency; Peru needed dollars, not Bolivian pesos, to buy manufactured goods and to pay its debt service. In addition, within each RTA the stronger economies tended to swamp the weak; El Salvador's industry boomed as it exported to the more backward Honduran and Nicaraguan economies, which ran up large and unpaid debts.

So why have Latin Americans turned again to RTAs as part of the solution to their troubles? Supporters of the new RTAs argue that they share a fundamentally different purpose from their forebears. The new generation of agreements aims to reap the benefits of an expanded domestic market *in order* to increase exports to the world outside. Where once they were merely a defensive laager of uncompetitive nations, RTAs are now portrayed as an 'export platform' from which to sell goods to outside markets, principally the US. Optimists also see them as a stepping stone to ever-broader integration, as the different areas join up to form a single hemispheric or preferably world free trade area, such as that envisaged by the GATT process. Tariff reductions within the RTAs are merely complementary to (and slightly greater than) the general tariff reductions taking place under structural adjustment.

Table 6.1: Main trading partners for largest Latin American economies, 1983 and 1993 (as percentage of total trade)

	Argentina		Brazil		Mexico[1]		Venezuela		Latin America and Caribbean	
	1983	1993	1983	1993	1983	1993	1983	1993	1983	1993
Exports to										
USA	10	9	23	21	58	78	31	47	38	43
Japan	5	4	6	6	7	2	3	2	5	4
EC/EU	24	25	29	26	18	6	22	8	22	17
Latin America	14	39	10	25	8	4	21	38	14	21
Imports from										
USA	22	23	16	22	61	68	47	40	31	43
Japan	7	4	4	5	4	7	5	6	5	7
EC/EU	27	25	13	21	15	12	22	21	17	19
Latin America	33	31	15	18	4	7	14	18	24	19

Source: IMF, *Direction of Trade Statistics Yearbook*, Washington, DC, 1990 and 1994.
[1] Includes *maquiladora* trade.

The new enthusiasm for RTAs has also been driven by fear. In the early 1990s, as the Uruguay round of GATT world trade talks dragged on with little sign of success, the US, Germany and Japan showed signs of retreating into regional agreements to become the nuclei of three world trading super-blocs. RTAs offered a regional insurance policy for anxious Latin Americans, and also increased their bargaining power as they queued up to be next in line after Mexico to join NAFTA. The unattractive alternative was to be frozen out of the main trade and investment flows of the world economy, like much of Africa.

In the face of recession and rising protectionism from the industrialized economies against Latin America's manufactured exports, and low commodity prices for their primary exports, RTAs within the region had other advantages. The outside world's main interest in trading with Latin America is to gain access to its raw materials, but when Latin American countries trade with each other, there is usually a much higher proportion of manufactured goods involved. In 1992, 56 per cent of intra-regional trade was in manufactured goods,[36] compared to barely a third of its trade with the outside world. RTAs can therefore help stimulate the industrialization process.

In addition to reviving existing, but moribund, RTAs, numerous new ones have been created (see Table 6.1), notably the giant of Latin American integration, Mercosur (*El Mercado Común del Sur*), bringing together two big fish – Brazil and Argentina – and two minnows – Uruguay and Paraguay. Established by the Treaty of Asunción in March 1991, Mercosur planned for a common market between all four members by 1996. Even before Mercosur came into force, the region was already the fastest-growing part of Latin America, registering a collective 5.2 per cent growth figure in 1993. In the period 1990-93, the Mercosur countries accounted for over half (51.9 per cent) of Latin America's output.[37]

Although Mercosur has led to a boom in trade between the four member countries from \$4.2bn in 1990 to \$9.6bn in 1994[38] and a proliferation of mergers and joint ventures between companies from different Mercosur members, there have been sporadic outbursts of tension, particularly over Brazil's surging exports to Argentina. President Menem's decision to raise some tariffs against Brazilian imports in late 1992 suggested that the problems which dogged the first generation of RTAs have not disappeared. Delays and disagreements have led to extensions of the timetable; for example, a common external tariff on capital goods and computers will now not come into force until the year 2006.

Thanks to a combination of RTAs and the recovering regional economy, intra-regional trade more than doubled between 1987 and 1992, to reach \$24.5bn, representing 15 per cent of the region's total trade.[39] As a proportion of total trade, however, the recovery only restored intra-regional trade to the levels that Latin America had enjoyed on the eve of the debt crisis.

Table 6.2: Main current regional trade agreements in Latin America and the Caribbean (excluding NAFTA and the World Trade Organisation)

Andean Pact: Founded in 1969 by Bolivia, Colombia, Chile, Ecuador and Peru. Venezuela joined in 1973 and Chile left in 1976. Went into decline during 1980s, but revived in early 1990s when Venezuela, Colombia, Ecuador and Bolivia agreed on a common external tariff in 1993, with the aim of eventually forming a customs union which would also include Peru. Regular disagreements between member states have impeded the integration process.

Caribbean Common Market (CARICOM): Formed in 1973 by Barbados, Guyana, Jamaica and Trinidad, later joined by the rest of the English-speaking Caribbean. In 1988 the original members (except the Bahamas) started to remove controls on trade which had sprung up during the debt crisis. In 1992 eight member states agreed on a common external tariff which would be reduced over time. The following year, the group also announced plans to move towards a single currency.

Central American Common Market (CACM): Created in 1963 by Guatemala, Costa Rica and Nicaragua and subsequently joined by Honduras and El Salvador. Honduras withdrew in 1970 when it became clear that the larger economies were benefiting at the expense of the weaker ones. In 1980s escalating regional tension forced it further into crisis. Revived in the 1990s, when Guatemala, El Salvador, Honduras and subsequently Nicaragua formed a free trade area in 1993 with a common external tariff on imports from outside the region. Costa Rica and Panama may also join, although both have reservations about the process.

Group of Three (G3): In 1993 the presidents of Colombia, Venezuela and Mexico signed a free trade agreement to come into force in 1994 for an initial ten year period.

Latin American Integration Association (LAIA): Formed in 1981 out of the remnants of the Latin American Free Trade Area (LAFTA) to provide a framework for trade agreements between various groups of countries within the area.

Organisation of Eastern Caribbean States (OECS): Existing within CARICOM, the OECS is a group of small island economies which currently operates the only true common market in Latin America and the Caribbean. Has continued uninterrupted since its foundation in 1968. The OECS operates a single currency, the EC dollar.

Southern Cone Common Market (Mercosur/Mercosul): Signed in 1991 by Argentina, Brazil, Paraguay and Uruguay. Formed common market from 1 January 1995, although protection in some sectors (cars, computers) will be phased out over a longer period of time. Chile is currently seeking associate status with Mercosur.

Note: In addition to these main groupings, there are numerous bilateral accords.

Sources: CEPAL, *Desarrollo Reciente de los Procesos de Integración en América Latina y el Caribe* (mimeo), Santiago, 5 May 1994; David Woodward, *Regional Trade Agreements in Latin America and the Caribbean* (mimeo), report written for Oxfam, Oxford, 1993.

NAFTA

The border at night is a battle of lights. On the Mexican side, the feeble yellow glow of countless single bulbs marks Tijuana's shanty towns. They are dwarfed in intensity, if not in number, by the neon billboards of the motels and burger bars which light up the night on the US side.

By day, the contrast is even starker. Tijuana's dusty sprawl covers every square inch of the hillsides, right up to the border fence. From their backyards, the shanty town residents look out on the bare, scrub-covered hills of Southern California. Separating the two worlds is *la linea*, the frontier.

Tijuana on the US-Mexican border is a unique eyeball-to-eyeball confrontation between First and Third Worlds, a town where dollar and peso are interchangeable, a brothel and booze resort built during the Prohibition years to service US marines from the San Diego naval base. It also serves as a prototype for the future relationship between the two countries, enshrined in the North American Free Trade Agreement signed by the presidents of the US, Mexico and Canada in October 1992. Some critics believe NAFTA will turn the whole of Mexico into a giant Tijuana.

On New Year's Day 1994, NAFTA came in with a bang. Unfortunately for the Mexican government's public relations team, it was the sound of gunfire in the southern state of Chiapas, as 2000 fighters of the previously unknown Zapatista National Liberation Army rose in rebellion against the oldest one-party state in the world. The uprising was an extraordinary hybrid of ancient and modern. Exhausted Indian fighters speaking little Spanish slumped next to their barricades in San Cristobal de las Casas while a few yards away, tourists queued up to take cash out of the automatic teller machine. The largely indigenous rebels were protesting age-old grievances such as the discrimination against Mexico's large Indian minority, but the trigger for the uprising was the silent revolution: the government's reversal of their constitutional right to communal land, and NAFTA, which they described as a 'death certificate for the indigenous peoples'.[40]

NAFTA is a very different entity from the proliferating Latin American RTAs. It is the first-ever RTA between a First and Third World economy and, in the words of one writer, 'a crucible in which advanced technology, subsistence farming, global finance capital, massive under-employment and contrasting legal and political systems are mixed for the first time'.[41] Whereas Latin American RTAs are, at least to some degree, a marriage between equals, the disparities within NAFTA are stark. The US economy is over 20 times larger than Mexico's and the technological gulf is even wider.

Table 6.3: What is NAFTA?[42]

The North American Free Trade Agreement gradually eliminates almost all trade and investment restrictions between the US, Canada and Mexico over 15 years. Side agreements, concluded in August 1993, require the enforcement of some environmental and labour laws, under penalty of fines or sanctions.

The US and Canada entered an RTA in 1989, and the pact thus mainly affects their trade and investment with Mexico. NAFTA came into effect on 1 January 1994.

General provisions
- *tariffs will be reduced over 15 years, depending on sector;*
- *foreign investment restrictions will be lifted in most sectors, with the exception of oil in Mexico, culture in Canada, and airlines and radio communications in the US;*
- *immigration is excluded, although restrictions on the movement of white collar workers will be eased;*
- *any country can leave the treaty with six months' notice;*
- *the treaty allows for the inclusion of any additional country;*
- *government procurement will be opened up over 10 years, mainly affecting Mexico, which reserves some contracts for Mexican companies;*
- *dispute resolution panels of independent arbitrators will resolve disagreements arising out of treaty;*
- *some tariffs will be allowed if a surge of imports hurts a domestic industry.*

Sectoral provisions
- *agriculture: most tariffs between US and Mexico will be removed immediately. Tariffs on 6 per cent of products — maize, sugar and some fruit and vegetables — will be fully eliminated only after 15 years;*
- *automobiles: tariffs will be removed over 10 years; Mexico's quotas on imports will be lifted over the same period; cars will eventually have to meet a 62.5 per cent local content rule to be free of tariffs;*
- *energy: Mexico's ban on private-sector exploration continues, but procurement by Pemex, the state oil company, will be opened up to US and Canada;*
- *financial services: Mexico will gradually open its financial sector to US and Canadian investment, eliminating barriers by 2007;*
- *textiles: the treaty eliminates Mexican, US and Canadian tariffs over 10 years. Clothes eligible for tariff breaks must be sewn with fabric woven in North America;*

- *trucking: North American trucks can drive anywhere in the three countries by the year 2000.*

Side agreements
- *environment: the three countries are liable to fines, and Mexico and the US to sanctions, if a panel finds repeated non-enforcement of environment laws;*
- *labour: countries are liable for penalties for non-enforcement of child, minimum wage and health and safety laws.*

Other deals
- *the US and Mexico will set up a North American Development Bank to help finance the clean-up of pollution along the US-Mexican border;*
- *the US will spend about $90m in the first 18 months of NAFTA, retraining workers losing their jobs because of the treaty.*

At the heart of NAFTA lies the growing incompatibility between nation states and the workings of international companies. In many ways NAFTA is a misnomer, since the bulk of the text concerns investment rather than trade, and in almost every case, it concerns Mexico, rather than the US or Canada.[43] NAFTA opens up formerly protected areas such as mining and (partially) petroleum, it binds Mexico into strict new patent rules for pharmaceuticals and computer software and prevents Mexico from trying to delay or obstruct the repatriation of profits by transnational companies. In short, Mexican law will have to treat US and Canadian businesses exactly like Mexican companies. Mexico's 2000-mile border with the US ceases to exist for investors, though not for Mexico's would-be migrant workers, who if anything will find it harder to get across.

In addition to its growing role as a cheap labour 'export platform' from which transnational corporations can export their products back to the US, Mexico also constitutes an attractively large and willing market for US companies. By 1993, the average Mexican already spent $450 a year buying US products, four times more than Japanese consumers.[44]

Besides the long-term influence of globalization and the needs of transnational corporations and other US investors, a number of other more short-term considerations pushed Mexico's President Carlos Salinas de Gortari to drop his previous objections to an RTA with the US and Canada.

In February 1990, when Salinas was invited to speak to the annual World Economic Forum in Davos, Switzerland, he had trouble filling the room, while speeches by Poles and Russians produced packed houses.[45] The experience drove home the point that Mexico could expect little investment or interest from outside the Americas. On the plane home, Salinas concluded that Mexico had to push for an RTA, even though a year earlier, he had gone on record opposing the idea.[46] Months later, the negotiations began.

Although Salinas and his predecessor Miguel de la Madrid had pushed through a free market/free trade transformation of the Mexican economy since the debt crisis hit in 1982, there was as yet nothing to stop future presidents reversing the process. Now, NAFTA will 'lock-in' Mexico to an agreement with the US by making it much more costly to revert to statist or protectionist models. It also locks in the US at a time of rising protectionist sentiment in Washington, thereby ensuring that Mexico will be inside the fold should the US ever return to its isolationist past. With each year that passes under NAFTA, the three economies will become more integrated, and the economic and political price of prising them loose will rise ever higher.

The rest of Latin America has watched the coming of NAFTA with anxiety. Although the US has always stressed its intention that the agreement should be but the first step on the road to creating a free trade area 'from Alaska to Tierra del Fuego', the initial impact on other countries in the region was negative. Governments in Central America and the Caribbean are particularly vulnerable. Within months of NAFTA coming into effect, they had seen textile factories, which formed a crucial part of their drive for non-traditional exports in the 1980s, relocating to Mexico. US imports from Central American and Caribbean producers must pay tariffs of between 17 and 21 per cent, while under NAFTA the tariff on Mexican-produced clothing will sink to zero by 1997. In 1993, the year before NAFTA came into effect, Mexico's garment exports to the US grew more slowly than those from Central America and the Caribbean. In the first quarter of 1994, Mexican exports easily outstripped the opposition, rising by 39.2 per cent, while sales from Central America and the Caribbean increased by only 9.9 per cent.[47]

Locking in neo-liberal reforms via NAFTA makes Mexico a far safer prospect for foreign investors deciding where to locate their factories and banks, or whether to make loans or buy shares in Mexican companies. Salinas hoped that NAFTA would guarantee the long-term inflows of capital he needed to upgrade the Mexican economy and initial results seemed to bear him out.

Until its crash in early 1995 (see p. 85), Mexico was Latin America's investment magnet, accounting for $20bn of the roughly $57bn that entered the region in 1994.[48] The start of NAFTA ensured that even the political chaos that bedevilled Mexico in the early months of the 1994 election year caused only a temporary interruption in the cascade of dollars. Over the first six months of the year, despite the Chiapas uprising and the assassination of the main presidential candidate, foreign direct investment rose by 25 per cent over the same period of 1993 and the dollar inflow to the stock market rose by nearly half.[49]

Those hoping to extend NAFTA to the rest of the region received a boost in December 1994, when President Clinton went to Miami to host the 'Summit of the Americas' with every Latin American head of state bar Fidel Castro. Despite earlier fears that rising protectionism within the US might prevent any further agreements, the summit agreed to establish a 'Free Trade Area of the Americas' by the year 2006. In a separate announcement, the NAFTA members also announced the beginning of talks with Chile over its accession to the agreement. Clinton predicted that at current trends, the hemispheric RTA would by then be 'the world's largest market – more than 850 million customers buying $13 trillion of goods and services.'[50] Paradoxically, Clinton's humiliating defeat in the Congressional mid-term elections the previous month had eased the path to integration, since in the US Republicans tend to be less suspicious of free trade than Democrats.

Despite the statements made in Miami, however, the 2005 deadline for the completion of negotiations is not binding, and the fate of the Free Trade Area of the Americas is bound to be hostage to political developments in the intervening years.

NAFTA will undoubtedly change the face of Mexico. After two centuries of national defeat in its sporadic conflict with the US (Mexico lost half its territory to Washington in the last century), the PRI has now accepted the inevitable, tying its economy, seemingly for ever, to the coat-tails of its giant neighbour. In the economic shake-out which this will entail, some firms will go under, while others thrive. More broadly, NAFTA like the other neo-liberal reforms of the last 15 years, will create new fault-lines running through Mexican society, separating new generations of haves from the ever-growing masses of the have-nots.

Table 6.4: Winners and losers under NAFTA

Politicians and pressure groups have conducted the heated debate over NAFTA in terms of which countries will win or lose from the deal, but in fact all three countries contain both winners and losers. Assessments of NAFTA are more about positions in the economic pecking order than about nationality. Opponents have dubbed the agreement a corporate bill of rights which seeks to maximize business profits by setting worker against worker.

Winners

In the US and Canada:
* *transnational companies can cut costs by relocating to Mexico;*
* *transnational companies with factories already in Mexico will obtain permanent guaranteed access to the US market;*
* *many US firms will gain improved access to the growing Mexican market. US food and drink companies are investing in huge numbers to produce for the Mexican market. In the first six month of NAFTA, US exports to Mexico rose by 17 per cent to reach $24.5bn, and the US was expected to record a $2.1bn trade surplus with Mexico in 1994, $0.5bn higher than the year before;*[51]
* *US consumers will benefit from cheaper Mexican imports in areas such as agriculture.*

In Mexico:
* *thousands of the urban un- or under-employed will find jobs in new factories or incoming US service industries;*
* *large Mexican exporters will be able to take advantage of improved access to the US market;*
* *Mexican entrepreneurs linked to transnational companies (e.g. those employed by or running industrial parks for* maquiladora *plants);*
* *Mexican consumers will benefit from cheap imports from the US – everything from US agribusiness-grown maize produced at a fraction of the cost of peasant-produced Mexican maize, to computers;*
* *Mexican consumers will also see results from new forms of US investment in Mexico, from new insurance and banking services to fast-food chains such as Kentucky Fried Chicken or even, in a Mexican version of 'sending coals to Newcastle', Taco Bell and Pancho's Mexican Buffet.*[52]

Losers

In the US and Canada:

* *workers thrown out of jobs as their factories move south of the border (Ross Perot's famous 'giant sucking sound' of disappearing jobs);*
* *workers elsewhere who are forced to accept lower wages by companies threatening to relocate;*
* *auto and petroleum exporters in Canada suddenly faced with competition from Mexico for the US market;*
* *in Canada, NAFTA continues the pressure created by its earlier bilateral RTA with the US to dismantle its superior welfare state (seen by the RTA as an unfair trading subsidy). Both NAFTA and the earlier RTA have provoked widespread opposition in Canada.*

In Mexico:

* *peasant farmers, especially 1.6 million maize growers who will be put out of business by imports from massive US farms which are 4 to 6 times more productive than small, under-funded Mexican peasant producers;* [53]
* *small 'artisan' producers will be wiped out by mass-produced US imports;*
* *industries set up in the days of import substitution, supplying the domestic market. Some of these are out of date and inefficient and will be undercut by US imports. However, many have already gone bust due to trade liberalization in the 1980s.*

Notes

1 *Guardian* (London), 13 August 1993.

2 CEPAL, *Anuario Estadístico de América Latina y el Caribe 1992* (Santiago, 1993).

3 Bradford Barham, Mary Clark, Elizabeth Katz and Rachel Schurman, 'Non-traditional agricultural exports in Latin America', *Latin America Research Review*, Vol.27, No.2 (Albuquerque, NM, 1992), p.48.

4 Sarah Stewart, *Colombian Flowers: The Gift of Love and Poison* (mimeo) (Christian Aid, London, 1994), p.3.

5 *NACLA Report on the Americas* (New York, November/December 1994), p.27.

6 *Ibid.*, p.24.

7 *Multinational Monitor* (Washington, DC, July/August 1993), p.21.

8 Barham *et al.*, *op. cit.*, p.47.

9 IDB, *Economic and Social Progress in Latin America 1992 Report* (Washington, DC, 1992).

10 Kevin Watkins, *Fixing the Rules: North-South Issues in International Trade and the GATT Uruguay Round* (London, 1992), p.13.

11 UNCTAD, *Trade and Development Report 1993* (New York, 1993), p.28.

12 Fernando Fajnzylber, *Unavoidable Industrial Restructuring in Latin America* (Durham, NC, 1990), p.143.

13 *Financial Times* (London), 15 June 1994.

14 Author interview (San José, NM), October 1988.

15 Jane Bussey, 'NAFTA: a bid to bridge the US-Mexico chasm', *Miami Herald*, 18 October 1993.

16 Report by Instituto Nacional de Estadística Geográfica e Informática (Mexico City), June 1994.

17 Latin America Monitor, *Mexico* (London, October 1994), pp.5–6.

18 IDB, *Economic and Social Progress in Latin America 1992 Report* (Washington, DC, 1992).

19 '4 ways to improve your bottom line performance in Latin America' (Economist Intelligence Unit, London, 1992).

20 Augusta Dwyer, *On the Line: Life on the US-Mexican Border* (London, 1994), p.66.

21 'Free trade: The ifs and buts', *Resource Center Bulletin* (Albuquerque, NM, Spring 1993).

22 Harry Browne, *For Richer for Poorer: Shaping US-Mexican Integration* (London, 1994), p.78.

23 *Caribbean Update* (Maplewood, NJ, February 1993).

24 James Ferguson, *Dominican Republic: Beyond the Lighthouse* (London, 1992), p.66.

25 CEPAL, *Anuario Estadístico de América Latina y el Caribe 1993* (Santiago, 1994), p.74.

26 IMF, *International Financial Statistics Yearbook 1994* (Washington, DC, 1994).

27 Jackie Roddick, *The Dance of the Millions: Latin America and the Debt Crisis* (London, 1988), p.47.

28 *CEPAL Review* No.50 (Santiago, August 1993), p.44.

29 CEPAL, *Panorama Económico de América Latina 1994* (Santiago, September 1994), p.8.

30 IMF, *Direction of Trade Statistics Yearbook* (Washington, DC), 1993 and 1989.

31 Oxford Analytica, *Latin America in Perspective* (Boston, MA, 1991), p.236.

32 R. Ffrench-Davis and Manuel Agosín, 'Liberalización comercial y desarrollo en América Latina', *Nueva Sociedad*, (Caracas, September/October 1994).

33 *Newsweek* (New York), 12 December 1994, p.16.

34 *Financial Times* (London), 2 September 1994.

35 David Woodward, *Regional Trade Arrangments in Latin America and the Caribbean* (mimeo), report written for Oxfam (Oxford, 1993), p.5.

36 GATT, *International Trade 1993* (Geneva, 1993), p.16.

37 Latin America Monitor, *Southern Cone* (London, December 1994), p.6.

38 CEPAL, *El Dinamismo Reciente del Comercio Intrarregional de la Asociación Latinoamericana de Integración* (Santiago, 23 August 1994), p.3.

39 CEPAL, *Anuario Estadístico de América Latina y el Caribe 1992* (Santiago, 1993).

40 *Guardian* (London), 3 January 1994.

41 Browne, *op. cit.*, p.3.

42 *Financial Times* (London), 17 November 1993.

43 William A. Orme Jr, *Continental Shift: Free Trade and the New North America* (Washington, 1993), p.89.

44 *The Economist* (London), 9 October 1993), p.93.

45 Orme *op. cit.*, p.22.

46 Stephanie Golob, 'Explaining NAFTA', panel at conference of the Latin American Studies Association (Los Angeles, CA, September 1992).

47 *Financial Times* (London), 11 October 1994.

48 CEPAL, *Balance Preliminar de la Economía de América Latina y el Caribe 1994* (Santiago, December 1994), p.2.

49 CEPAL, *Panorama Económico de América Latina 1994* (Santiago, September 1994), p.55.

50 *Financial Times* (London), 12 December 1994.

51 *Financial Times* (London), 26 August 1990.

52 *Latinamerica Press* (Lima), 4 February 1993, p.2.

53 Woodward, *op. cit.*, p.35.

CHAPTER 7

For and Against

The Politics of Neo-Liberalism

In the grimy, polluted Chilean capital of Santiago, the campaign billboards for the presidential elections of December 1993 were instantly forgettable – grey men in dark suits looked sternly out like disapproving bank managers. Both main candidates were promising more of the same – continuity with the neo-liberal policies first put in place by General Augusto Pinochet when Chile was an altogether more turbulent place.

In the same week that Chile was selecting its new bank manager, rioters were sacking the impoverished town of Santiago del Estero, across the Andes in Argentina. The provincial government ignited the protest, in which four died and fifty were injured, when it announced that, owing to central government cutbacks, it had run out of cash and could not afford to pay public employees their wages for September and October, and that only half of November's pay packet would be paid. When provincial deputies then voted themselves a large pay increase, the town exploded.[1]

At the other end of the continent, in Mexico, trouble was brewing in another of neo-liberalism's purported success stories. On New Year's Day 1994, an Indian revolt erupted in Mexico's southernmost state, Chiapas. On the very day that the North American Free Trade Agreement came into effect, popular rage at the social impact of the structural adjustment programme shook the foundations of the Mexican state.

Consensus, urban riots or rural revolt, the contrasts of Mexico, Argentina and Chile in the mid-1990s exemplify the range of political models and processes that have accompanied the silent revolution. In the 1970s, when General Pinochet was ruling Chile, it was commonly believed that his brand of radical free-market reforms could only be achieved through dictatorship and repression to quell the fierce public resistance that was bound to occur. Yet in June 1993, 20 years after the coup that brought Pinochet to power, the people of Bolivia elected the architect of the country's structural adjustment to be the new president.

Gonzalo Sánchez de Losada, 'Goni', a mining entrepreneur whose US upbringing has left him speaking Spanish with a gringo accent, took the helm promising privatization and business efficiency instead of the corruption and incompetence of 'the politicians'. How has free-market ideology become electable in the intervening decades?

The roots of this political turn-around lie in the collapse of the previous economic system, import substitution, the perceived failure of the attempt to find less painful 'heterodox' forms of adjustment in the mid-1980s and the broader ideological impact of the disintegration of state-run economies in Eastern Europe. The traumas of the debt crisis and hyper-inflation have increased voters' readiness to grapple with the market, while renewed capital inflows in the early 1990s have allowed politicians to experiment with less painful forms of structural adjustment. They have been backed by powerful Latin American business groups who previously benefited from import substitution, but increasingly believe that their future prosperity depends on a full engagement with the new globalized economy. Moreover, voters have rarely been given a clear choice. Since the late 1980s, numerous presidents have been elected on anti-neo-liberal platforms, only to perform abrupt U-turns on taking office.

Military and markets

The Chilean military espoused a particularly brutal form of economic Darwinism. When asked about the high bankruptcy rate caused by the government's adjustment policies, Pinochet's colleague in the junta, Admiral Merino, replied, 'Let fall those who must fall. Such is the jungle of ... economic life. A jungle of savage beasts, where he who can kill the one next to him, kills him. That is reality.'[2]

Faced by a labour force accustomed to secure, unionized jobs, Pinochet's bloody repression of the trade union movement played an essential part in the 'adjustment' process. 'If he hadn't killed all those people, the economy wouldn't be where it is today,' admits Luz Santibañez, a former exile in Scotland who now runs her own clothes workshop in Santiago.[3] The final death toll is still unknown, but the most recent upward revision in early 1994 put at 3100 the number of people slaughtered to clear the way for the new Chile.[4]

Elsewhere, however, the military has never been an automatic ally of the market (Pinochet himself hesitated for almost two years before finally adopting the neo-liberal creed). In Brazil, the military government that took power in 1964 ran up the Third World's largest foreign debt by its massive support for infrastructure and state companies, while also opening up key sectors of the economy to investment by transnational corporations. In Argentina, the juntas after 1976 destroyed much of the country's industry by abandoning all protection for local producers, but never considered privatizing the military's mighty industrial complex. In Paraguay, the Generalísimo, Alfredo Stroessner, built his 35-year rule on a combination of brutality and graft, buying the army's support with the proceeds from smuggling goods into Paraguay from neighbouring Brazil and Argentina.

Nor, for that matter, has big business been a keen supporter of deregulation. Import substitution enjoyed considerable support from both transnational corporations and local manufacturers, both of which produced goods for the local market. Safe from competition from better, cheaper goods produced elsewhere, they were able to foist shoddy, overpriced products on generations of Latin American consumers. In most countries, the market was controlled by a few large companies, who were able to avoid internal competition by fixing prices among themselves. However, as the globalization of the world economy got under way, other groups of entrepreneurs have become increasingly determined that Latin America should redirect its economies towards exports and free trade. The two groups have often come into conflict (often via their political proxies), but the debt crisis, increased influence of outside forces like the IMF, and the collapse of import substitution has decisively weakened the hand of the older generation of industrialists.

Military government in Latin America carries the seeds of its own destruction. Power politicizes and fragments the military institution itself, and the population's anger at the generals' authoritarian ways grows as the military fails to deliver on its initial promises of efficient management and economic boom. In the late 1970s and early 1980s this process coincided with the death throes of import substitution and the onset of the debt crisis. Latin America in the early 1980s therefore experienced an historical anomaly; whereas in the past, economic recession has provoked military unrest and seizures of power, when the debt crisis hit in 1982, the military were already in full retreat to the barracks. A new generation of civilian governments took office as their economies were collapsing around them. The suffering of the 'lost decade' has had a profoundly negative impact on the continent's return to democracy, but it has not led to a swift return to military rule.

In the immediate aftermath of the Mexican crisis of August 1982, government after government accepted IMF tutelage and applied its standard shock treatment to stabilize the economy. However, when it became clear that the result was often *destabilization* of the economy through a lethal combination of inflation and recession, several governments broke ranks and began looking for an alternative and less painful means of stabilizing the economy. The resulting heterodox packages led to a brief recovery, before most of them collapsed in a welter of hyper-inflation.

The failure of the heterodox shock programmes left neo-liberal structural adjustment as the undisputed orthodoxy, and political parties of all stripes from the Sandinistas to El Salvador's right-wing ARENA party have signed up for the treatment since the late 1980s. They have faced an acute political quandary: how can a party hope to be elected if its policies are guaranteed to inflict an instant and devastating blow to the standard of living for the population? Peru's Fujimori explained his dilemma, saying 'It's very difficult and terribly unpopular to apply stabilization measures in an impoverished country like Peru, but it would be even harder to lead the country towards social and national disintegration through economic ruin.'[5]

Whether through bad faith, or the recognition upon taking office that the external forces pressing for adjustment were overwhelming, some of the men who subsequently became the darlings of the neo-liberals won the presidency by campaigning on an anti-neo-liberal platform, then performing a policy somersault on coming to power. Taking office in 1989 and 1990, Peru's Alberto Fujimori, Argentina's Carlos Menem, Brazil's Fernando Collor de Mello and Venezuela's Carlos Andrés Pérez all performed sharp economic U-turns immediately after being elected on anti-austerity platforms.

To do so, they have all been forced to ride roughshod over democratic institutions, using the traditional Latin American technique of governing by decree in order to bypass congressional opposition. Argentina's President Menem announced as many decrees during 1989–92 as were issued by all of his civilian predecessors since 1922 put together.[6] Civil rights have also taken a battering. In Bolivia, the government attempted to defuse union opposition to the 1985 structural adjustment decree by declaring a state of siege and imprisoning 143 strike leaders in Amazonian internment camps.[7] In Colombia, the government used anti-terrorist legislation in 1993 to try 15 trade union leaders opposing the privatization of the state telecommunications company.[8] In the most extreme example, Peru's Alberto Fujimori dealt with a troublesome Congress by simply dissolving it in April 1992 (with army support) and seizing emergency powers in what was billed a 'self-coup'. Elsewhere, 'telepopulist' presidents like Collor have taken to the media to sell their policies direct to the electorate, building on Latin America's long love affair with the *caudillo*, the strongman on horseback (in Collor's case updated to a Ferrari) who would come to the rescue of his people.

Even in their own terms, the four U-turn specialists have achieved mixed results. Menem and Fujimori have both led their countries swiftly from stabilization to renewed growth and were both rewarded with re-election in 1995, but in Brazil and Venezuela, Collor and Pérez's economic failure, autocratic habits and corrupt practices ensured they were both publicly vilified and impeached when only half-way through their terms in office. Ironically, Collor had come from nowhere to win Brazil's elections in 1989 by promising to stamp out corruption in government. Collor's stabilization plan was doomed from the start by Brazil's highly decentralized political system, which severely restricts the president's ability to control public spending or anything else. One observer even sees the existence of a political system with a strong president as the essential precondition for successful adjustment.[9] Only then can swift and initially unpopular measures be forced through quickly enough to allow time for a return to growth, restoring public belief in the president.

Winning support for neo-liberalism

The real extent of public support for neo-liberal reforms is still hard to gauge precisely because so few presidential candidates have stood on an openly neo-liberal ticket. The fact that they have not suggests that politicians at least believe that open support for the market remains an electoral liability. In one of the few cases when voters were asked specifically to endorse a neo-liberal programme, the Uruguayan government held a referendum in 1992 which it expected to rubber-stamp its plans to privatize five state companies. Instead, to the neo-liberals' dismay, the Uruguayan public voted overwhelmingly (72 per cent) against privatization. In Uruguay, as the *Financial Times* commented, 'Slogans like "solidarity" and "unity" still carry real weight,'[10] although the *FT* took this as a sign of the Uruguayan people's 'unyielding conservatism' rather than anything more positive.

Since the late 1980s, following the collapse of both the Berlin Wall and the attempts at a heterodox alternative to structural adjustment, the 'there is no alternative' rhetoric so successfully employed by Mrs Thatcher has rung true for many voters. Resignation to the inevitability of adjustment hardly constitutes real support, but Presidents Fujimori and Menem have persistently won high approval ratings *since* executing their U-turns, while the election of Sánchez de Losada in Bolivia in 1993 shows that neo-liberals can become electable.

Support, or at least acquiescence, is easier to obtain in countries which have been through the trauma of hyper-inflation, as in Nicaragua, Peru, Bolivia and Argentina. The best-known example of the profound impact of hyper-inflation on a nation's political culture is the rise of Hitler in Germany in the 1930s, following the economic crisis of the Weimar Republic. Where a government is able to stabilize the economy and eradicate inflation, the population is often willing to support it, even at the cost of recession and increased poverty, as in Peru under Fujimori.

The 1994 elections in Brazil gave a graphic demonstration of the importance attached by the poor to ending inflation. With four months left before polling, the candidate of the left-wing Workers Party (PT) was over 20 points in the lead in the opinion polls and looked certain for victory. In July the *Real* plan, a new economic package drawn up by then Finance Minister Fernando Henrique Cardoso, was introduced, cutting inflation from 50 per cent a month to 1 per cent in the space of three months.[11] Cardoso then went on to run for president in October. He clearly recognized the devastating impact of inflation on the lives of the poor, commenting during the campaign, 'If I were the devil and wanted to invent a tool to punish the poor, that tool would be inflation.'[12] On 3 October the poor multitudes of the shanty towns proved him right, electing Cardoso by a landslide. Equally, the fact that Venezuela had not undergone the ravages of hyper-inflation could explain the lack of support for Carlos Andrés Pérez's adjustment programme following his election in 1988, which led to the bloody protests and repression of the *Caracazo*. Venezuelans had not suffered enough to convince them of the need to swallow the neo-liberal medicine.

The degree of political opposition to a stabilization and structural adjustment programme is also affected by the degree of pain involved, since some adjustments are more painful than others. One of the key factors in determining the pain level is the availability of international capital. Countries which stabilized in the mid-1980s did so in an international climate where virtually no one was interested in lending to Latin America. But by the end of the decade, Latin America was back in the good books of international lenders, and pickings were thin back in the US and Europe. Since then, countries like Argentina have led the boom in investor interest in 'emerging markets' and have been able to count on massive international capital inflows to ease the pain of adjustment, especially if they go on privatization sprees to attract foreign investors. In Argentina, large capital inflows have paid for imported machinery to upgrade productivity in the factories, while also creating an overvalued peso which has depressed the price of imports, keeping inflation down without the need to provoke a recession. President Menem was able to stabilize the economy in 1990 without going into recession, then move swiftly towards high economic growth.

Economic growth based on a massive trade deficit and capital inflows is not sustainable in the long term (except, perhaps, in the case of the United States), as the Mexican crisis of 1995 made painfully clear. For the foreseeable future, Latin America has ceased being the flavour of the month for international investment, and the region will have to return to more painful forms of adjustment. Nevertheless, from the late 1980s until 1995, capital inflows made the initial phase of adjustment much less painful and politically costly than the kind of recession which adjustment brought to Chile in 1975, when GDP fell by 13 per cent in a single year and unemployment rose to 20 per cent.[13] No government other than a dictatorship could have survived that kind of disaster.

The political conditions for successful stabilization can differ from those needed for longer-term structural adjustment and a return to export-led growth. Stabilization requires little more than the absence of effective opposition as the government axes public spending, clamps down on consumption and brings inflation under control. The best time for such steps is usually in the honeymoon period immediately after an election victory, while the new president's prestige is at its highest, the opposition is demoralized and there is still plenty of time to get the most painful part of the stabilization over with before the next election.

Adjustment and an eventual return to growth are altogether more complex tasks, as a former Venezuelan industry minister explains:

> *Stabilization programmes are difficult and politically costly to launch, but their technical and administrative requirements are much simpler than those of structural reforms. In most countries, the executive branch of government has the power to cut public budgets unilaterally, liberalize prices, devalue the local currency and tighten the money supply. In contrast to those 'decree driven' measures, structural changes like privatization, the restructuring of social security systems, tax reform, and the institutional transformation of industry, agriculture and higher education require more than the stroke of a pen and are immensely more complex. The public bureaucracy, Congress, the courts, state and local governments, political parties, labour unions, private sector organizations and other interest groups all get involved in the process ... the debate ... can seem endless.[14]*

Touting for private-sector investment, whether domestic or foreign, means building business confidence in the government's plans. This, in turn, means guaranteeing efficient government and political and social stability. Countries such as Nicaragua (after 1990) and Bolivia have proved highly successful at curbing inflation, but have been unable to attract significant amounts of foreign investment. Political and social unrest caused by the stabilization effort, combined with the level of incompetence and corruption in government, have deterred foreign investors and left the economies struggling to recover from the ravages of stabilization.

To avoid such unrest and instability, a degree of social consensus on the need for market reform seems essential. That consensus has been easiest to achieve in the old corporatist countries such as Mexico, where the government traditionally controls the trade unions and other likely sources of opposition.

Reversing the revolution

Diego Zapata looks nothing like his grandfather, General Emiliano Zapata, Mexico's revolutionary icon. The portraits which line his grandson's grimy front room show a solemn, handsome young man sporting the famous droopy moustache, bandoliers, sombrero and sword. Diego, on the other hand, is a 63-year-old peasant with an unshaven, lived-in face, who is clearly annoyed at being woken from his siesta. He lives in the village of Anenecuilco, birthplace of his famous forebear.

He talks fondly of his grandfather, 'El General', but Diego's face hardens at the mention of the current Mexican president, Carlos Salinas. He was unimpressed when Salinas dropped in to inaugurate the new Zapata museum, even though the president bought the village a new statue of its most famous son, which now stands in the neat palm-lined village square, opposite the Zapata pharmacy and the Zapata kindergarten. 'They come here and talk marvels about Zapata but it's just politics. The General wanted to give land to the peasants, now Salinas is doing the exact opposite,' he says.

Everyone is a Zapatista in Mexico, where the old guerrilla hero is revered as the spiritual leader of the chaotic Mexican Revolution of 1910–17. Much like Sandino in nearby Nicaragua, Zapata mobilized the masses for revolution, and was then assassinated before his image could be tarnished by compromise or old age. Zapata's death in 1919 is seen as part of the wider betrayal of the revolution's ideals which left Mexico in the hands of the aptly-named 'Institutional Revolutionary Party', or PRI. The PRI has turned Mexico into the world's oldest one-party state, keeping a tight grip on power since 1929, through a blend of fraud, bribery, violence and appeals to revolutionary nationalism.

Zapata's cry of 'Land and Liberty' still strikes a chord with Mexico's dispossessed. In the decades after the revolution, many large ranches were handed over to the peasants, but the cream of the agricultural land stayed in the hands of the wealthy. Now the PRI has reversed even that land reform, allowing market forces in to demolish the communal land-owning structures put in place by the revolution. 'The ones with the money will end up with the land, just like before,' grumbles Diego. Along the way the government's claim to be the true inheritors of the revolution has become increasingly untenable.

Its octopus-like control over every aspect of society has enabled the PRI successfully to coerce, coopt and divide potential opposition since

President Salinas embarked on his sweeping structural adjustment programme in the late 1980s. One critic of the ruling party acerbically observes, 'The PRI's *raison d'être* is to help the government avoid the irritations of democracy.'[15]

As leader of what the Peruvian novelist Mario Vargas Llosa has famously described as 'the perfect dictatorship', Salinas could rely on the PRI's control of trade unions, peasant organizations, the media and just about everything else to smooth the way for privatization, government cutbacks and free trade. Nicholas Scheele, director of Ford Motor Company's Mexican operations, was very appreciative. 'It's very easy to look at this in simplistic terms and say [union corruption] is wrong, but is there any other country in the world where the working class ... took a hit in their purchasing power of in excess of 50 per cent over an eight-year period and you didn't have a revolution?'[16] Still, the PRI has not remained in power since 1929 by taking things for granted, and as a further guarantee, Salinas also embarked on the National Solidarity Programme (Pronasol), a massive social compensation effort to ease the impact of adjustment on the poor.

Salinas understood the breadth of the undertaking, and even attempted to rewrite the historical iconography of the Mexican revolution. In 1992, the then education secretary Ernesto Zedillo caused a national furore by trying to revise Mexico's primary school textbooks.[17] Overnight, pre-revolutionary dictator Porfirio Díaz was transformed from archetypal bloated plutocrat to misunderstood modernizer and Zapata's revolutionary agrarian reform plan suddenly disappeared from the textbooks. So blatant was the effort that Zedillo was forced to withdraw the texts, although his blunder did not prevent him from taking over the presidency from Salinas when the PRI won yet another election in 1994. Zedillo promptly named a cabinet stuffed with young foreign-educated economists to continue Salinas' market crusade.

Salinas watched events in Russia and drew a simple conclusion; Gorbachev's mistake had been to put political reform (*glasnost*) before economic restructuring (*perestroika*). The PRI opted for immediate radical economic adjustment, while keeping the lid on protest and deferring political reform, preferably for ever, or at least until it was safe to do so without the risk of losing power. Roberta Lajous, the PRI's Secretary of International Relations, may look modern, in her office wear of black leather trousers and bouffant blonde hair, but her politics are definitely in the PRI tradition. 'We are not going to throw away the corporatist structure as long as it's useful. Not for votes, but to help the government implement policy. We'd never have been able to carry out the reforms without pyramidal structures.'[18]

The Zapatista uprising in early 1994 forced the PRI to take serious steps along the road of democratic reform before the elections in August, making them the most democratic poll this century. Proving its extraordinary ability to defy history, the PRI won by a landslide, bolstered by years of carefully targeted social spending, its domination of the media and the support of virtually every millionaire in Mexico. The assassination of the PRI's presidential candidate in the first days of the campaign paradoxically helped the PRI's campaign by creating a climate of insecurity. Mexicans voted for business as usual, fearing the chaos that could result from ending the PRI's 65-year reign.

Outside the country, the uprising received a great deal of media coverage, but did not seem to worry foreign investors over-much. In a survey in May 1994 of senior US executives, 97 per cent said they were aware of political unrest in Mexico, but 87 per cent said it would not influence their companies' plans to conduct business there. The *Financial Times* concluded that 'A strong labour movement would be far more likely than a dozen bands of Zapatista rebels to turn US companies off Mexico.'[19]

In the longer term, however, it is hard to see how the PRI can cut back on the role of the state and open the economy up to market forces without eroding its ability to maintain political control. In the past, its power has been based on massive state spending through a corporatist network of state-sponsored trade unions, peasant associations and other groups. Now that cutbacks in state spending have reduced that option, it seems unlikely that the PRI can stifle change for ever, especially if the economy fails to sustain its faltering recovery of the early 1990s. The PRI's fate clearly hinges on NAFTA's impact on Mexican wages and job prospects, yet in NAFTA's first year, the PRI was showing signs of severe internal division between the neo-liberals and those they labelled the 'dinosaurs': old-style politicians who feared the loss of party power implicit in the reforms. The divisions exploded into the public domain following the assassination of several high-ranking PRI officials, and subsequent allegations that the 'dinosaurs' had had a hand in the killings and had blocked the subsequent investigations.[20]

The PRI was able to hold things together by pursuing the soft option of using an overvalued peso to hold down inflation, while relying on massive inflows of foreign capital to bridge the resulting trade deficit. But when foreign investors took fright in late 1994, provoking a foreign exchange crisis and a collapse of the peso, Salinas's successor, Ernesto Zedillo, was forced to turn to President Clinton and the IMF for an unprecedented $50bn rescue package. In return, he had to promise to return to the old ways of using domestic austerity to get inflation back under control, meaning another fall in real wages, which had only just begun to recover from the recession of the 1980s. The crisis promises a severe examination of the PRI's remaining corporatist strength, in particular testing whether it can force the trade union rank and file to accept yet more austerity when the promised benefits recede ever further into the distance.

Elsewhere in the region, other governments have imitated the PRI's methods. In Argentina, Carlos Menem has used his Peronist Party's control of the trade union movement to good effect, while the post-Pinochet Christian Democrat governments in Chile have been helped by their party's dominant position in the trade union movement.

The political conditions required for a successful stabilization and adjustment programme reveal the silent revolution's impact on the wave of democratization of the 1980s. Successful adjustment is easier when there is a strong, centralized presidency able to overrule Congress and when the government controls the trade union movement and other sources of potential opposition. Autocratic presidents who ignore or dissolve parliaments and tear up their campaign promises and manifestos the day after the election hardly help build the institutions of a stable democracy, still less the kind of democracy which actively involves its citizens.

The cruel twist of history that made the debt crisis and structural adjustment coincide with Latin America's return to (more-or-less) democratic rule provoked a sharp decline in the credibility of political parties in particular and politicians in general. In the political vacuum created, people have turned not just to local grassroots organizations, but to a new generation of Latin America's traditional *caudillos*, men like Bolivia's brewing magnate Max Fernández or media star 'Compadre' Carlos Palenque, who use their wealth and radio and TV chat shows to reach out directly to the battered and disoriented communities of the shanty towns. In Peru, President Fujimori revealed the nature of modern, technocratic *caudillismo*, saying, 'One of my goals is total independence – from political parties, from institutions – so I don't have any obligations. This distancing has helped me get closer to the people.'[21]

According to the silent revolution's critics, structural adjustment has ripped the heart out of democratization, turning what could have been a flowering of political and social participation into a brand of 'low-intensity democracy'. In the words of one critic of the Chilean transition from dictatorship to electoral democracy, 'The peaceful co-existence of export-oriented accumulation and elected regimes hinges on the ability of the political class and ruling élites effectively to disembowel the democratic political system.'[22] The traffic has not been all one way, however, and even low-intensity democracy is better than no democracy at all. The impeachment of Collor and Pérez and steps towards political reform in Mexico are signs that those in power must at least take note of the opinions of their people, but this is hardly the democracy for which thousands of men and women laid down their lives in the 1970s in their fight to rid the continent of military dictatorship.

Opposition and protest

The roadblock is a couple of tree trunks and a few boulders, cutting off the dirt road to Potosí where it passes through the scattered huts of another bleak Bolivian *altiplano* village. In the dusty school hall a young man reads out a communique to the growing number of trapped truck and bus drivers. He says the local peasants union is cutting the roads in protest at the government's deal with Lithco, a US transnational mining company, which allows it to exploit Potosí's vast salt lake for virtually nothing in return. A woman warns, 'They're stoning people at the next *bloqueo*. People are drunk. You must go back to Sucre.' Potosí, the poorest department of the poorest nation in South America, has watched its mineral wealth leave for 500 years. 'We don't want the same thing to happen with lithium as happened with our tin and silver,' says one leader of the protest, 'Whatever transnational comes will rob us, we just want them to rob a little and not take everything.'[23]

More than a decade after the Mexican debt crisis paved the way for the silent revolution, there are relatively few islands of political calm in Latin America's troubled continent. Chile, Costa Rica perhaps, but elsewhere social and political unrest have become the norm, as continued opposition to the impact of structural adjustment has sputtered and occasionally ignited in sporadic riots, strikes, rural uprisings, land takeovers and, increasingly, electoral victory for presidential candidates promising to soften the impact of adjustment. In general, however, the opposition is scattered and incoherent, dogged by its lack of a coherent alternative. Grassroots political leaders and intellectuals alike bemoan the opposition's inability to move from *protesta* (protest) to *propuesta* (proposal). The scattered nature of protests also means that many of them escape the attention of the world's press, contributing to a misleading impression of social stability in the region.

Establishing who is worst hit by adjustment and any likely political response is complicated, since most people both win and lose from the changes, and their opposition or support for the measures depends on how they subjectively weigh up their gains and losses. Workers may face wage cuts and deteriorating social services, but be sufficiently relieved at lower inflation to re-elect the president. The middle class may mourn their lost job security, yet welcome the fact that their phone now works following privatization and they can buy imported food and modern consumer goods in the shops thanks to trade liberalization. Furthermore businesses, including transnational corporations, frequently pay lip service to the virtues of free trade, while lobbying behind the scenes to keep the protection they enjoyed under import substitution.

Turning opposition into a serious political force has been hampered by the very impact of the adjustment process, which has weakened many of its natural opponents. In the shanty towns, women who led the grass-roots social movements which were instrumental in driving the military from power now exhaust themselves in the struggle to feed and clothe their families in increasingly hostile conditions, leaving little time for community activism beyond that strictly necessary to their 'survival strategies'. Government cuts have targeted the most unionized sector of the workforce, public employees, while overall casualization policies have drastically weakened the bargaining power of industrial unions. On the positive side, the decline in government backing for 'official' trade unions has encouraged a resurgence of more democratic and independent unions such as those involved in founding Brazil's Workers Party.

In Chile, adjustment has created an atomized society, where increased stress and individualism have damaged its traditionally strong and caring community life. According to press reports, suicides have increased threefold between 1970 and 1991 and the number of alcoholics has quadrupled in the last 30 years. Community leaders in Santiago's working-class *poblaciones* say family breakdowns are increasing, while opinion polls show the current crime wave to be the most widely condemned aspect of life in the new Chile. 'Relationships are changing,' says Betty Bizamar, a 26-year-old trade union leader. 'People use each other, spend less time with their family. All they talk about is money, things. True friendship is difficult now. You have to be a Quixote to be a union leader these days!'[24]

With political parties battered by their lack of prestige and frequent irrelevance to national politics, as well as their lack of an alternative to the neo-liberal recipe, much of the real opposition to adjustment has taken place elsewhere. In the cities riots and strikes have punctuated the adjustment process; in the countryside land takeovers and occasional uprisings have occurred in countries such as Ecuador and Mexico, while at an organizational level a plethora of institutions including Non-Governmental Organizations (NGOs), trade unions, peasant, Indian and women's organizations and Latin America's ever-active intellectuals have stubbornly opposed the neo-liberal crusade.

Those protesting at the social costs of adjustment have received strong backing from the radical wing of the Catholic Church, which has repeatedly attacked the social injustice of the market. At the meeting of the Conference of Latin American Bishops in Caracas in March 1993, the

Bishop of Cali in Colombia, reflected 'In Latin America the economy is doing well, but the peoples are doing badly: you must not worship neo-liberalism because it is inhumane, unacceptable, because it cares only about economic success and does not put human beings at the centre of things.'[25]

Table 7.1: Latin American Austerity Protests 1976–94[27]

Country	Date	Action	Severity	Precipitating events
Argentina	1982 to 1985	Demonstrations by labour unions, strikes and looting	Hundreds arrested	Price increases, inflation and austerity policies
	1988	General strike, street violence and looting	Over 100 wounded	Government anti-inflation plan
	1989	Food riots and looting. Women march into supermarkets, load up trolleys and walk out without paying	14 dead, over 80 injured, thousands of arrests	Outbreak of hyperinflation
	1993	Riots in Santiago del Estero	4 dead, 50 injured	Provincial government unable to pay wages to state employees due to cuts demanded by central government
Bolivia	1983 to 1987	General strikes. Street violence, looting and protest marches	c10 killed, 1500 arrested. Closure of mines, banks, shops, industry and universities	Proposed austerity package to increase prices of gasoline and food. Unemployment and devaluation
	1990	Strikes by trade unions and 'civic strikes' by local population		Sale of lithium deposits and 4 oilfields to transnational corporations
	1992	Wave of strikes and hunger strikes by miners, oil workers, and La Paz residents		Privatization programme and wage controls imposed under agreement with IMF
	1993	Series of general strikes		Incoming government proposals for privatization and cutting state payroll

Country	Date	Action	Severity	Precipitating events
Brazil	1983	Riots over food prices, looting of super-markets. Political protests	2 killed, 130 injured, 566 arrested	Devaluation, removal of subsidies, price increases
	1986 to 1987	Violence, looting and vandalism. Peaceful general strike	Tens of injuries, 30 arrested	Renewed austerity, tax and price increases
	1990	1.5 million workers on strike, mainly among public sector		Collor shock programme, threatening 200,000 public-sector dismissals
	1992	Wave of looting in Rio supermarkets and hunger riots in North-east		Inflation and death from starvation of 38 children in Pernambuco state
Chile	1983 to 1985	Regular political protests, general strikes	30–60 killed, over 1000 arrests and several thousand detained	Devaluation, removal of subsidies, privatization
Cuba	1994	Demonstrations and riots	35 injured	Price rises and growing poverty
Dominican Republic	1984	Demonstrations and riots, attacked by troops	112 civilians killed, 500 wounded	Price rises following IMF agreement
	1990	Strikes, riots and demonstrations	12 killed, 100 injured, 5000 arrests	Fuel price rises and other austerity measures
Ecuador	1982 to 1987	General strikes, street violence and protests	Schools and universities closed. 7 killed, 50 wounded and 500 arrested	Price increases and removal of subsidies on flour and gasoline
	1989	5 days of riots led by students	One killed	Price rises in public transport
	1991	4 days of riots	One killed, over 30 injured	Public transport fare increases
El Salvador	1985 to 1986	Large protests by workers, students and teachers, public employees	Strikes, hospital taken over and 15 arrests	Price rises and university cuts. Later devaluation and austerity package
Guatemala	1985	Riots, looting, protests and strikes	2–10 killed, 1000 arrested. Troops invade university	Increase in bus fares, bread and milk prices

Country	Date	Action	Severity	Precipitating events
Mexico	1986	20–50,000 people in frequent protests	Some injuries	September 1985 earthquake and austerity
	1994	Guerrilla uprising, followed by spate of land invasions and reprisals	At least 107 dead	Triggered by reversal of agrarian reform laws, the start of the North American Free Trade Agreement, and discrimination against Indians
Nicaragua	1990	Strikes and rioting	6 dead, 150 injured	Incoming government's proposals for mass lay-offs and the reversal of Sandinista laws on nationalization and redistribution of land and property
Panama	1983 and 1985	General strike, protests, National Assembly occupied	Tens of injuries, 30 arrested	Freeze on public-sector wages and cuts in business subsidies
	1992	Riots and looting in port city of Colón	One killed, dozens injured	Unemployment
Peru	1976 to 1985	Street riots and protests in Lima spreading to other cities. General strikes	21 killed and 'dozens' injured. 200 union officials arrested, 300–800 others arrested	Petrol and food price increases, removal of subsidies, unemployment
	1991	Strikes, demonstrations, riots and looting	Several killed, peasant and teachers' union leaders 'disappeared' by the army	Incoming President Alberto Fujimori's 'Fujishock' austerity programme
Venezuela	1989	Riots and looting	300–1500 killed, depending on source	Public transport fare increases as part of IMF package – letter of intent signed after the first day of rioting
	1991	Demonstrations and riots	7 killed	Privatization, state cutbacks and dismissals, gasoline price rises

One study of Latin American austerity protests from 1982 to 1986,[26] sometimes known as 'IMF riots', found that urban strikes and demonstrations, usually violent and often ending in looting, erupted against stabilization measures in Peru, Jamaica, Argentina, Ecuador, Bolivia, Chile, Brazil, the Dominican Republic, Haiti, Guatemala, El Salvador and Mexico. Since 1986, sporadic protests have continued in many urban areas, notably in Venezuela (1989), Argentina (1993) and Bolivia (1993). For a fuller list, see Table 7.1 (p. 167).

The extent of this kind of spontaneous protest depends on the existing political situation. Where countries have an established guerrilla movement, media reporting of events in these countries can distort the picture by confusing anti-government and pro-rebel protests. Guerrilla movements also channel protest into increased support for insurgencies, rather than one-off protests. This may explain why some of the countries best known for violent rebellion (Colombia, Guatemala, El Salvador) are missing from the table.

During the unrest, hundreds of protesters have been killed and thousands arrested in a continent-wide tide of protest. Typically the measures leading to unrest are those most directly affecting the poor: cuts in government food subsidies, price rises on public transport, the sacking of state employees. The main people protesting are the urban poor, who descend from the surrounding shanty towns to demonstrate in, and occasionally loot, the rich city centres. The looting is usually a response to police violence and is discriminating: 'In cases of riot, the targets of attack are selective and meaningful: affluent supermarkets in Rio, clothing and appliance stores in São Paulo, private automobiles and gas stations in Kingston, government offices in Chile, banks in Brasília, police stations in Haiti and the Dominican Republic.'[28] In countries with a strong trade union movement, these usually take the lead in calling strikes and demonstrations, which are often supported by other groups, such as students, left-wing political parties, or the urban poor.

The most bloody of the riots occurred in the Venezuelan capital of Caracas, when the incoming president Carlos Andrés Pérez doubled the price of petrol:

> As people flagged down buses, the drama began. Bus drivers angrily insisted that they had had to double fares over the weekend because Pérez had doubled the price of petrol. Students were told that their discount cards were no longer valid. The first violence erupted at the Nuevo Circo bus station in the city centre. Rocks and bricks were thrown, roadblocks went up, buses were set on fire.
>
> Within hours Caracas was gripped by insurrection. People streamed

down from the slums to help themselves to food, clothes and anything else from the shops whose windows they smashed. Some police and troops tried to intervene. Others actively helped the looters. Fabricio Ojeda, a journalist from El Nacional, reported that grateful slum-dwellers passed soldiers presents through the smashed-in shop windows. People careered along the main streets of Caracas, pushing supermarket trolleys crammed with loot or dragging entire beef carcasses from butchers' shops. As news of the caracazo reached other towns in Venezuela, similar riots broke out.

Eventually, on Wednesday, a massive military presence retook control of Caracas. By then, many shops and entire streets were in ruins. The army arrested thousands of people as they swept through the shanty towns searching for stolen goods. In the course of the following week, perhaps 1500 people died at the hands of the military, although the government admitted to only 287. Soldiers opened fire without warning in poor barrios, people who appeared suddenly at windows were shot dead by nervous troops. Many bodies were later found in unmarked graves. Caracas, said El Nacional, had become Beirut, an urban killing field.[29]

In the countryside, opposition has been less frequent, perhaps not surprising since it is the urban poor that has been worst hit by adjustment. When rural protests do erupt, however, they are are often spectacular, especially when combined with the burgeoning indigenous movement.

The impact of neo-liberalism has played an important role as a catalyst for the continent-wide resurgence of the indigenous protest movement in recent years. In Ecuador, the drive for dollars led the government to encourage transnational oil companies to drill for oil on indigenous lands. Rivers and streams which are traditional fishing grounds have turned black with oil. The indigenous groups have responded with a sophisticated international campaign, involving an international boycott and court action against Texaco in a New York Federal Court in 1993.[30]

Even more explosive has been the reversal of previous government commitments to indigenous forms of communal land ownership. The Mexican government's decision to alter the constitutional commitment to communal *ejido* land ownership precipitated the Zapatista uprising in the southern state of Chiapas in 1994, while a similar decision in Ecuador in June of the same year also provoked nationwide protests in a well-organized 'Uprising for Life'. This indigenous protest campaign paralysed a large part of the country for over a week. The Ecuadorean government, like the Mexican, had proposed legislation effectively abandoning its agrarian reform programme and surrendering the countryside to market forces.

With its focus on individualism and the market, the silent revolution stands diametrically opposed to the indigenous traditions of community, subsistence agriculture and reciprocal aid. Indigenous groups have condemned the cultural impact of neo-liberalism. In the spring of 1993 the annual congress of Mexico's *brujos* or shamen, passed a resolution condemning NAFTA, saying it would 'bring a cultural invasion that could adulterate the roots of our knowledge'.[31]

The damage inflicted by structural adjustment also extends to traditional indigenous sources of income, such as craftwork, as the Lima-based magazine *Latinamerica Press* reported in 1993:

> *'Who is going to buy this for $5 now that they can get a Barbie for $7?'* asks Augustina Mondragón, director of a cooperative of Mazahua Indian women. She shows an olive-coloured rag doll dressed in typical costume. 'I don't think free trade is going to be very good for the Mazahuas,' she adds.[32]

Nevertheless, in the run-up to the start of NAFTA, Superbarrio, the larger-than-life leader of the protest movement in the shanty towns of Mexico City, was grimly optimistic, 'I can't see much difference between what Columbus did to us and what the free trade treaty is going to do ... The culture of the US is consumerism. Our civilization is founded on reflection and history. But ours is the stronger.'[33]

From barricades to ballot box?

A decade of sporadic protests against the impact of neo-liberalism has achieved mixed results. In countries such as Bolivia, Nicaragua, Brazil or Venezuela, protests have managed to stall the privatization programme and other parts of adjustment packages. Elsewhere, as in Argentina or Mexico, power is so centralized in the president that protesters have had little chance of deflecting him. Individuals and organizations protesting against adjustment have been handicapped by their lack of a concrete alternative to the neo-liberal recipe, which means that successful protest tends to produce a policy vacuum and economic stagnation, rather than anything more positive, undermining the validity of the protesters' criticisms and eventually laying the basis for another round of adjustment measures.

One of the protesters' chief failures has been to turn opposition into victory at the ballot box. Throughout the silent revolution, Latin American elections have exhibited what one Mexican author described as 'apparent schizophrenia. Right-of-center, pro-business regimes are voted in at national level, while left-of-center, socially oriented administrations are elected at a municipal one.'[34] In Brazil, the Workers' Party has achieved some notable successes in local government after winning control in 1988 of the town halls of massive cities such as São Paulo,

Santos and Porto Alegre. In 1992 it extended its control to 55 towns and cities (although it lost São Paulo) giving it the second largest municipal vote in the country.[35] Since 1988, the Uruguayan capital of Montevideo has been in the hands of the *Frente Amplio* (Broad Front) of left-wing parties and other organizations. Similar victories have since occurred in Asunción and Caracas. In Argentina in 1994, in the midst of Carlos Menem's neo-liberal boom, the population of Buenos Aires chose the left-wing *Frente Grande* (Big Front) coalition to run their city of 10 million people.

The left has thus won a degree of local power, without gaining corresponding control of resources, since neo-liberal central governments have been in charge of taxation and setting national budgets. Within these constraints, however, the left has been able to lay the basis for a new kind of participatory politics, encouraging the explosion in grassroots movements and, along the way, acquiring an invaluable reputation for honesty and efficiency in local government.

Despite the alternative visions on offer at a municipal level, opponents of neo-liberalism have still to make the leap from protest to power at a national level. By 1995, scattered opposition nevertheless was showing signs of making a limited political impact at national level. In several countries, new elections have brought to power presidents whose rhetoric is sharply different from that of the neo-liberals of the late 1980s. All espouse ideas associated with the 'social market', re-emphasizing the role of government in educating and caring for its citizens. Some, like Colombia's Ernesto Samper, are modernizers along the lines of Chile's Patricio Aylwin, adding renewed emphasis on social spending and poverty relief to a basically neo-liberal core which includes plans for widespread privatization and falling inflation.[36]

In Venezuela, Rafael Caldera, an old-time populist, won the election in late 1993 on a combination of nostalgia for the lost security of Venezuela's oil boom years and contradictory promises to cut inflation and the fiscal deficit, and increase spending while simultaneously rescinding sales taxes.[37] His election was hardly evidence of an emerging alternative to neo-liberalism; when asked shortly before the election which market reforms he planned to jettison and which he would keep, he replied with unusual frankness, 'I wish I knew'.[38] In any event, he was promptly derailed by a banking crisis not of his own making, which he dealt with by reimposing exchange and price controls. When the initial crisis was over, Caldera's recovery package promised a prompt return to the market. This included cuts in state subsidies on fuel, a stepped-up privatization programme including further openings for foreign investors in the all-important oil sector, and labour reforms to reduce severance payments to employees.[39] If he carries any of it out, he will end up resembling other U-turn presidents in Peru and Argentina, although perhaps with more excuses than most.

Presidents of more moderate rhetoric have also been elected in Uruguay and the Central American republics of Costa Rica, Honduras and Panama. Despite their campaign promises, these small economies are much more dependent on the international financial institutions than larger countries like Colombia or Venezuela, and all three of the new Central American presidents (José María Figueres in Costa Rica, Roberto Reina in Honduras, and Ernesto Pérez Balladares in Panama) were promptly embroiled in negotiations with the international financial institutions which left them little room for manoeuvre.

Moreover, the big prizes continue to elude the left's grasp. In Mexico the population opted for continuity in August 1994, electing Ernesto Zedillo, the greyest of grey technocrats, to continue the country's *de facto* integration with the US. The left, in the person of Cuauhtémoc Cárdenas, trailed in a poor third. In Brazil, the Workers Party's initial lead in the opinion polls was wiped out when then Finance Minister Fernando Henrique Cardoso's *Real* plan succeeded in curbing inflation, at least until the poll on 3 October. Despite losing, the PT may prove at least to have done Brazil a favour by forcing the right to accept Cardoso as a 'lesser evil' than Lula. Cardoso, a former left-wing sociology professor, came to power in Latin America's largest economy with few illusions about neo-liberalism. 'If you leave it to the markets to resolve social problems, it won't work', he said, 'The market solves some problems, but not that of poverty. You have to have a state and an effective reform of the apparatus of that state.'[40]

Undermining the campaigns of both Cárdenas and Lula was their lack of a coherent national or regional alternative to the neo-liberal programme. Cárdenas was far more convincing when assailing the PRI's abandonment of the poor than when trying to say what *he* would do in government. Lula's campaign was crippled when he opposed the hugely popular *Real* plan, yet had little to offer in its place except vague calls for the 'democratization of the state' and an unconvincing promise that the PT would generate eight million jobs in its first term in office.[41] The silent revolution's failure to trickle down to the forgotten masses of the region could not turn into a successful political counter-attack until its opponents could come up with a new 'common sense' to challenge that of the market. It is to this all-important search for alternatives that we now turn.

Notes

1 Latin America Monitor, *Southern Cone* (London, January 1994), p.3.

2 *Ercilla*, 23 March 1977, cited by Vergara, *Auge y caída del neoliberalismo en Chile* (Santiago, 1983), p.96.

3 Author interview (Santiago), September 1993.

4 *Guardian* (London), 15 June 1994.

5 *El País* (Madrid), 8 April 1991 (author's translation)

6 George Philip, 'The new economic liberalism and democracy in Latin America', *Third World Quarterly*, Vol. 14, No. 3, (Abingdon, 1993), p.567.

7 *NACLA Report on the Americas* (New York, July 1991), p.12.

8 *Latinamerica Press* (Lima), 25 March 1993, p.3.

9 Philip, *op. cit.*, p.568.

10 *Financial Times* (London), 7 June 1993.

11 *The Economist* (London), 1 October 1994.

12 *Ibid.*

13 Joseph Collins and John Lear, *Chile's Free Market Miracle: A Second Look*, Chapter 3 (Oakland, CA, 1994).

14 Moisés Naim, 'Latin America: post adjustment blues', *Foreign Policy* Vol. 92 (Washington, DC, Fall 1993), p.138.

15 Adrián Lajous, author interview (Mexico City), September 1992.

16 *Wall Street Journal* (New York), 5 February 1991.

17 *Latinamerica Press*, (Lima), 10 December 1992.

18 Author interview (Mexico City), September 1992.

19 *Financial Times* (London), 26 August 1994.

20 *Financial Times* (London), 1 December 1994.

21 *Newsweek* (New York), 22 July 1991.

22 Fernando Leiva, correspondence with author, 10 November 1994.

23 Author interview (Potosí), April 1990.

24 Author interview (Concepción), September 1993.

25 Bulletin of Centro Regional de Informaciones Ecuménicas (Mexico City), 3 May 1993, p.4.

26 John Walton 'Debt, protest and the state in Latin America' in Susan Eckstein (ed.), *Power and Popular Protest: Latin American Social Movements* (Berkeley, CA, 1989).

27 Sources: J. Walton, *op. cit.*; *Boletín de Derechos Humanos y Coyuntura* (Provea, Caracas); Caribbean Insight; Economist Intelligence Unit; Latin American Monitor; Latin America Newsletters Regional Report; Latin America Press; Deborah Poole and Gerardo Rénique, *Peru: Time of Fear* (London, 1992); James Ferguson, *Dominican Republic: Beyond the Lighthouse* (London, 1992).

28 Walton, *op. cit.*, p.318.

29 James Ferguson, *Venezuela in Focus* (London, 1994), p.5.

30 *NACLA Report on the Americas* (New York, September/October 1994).

31 *Latinamerica Press* (Lima), 28 January 1993, p.3.

32 *Ibid.*, p.3.

33 *Latinamerica Press* (Lima), 4 February 1993, p.2.

34 Jorge Castañeda, *Utopia Unarmed: The Latin American Left after the Cold War* (New York, 1993), p.367.

35 Sue Branford and Bernardo Kucinski, *Brazil: Carnival of the Oppressed. Lula and the Brazilian Workers' Party* (London, 1995), p.115.

36 Latin America Monitor, *Andean Group* (London, December 1994), p.5.

37 Latin America Monitor, *Andean Group* (London, various months).

38 *The Economist* (London), 11 December 1993.

39 *Financial Times* (London), 14 September 1994.

40. *Guardian* (London), 3 October 1994.

41 Branford and Kucinski, *op. cit.*, p.94.

CHAPTER 8

Other Paths

The Search for Alternatives

Despite the ornamental lake, graced by a pair of Chilean black-necked swans, the squat grey concrete bunker is probably the ugliest building in Santiago. It houses the UN's Economic Commission on Latin America and the Caribbean (ECLAC, better known by its Spanish acronym CEPAL), and hundreds of economists stroll its corridors, chatting and arguing in a bewildering range of languages.

The bunker design is appropriate, for CEPAL has been one of the few intellectual redoubts against the neo-liberal tide which has swept across Latin America over the last 20 years. If by the early 1990s, the neo-liberal model was still very much the regional orthodoxy, its shortcomings were becoming ever more obvious. As grassroots rejection of the neo-liberal crusade has grown, it has become ever more necessary to find a credible alternative which can both channel protest into positive action and attract new support. If not, the opposition movement runs the risk of being branded as dinosaurs, clinging to the vested interests of the old order. Now CEPAL is leading the effort to define a new economic model which will put the continent on a path to long-term sustainable development. Other sources of inspiration have come from the study of Asian economies such as South Korea or Taiwan, which have succeeded in industrializing with a high degree of social equity. At the grassroots, Latin America's burgeoning network of social movements and Non-Governmental Organizations (NGOs) have been active in criticizing the neo-liberal model and searching for sustainable alternatives at the community level.

Any discussion of 'alternatives to neo-liberalism' must first clearly identify the enemy. Although the core of neo-liberal thinking is largely unvarying, the theory has acquired many different practical forms during its implementation in Latin America. Geography (for example proximity to the US), the state of the world economy at the time of adjustment, the size of the domestic market, the availability of natural resources or a skilled workforce, the capacity of the civil service, and the prior existence (or absence) of a dynamic local private sector, besides the political preferences of different presidents, all influence the way neo-liberal ideas are put into practice.

Furthermore, neo-liberalism has evolved over time, passing from its 'savage capitalism' phase at the start of the debt crisis, in the heyday of Ronald Reagan and Margaret Thatcher, to a kinder, gentler neo-liberalism in the 1990s. To varying extents, neo-liberals have rediscovered the issue of poverty, and the need to educate their citizens. At least at the level of rhetoric, few politicians would now admit to being a neo-liberal, as the 'social market' has become the catchphrase of the caring 1990s. The combination of change and continuity is best illustrated by Chile, where the savagery of the Pinochet dictatorship has been replaced by the consensus of the Aylwin and Frei governments, which have achieved a measure of tax reform and impressive degrees of poverty relief.

Nevertheless, the underlying economic model has hardly changed; despite the superficial variations, there is clearly an ideological and intellectual core to the silent revolution.

Over the continent as a whole, the rhetoric has changed far more than the reality. Poverty is still on the rise (Chile is the exception), market forces are boosting inequality in an already hugely unequal society and in most cases the 'social market' boils down to little more than *laissez-faire* capitalism plus a degree of poverty relief and some attention to improving health and education services, but within miserly limits on spending.

Although those proposing alternatives face governments who are energetically stealing their rhetoric, as the 1990s wear on, a growing chorus of individuals, parties, grassroots organizations and institutions have started to challenge the ideological dominance which enshrined neo-liberalism as the economic 'common sense' of the 1980s. It is fast becoming what one veteran British Marxist termed 'yesterday's truth',[1] although which, if any, 'big idea' is to replace it is still far from clear. Neo-liberalism may have many faces, but so too do the sources of alternatives. Here too, generalization is dangerous, not least in identifying any source of ideas as coming from 'the left', which in Latin America, as elsewhere, is an increasingly elusive and amorphous entity.

An important turning point in the search for alternatives took place in November 1992, thousands of miles to the north. Bill Clinton was elected on a programme which explicitly rejected Reaganomics and argued for a new enhanced role for the state. Just as the Chicago Boys had played Pied Piper to the continent's technocrats in the 1970s, the cluster of economists around President Clinton have made questioning the market a legitimate activity for economists and politicians everywhere. 'Today it is conservatives who have lost their intellectual energy. Over a dozen years of stunning political successes, they have had an opportunity to put many of their ideas into practice – and see them fail,' crowed one MIT Professor of Economics shortly after Clinton's victory.[2] The anti-Clinton landslide in the mid-term elections in late 1994 suggested that such an obituary was a little premature, but at least debate on the merits of alternative economic systems has now become a legitimate activity.

US policy-makers argue energetically for increased R&D, more government spending on infrastructure, and active government intervention in industrial planning, which they believe are essential to US economic recovery. In a speech to the annual meeting of the IDB in April 1994, US Treasury Under-Secretary for International Affairs Lawrence Summers even prescribed parts of the new medicine for Latin America. 'Markets alone, without government action, cannot bring the shared prosperity that we crave', he said. This was 'the core idea that animates Bill Clinton's presidency' and 'should be top of any agenda for Latin America and the Caribbean today'.[3] Summers, a former controversial top World Bank economist, called on the IDB to help restructure labour laws 'to ensure stronger, more independent labour unions' to protect workers' rights, including minimum standards for health and safety and to rewrite and enforce environmental protection laws.

However, the Clinton White House has largely failed to practise what it preaches. While it advocates 'managed trade' in its own dealings with countries like Japan, it is unwilling to countenance such activities from the South, for which it continues to prescribe large doses of free trade and deregulation. The flow of ideas from the North has nourished the debate, but the political pressures from Washington have continued to close it down.

Furthermore, the international financial institutions continue to use their power as the gatekeepers of world capital to force an outdated and damaging doctrine onto countries in the South. The debate over reform or abolition of the IMF, World Bank and other multilateral institutions is central to the discussion for alternative development models within Latin America, since the large lenders are now the chief intellectual repository of neo-liberal beliefs and currently enjoy a virtual right of veto over economic policy in many countries in the region.

State v market: the lessons of Asia

The World Bank and other proponents of market reform appear to have an important advantage over their critics; they have a success story to point to, in the shape of the 'Newly Industrializing Countries' (NICs) of East Asia, namely South Korea, Taiwan, Singapore and Hong Kong. These countries, the Bank argues, have got it right. Their sustained growth and industrialization based on exports, rather than protectionism and import substitution, prove once and for all what the free market can achieve once the state gets off its back. In its report on East Asia's spectacular achievements in poverty reduction, the World Bank attributes the successes to 'sound macroeconomic management ... improving the business-enabling framework, and liberalizing markets and prices', measures that the Bank says provide 'powerful incentives to private-sector led growth', along with other cherished Bank policies such as targeting health and education spending at the poorest groups.[4]

But a closer examination reveals that, far from demonstrating the virtues of liberalization and government non-interference, the East Asian NICs' successes have been based on a high level of state intervention in the economy, a fascinating duet between state and private sector, and many more restrictions on foreign capital than ever existed under import substitution in Latin America. Many of the lessons to be learned are anathema to the neo-liberal orthodoxy and could instead play a valuable part in the search for alternatives to the dogma of the silent revolution.

South Korea and Taiwan[5]

The two countries which allow the best comparisons with Latin America are Taiwan and South Korea, since the other two Asian 'tigers' (Singapore and Hong Kong) are too small to have much in common with economies the size of Mexico or Brazil.

After the Second World War, Taiwan and South Korea emerged from Japanese occupation with classic colonial economies restricted to exporting raw materials. After war and independence had shattered their former colonial ties, with an impact on their trade balance similar to the effect of the depression on Latin America, the two countries had little choice but to opt for an initial period of import substitution. When this showed signs of running out of steam in the late 1950s, the two countries switched to an all-out export drive based on manufactured goods. The results were extraordinary. Taiwan's exports rose 100 fold between 1965 and 1987, while South Korea's multiplied by 250 times over that period.[6] In 1965 South Korea and Argentina both had about 0.1 per cent of the world market in engineering products. Two decades later Argentina still had 0.1 per cent, but South Korea's share had gone up 20 times.[7] Taiwan, in many ways the star performer, can boast negligible unemployment, virtually 100 per cent literacy and the fairest income distribution in the world.[8] Furthermore by 1995 it had achieved all this without ever being a member of GATT – portrayed by the powerful nations as the prerequisite of trading success.

The lessons to be learned from the successes of the Asian NICs challenge the received wisdom on both sides of the state-versus-market debate in Latin America.

Foreign capital

Whereas policy-makers in Latin America have veered between blanket hostility to and uncritical infatuation with foreign capital, the NICs have proved able to work with foreign capital, while subordinating it to their national interests. Initially, foreign capital inflows in East Asia were largely in the form of government loans, which entered in large amounts immediately after the Korean war, but fell thereafter. Since government loans usually went to the recipient state, they were easy to control and direct towards priority export industries. In South Korea the government allows transnationals to invest only through joint ventures with Korean companies, while Taiwan is more open to foreign investment, but directs it to the benefit of the national economy, using a system of tax incentives which vary according to what the company is producing, how much it exports, and what proportion of local products it uses. There are no transnationals among the top ten largest companies in either country.

In Latin America, on the other hand, most foreign investment has been private – either direct investment by transnational corporations or loans from private banks. Unlike in Asia, transnationals play a leading role in many economies, exercising enormous influence over policy direction in pursuing their own, rather than the national, interests. Behind the transnational corporations stand powerful supporters, not least the US government and the international financial institutions, like the IMF and World Bank, as well as the transnationals' local employees and managers. All of them share and promote the transnationals' agenda on issues like free trade and deregulation.

Foreign capital inflows have fallen over time in East Asia. Both South Korea and Taiwan are now net capital exporters, and are becoming significant investors in parts of Latin America. Samsung and Lucky-Goldstar, South Korea's two largest conglomerates, have TV assembly operations in Mexico.[9]

In Latin America, however, foreign capital inflows rose inexorably until the onset of the debt crisis. After the capital famine of the 1980s, when Latin America exported much-needed capital to pay the interest on its foreign debt, renewed inflows of foreign capital are now being hailed as one of the proofs that Latin America's economy is on the mend. The East Asian experience suggests that Latin America's continued dependence on foreign capital is a sign of weakness, not strength, and is a serious obstacle to charting a path to sustained economic growth.

Investment and savings

Over the years, the Achilles' heel of Latin America's economy has been its inability to generate domestic savings and investment, a weakness which has been exacerbated by the investment famine of the silent revolution. An impoverished majority with nothing to spare and a small, rich élite addicted to a US consumer lifestyle and unwilling to pay even minimal taxes has meant that the region has always skimped on investment, much of which has been funded by foreign sources of capital. South Korea and Taiwan, on the other hand, have inexorably increased their levels of domestic savings over the years, thereby reducing their dependence on foreign capital. Taiwan has been so successful in accumulating capital that it now has the second-largest foreign currency reserves in the world, after Japan.[10]

Equality

One of the reasons for the NICs' success is distinctly unpopular with the neo-liberals – agrarian reform. Before industrialization began, sweeping land reforms in Taiwan (1949–51) and South Korea (1952–54) established an initial distribution of wealth and income far fairer than anything achieved in Latin America. One of the driving forces behind the reforms was the United States, desperate to head off the threat of communist revolt in the aftermath of the Chinese revolution. By comparison, the kind of reforms enacted in Latin America following the Cuban revolution ten years later were timid, systematically watered down by a stubborn land-owning aristocracy despite Washington's pressure for reform.

For the US, the geopolitical stakes were much higher in Asia, where the Chinese revolution was swiftly followed by wars in both Korea and Vietnam. Washington was therefore far more ready to provide large quantities of aid with few strings attached, and accept defiance on policy issues from the Asians; for example, Taiwan has systematically rebuffed US pressure to privatize state firms.

In Asia, agrarian reform created nations of small farmers who constituted a market for the initial phase of import substitution. Between 1952 and 1954 owner occupation of land in South Korea went up from 50 per cent to 94 per cent.[11] By contrast the gulf which has always divided rich landowners and landless peasants in Latin America is not only unjust, but greatly reduced the size of the internal market for the products of import substitution.

Later on, when the Asian countries switched to export-oriented industrialization, they gave priority to labour-intensive industry. This meant that the benefits of industrialization spread to the whole of society, and the region has maintained its equal distribution of income throughout its period of extraordinary growth. In Latin America, the decision to deepen import substitution based on capital-intensive industry, frequently owned by transnationals, created far fewer jobs, further skewing income distribution.

It is worth noting, however, that when the NICs' new entrepreneurs moved abroad, they left much of their concern for equality and improvement at home. Taiwanese factories in southern China are every bit as exploitative as US factories in Mexico, while Korean textile *maquiladoras* in Guatemala have become notorious for their harsh working conditions.[12]

State and private sector

In both Taiwan and South Korea, the state plays a leading role in directing national economic development, using its virtual monopoly ownership of the finance sector to guide investment. In South Korea, the state uses its financial muscle to push and prod the giant conglomerates, known as *chaebols*, along its chosen course. In Taiwan, the government uses its many state-owned companies and public research and service organizations to direct the economy. Taiwan proves that state ownership is not automatically an obstacle to success. At the end of the 1970s, state-owned enterprises accounted for a third of domestic investment, more than their counterparts in Brazil or Mexico.[13] When the Taiwanese government decides to encourage a new industry which either needs lots of capital (e.g. steel) or new technology (e.g. semi-conductors) state-owned companies move in and set it up, but then withdraw, handing it over to the private sector.

Protection for industry

Both regions have periodically protected local industries from foreign competition as part of their strategy for industrialization. However, the nature of Asian protection is very different from the Latin American variety. Whereas Latin America during import substitution opted for blanket protection across the whole of industry on a permanent basis, Taiwan and South Korea have used selective protection for key industries. They also make it clear from the beginning that protection is not permanent, but will be phased out according to a pre-determined timescale, by which time the industry will have to be internationally competitive to survive in the world market. In Latin America, only Brazil has opted for this model with some success in establishing a domestic micro-electronics industry, using selective and temporary protection along Asian lines since 1977.[14]

Politics and culture

One point of similarity which is rarely mentioned by the neo-liberals is the undemocratic political systems in the four countries. South Korea's drive for industrialization was launched following a military coup in 1961, just as Brazil's economic miracle followed the military coup of 1964. South Korea is if anything, the most brutal of the four regimes, and still regularly uses its Darth Vader-like riot police to crush protesters. Taiwan's one-party state, ruled by the Kuomintang (KMT) since 1947, bears a certain resemblance to Mexico's Institutional Revolutionary Party (PRI) which has clung doggedly to power since 1929. The similarity even extends to both parties' current difficulties in clinging to power while accommodating to growing opposition pressure for increased democracy.

However, the East Asian states have a far greater degree of autonomy than their Latin American equivalents. Japanese occupation in the Second World War conveniently destroyed the old landed oligarchy and allowed the post-war governments' technocrats to chart a new course, leading to the kind of economic success story associated with other war-flattened economies like Germany and Japan. In Latin America, the traditionally conservative class of large landlords retains enormous political influence, as do both foreign capital, the trade union movement built up under populism, and the new generation of grassroots 'social movements' which have sprung up since the 1970s. All these groups consistently challenge governments, forcing them into a higher degree of political and economic compromise than has been necessary in East Asia.

This raises uncomfortable questions for those seeking a more democratic alternative to neo-liberalism in Latin America – how is it that the most economically egalitarian and successful Third World economies are so authoritarian and undemocratic? Can long-term development along Asian lines be achieved only by shutting out the voices of the majority of the people? How can a more participatory model in Latin America avoid the pent-up demands of the poor from immediately forcing the government into over-spending and a re-run of the collapse of import substitution?

The commonplace cultural stereotypes of meek, hard-working Asians and lazy Latins conveniently ignore the Chinese Revolution or the right to rebellion enshrined in Confucian thought, not to mention the extraordinary degree of effort involved in so many Latin American households' daily struggle to survive in the era of adjustment. Nevertheless, cultural differences are significant in explaining the differences between the two regions' experiences. The Latin American élite idolizes the

North American way of life with its emphasis on consumerism and short-term rewards, whereas the East Asians are influenced by the more austere Confucian tradition. The Latin American élite's affinity to US values is such that it is often hard even to describe them as a 'national bourgeoisie' whose first allegiance is to their own country's development. They speak English, send their sons and daughters to colleges in the US, work for or in partnership with local transnational corporation subsidiaries, move their dollars around the world economy and even do their shopping in Miami.

Imports v exports

Although neo-liberals claim that Taiwan and South Korea are exemplars of 'export-led growth' and would never dream of indulging in import substitution, the truth is more complex. Both countries have alternated selective import substitution with export drives, in the process steadily developing their economies.

What *is* true is that both Asian economies are much more geared to exports than most of their Latin American counterparts. In 1992 the ratio of exports to GDP, a guide to the importance of trade to a given economy, was 30 per cent for South Korea[15] and an extraordinary 44 per cent for Taiwan.[16] In contrast, Mexico and Brazil's export/GDP ratios were just 14 per cent and 8.5 per cent respectively,[17] although this is partly explained by the tendency for larger countries to have a smaller export/GDP ratio. A further difference lies in Asia's concentration on promoting exports while keeping a number of controls on imports. Under import substitution Latin America largely neglected exports and controlled imports. After the onset of the debt crisis, under heavy pressure from Washington and the international financial institutions, it switched to wholesale liberalization of both imports and exports, allowing an influx of imported goods to swamp the benefits of its improved export performance.

There is a sharp contrast between East Asia, where governments have encouraged foreign trade, but maintained strict controls on foreign investment, and Latin America where trade has been controlled, but foreign investment allowed to go almost unchecked, acquiring enormous political influence. This is one lesson the neo-liberals have not learned. The main significance of the North American Free Trade Agreement (NAFTA) is not its commitment to free trade, but that it sweeps away almost all controls on foreign investment in Mexico.

The parting of the ways between the Asians and Latin Americans came in the late 1950s (see Figure 8.1), when both regions had come to the end of the first phase of 'easy' import substitution. At this point they

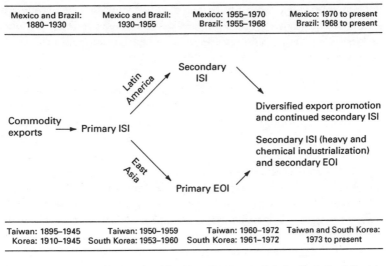

Mexico and Brazil: 1880–1930	Mexico and Brazil: 1930–1955	Mexico: 1955–1970 Brazil: 1955–1968	Mexico: 1970 to present Brazil: 1968 to present

Taiwan: 1895–1945 Korea: 1910–1945	Taiwan: 1950–1959 South Korea: 1953–1960	Taiwan: 1960–1972 South Korea: 1961–1972	Taiwan and South Korea: 1973 to present

Key: EOI = Export Oriented Industrialization; ISI = Import Substituting Industrialization

Figure 8.1: Paths of Industrialization in Latin America and East Asia

Source: Gary Gereffi and Donald L. Wyman (eds) *Manufacturing Miracles: Paths of Industrialization in Latin America and East Asia* (Princeton, NJ, 1990), p.18.

were able to produce less-complex manufactured goods like televisions and fridges, but had to confront their continued dependence on imported capital goods like turbines and cranes and intermediate inputs like iron and steel or chemicals. The Latin Americans chose to deepen import substitution by investing in industries to produce capital and intermediate goods. In doing so they believed they could generate sufficient foreign exchange to pay for essential imports by exporting abundant natural resources such as oil, minerals or agricultural commodities. Repeatedly in Latin American history this so-called 'curse of wealth' has allowed governments to go on plundering natural resources rather than undertaking long-term and equitable industrialization. By the early 1990s, some 63 per cent of Latin America's exports were still raw materials,[18] which in contrast make up only 7 per cent of South Korean exports.[19] The paradoxical legacy of Latin America's natural riches has been chronically underdeveloped and unequal societies.

East Asia had neither the internal market to justify further import substitution, nor the natural resources to pay for it, and therefore quickly opted to switch its emphasis to manufactured exports. It chose to rely on the intensive use of labour rather than the huge inputs of capital required for deepening import substitution, and so did not require massive inputs of foreign exchange. The resulting exports further improved the trade balance.

In the early years after East Asia and Latin America parted company, both prospered. From 1965 to 1973 Latin America's GDP grew by 7.4 per cent a year, while East Asia's growth reached 8.3 per cent.[20] It took the sudden oil price rise of 1973 to expose the underlying vulnerability of the Latin American model, and the resilience of the Asian export-led path.

The first stage of export-led growth came to an end in the early 1970s, by which time the NICs' rapid industrialization had soaked up all available labour and wage levels were starting to rise, damaging the competitivity of the labour-intensive export industries which had flourished in the first phase. Furthermore, recession and protectionism in the West in the wake of the OPEC oil price rise of 1973 hit the NICs' major export markets. Now that export-led growth had enormously enlarged the size of the internal market, the NICs were able to turn inwards for a further phase of import substitution aimed at building up heavy industries such as shipbuilding and chemicals. Korea ran up a large foreign debt in the process, but was able to service it throughout the 1980s because of its export strength. Later the NICs combined this second-stage import substitution with moving into new export fields, involving more capital and skills to produce more complex goods such as electrical equipment or cars, where know-how matters more than cheap labour. Wage levels were thus able to rise without unduly hitting competitivity.

As long as foreign loans were plentiful in the 1970s, Brazil and Mexico could go ever deeper into debt to keep the creaking wheels of import substitution turning, but when the loans dried up, the model collapsed. Their partial attempt in the 1970s at turning outwards and building up manufactured exports failed to produce the kind of transformation that would have been required to stave off the debt crisis.

East Asia's astute alternation between building up its export industries and promoting import substitution enabled it to develop an ever more complex and complete industrial apparatus, largely under national control. In contrast, Latin America during its import substitution period gave too much priority to imports, let itself be dominated by the demands of foreign capital, both creditors and transnational investors, and seemed to operate out of synch with the world economy. It tried to shift to exports when the world economy was in recession, and turned inwards when export markets were booming, whereas the policy changes of the Asian NICs expertly coincided with the ups and downs of the world economy.

But can Latin America follow in the footsteps of the Asian NICs, even if it tries to adopt their development models tomorrow? In the 1950s Taiwan and South Korea were of enormous geo-political importance to the US in the wake of the Chinese Revolution and Korean War. With Washington at the height of its power, aid flowed in abundance, and the governments had plenty of leverage in negotiations over its use. Forty years on, the US is the world's largest debtor, with an intractable fiscal deficit and little money available for aid. Apart from Mexico, Latin America carries little political weight in Washington, ranking well behind Eastern Europe and the Middle East.

The increasing fragility of the US economy has also led to growing protectionism against manufactured imports and heightened vigilance against attempts by Third World governments to regulate trade and foreign investment. The GATT agreement, NAFTA and other regional free-trade treaties all reduce the ability of Latin American governments to use selective state controls and subsidies to direct their economies in the manner of the Asian NICs. Many of these measures will now become crimes under free-trade agreements. Some writers even see the primary purpose of GATT and Washington's increased insistence on free trade as part of a strategy of 'global rollback', preventing Third World countries from industrializing, while forcing the already industrialized nations of the South and East to open up their economies to US exports and investment.[21]

Asia's success in recent years has in large part been built on its ability to absorb, adapt and improve the latest technology. This requires a skilled workforce, high levels of public and private spending on R&D, and the ability to identify emerging new technologies and assimilate them early enough to compete with rivals. As the pace of technological innovation accelerates, it will become increasingly hard for Latin America, which spends little on R&D and is chronically short of technical expertise, to jump aboard the moving train.

The Asian model's extraordinary ability to generate growth *with equity* shows little sign of being repeated in Latin America, where inequality has increased remorselessly both under import substitution and during structural adjustment. Agrarian reforms are being put into reverse in countries like Mexico, Ecuador and Nicaragua, leading to greater inequality, not less. In any case, now that Latin America is so overwhelmingly urban, agrarian reform can no longer alter radically the distribution of income in much of society. It remains to be seen whether the increasing emphasis on labour-intensive export industries demonstrated by the *maquiladoras* in Mexico and Central America leads to long-term improvements in living conditions, given that the pool of unemployed workers to be soaked up before wages will rise is far larger than in the Asian case. In addition the *maquiladoras* are under foreign, not Latin American control and are more likely to leave the country should wage levels eventually start to rise.

More generally, there is a fallacy of composition involved, both in terms of the market and the environment, in suggesting that all developing countries follow the NIC path. Firstly, the market for NIC products is limited to the economies of the North, and the more NICs there are, the more cut-throat the competition will be (and the greater are protectionist pressures likely to become in the importing countries). Taiwan and South Korea are both small countries, but when a goliath like China embarks on the NIC path, it is questionable whether the market is sufficient to allow it to achieve full NIC status, let alone whether there is any room left for any other country to join in. By early 1995 the initial signs of an escalating trade war between the US and China were already apparent, not least because China was running an estimated $30bn trade surplus with the US by 1994.[22] Given the poor environmental record of the NICs, and the increased use of fossil fuels and other non-replaceable inputs that their industrialization involves, there is also serious doubt that the planet could sustain the impact of another hundred NICs.

Despite these misgivings, the rapid rise in recent years of a second tier of Asian NICs such as China, Malaysia and Thailand has shown that there is still room for manoeuvre. Many of the measures used by the Asian NICs are still open to Latin America. In order to use them, however, the region's governments will have to shrug off the defeatism of the neo-liberals and start managing the economy again.

Cepalismo

Within Latin America, the debates over alternatives to neo-liberalism range across the political spectrum, from detailed technocratic tinkering to improve its efficiency and reduce its social cost, to clarion calls for a new utopia, junking the whole doctrine and starting from scratch to build a new 'popular economic alternative'.

Occupying the centre ground is CEPAL. In the 1960s, CEPAL was seen as the chief vehicle for import substitution, and its influence went into eclipse as the model collapsed. In the late 1980s, CEPAL's economists embarked on the long road back from the intellectual wilderness, pioneering the discussion on a new alternative, to which they gave the ugly and instantly forgettable name 'neo-structuralism'.

CEPAL agrees with the neo-liberals on the need for radical economic adjustment in Latin America, arguing that the continent missed the chance to adjust in the 1970s when plentiful supplies of foreign capital could have eased the pain. It accepts the need for avoiding giant deficits, whether in government accounts or in trade. However, it disagrees with the neo-liberal recipe on just about everything else.

The heart of the neo-structuralist alternative, laid out in detail in Appendix B (p. 244), is a redefinition of the goal of the economic model. Instead of neo-liberalism's single-minded pursuit of growth at any cost, CEPAL argues for the twin goal of combining growth with equity, a feat never achieved by any Latin American country,[23] but a central characteristic of successful newly industrialized economies in Asia and Europe. In the past, what can be loosely described as Latin America's populist left (led by men such as Peru's Alan García or Argentina's Juan Domingo Perón in his earlier years) has seemed almost exclusively concerned with redistributing wealth, omitting to say how it would generate it in the first place. The more clearly Marxist left, such as Nicaragua's Sandinista Front or the Cuban Communist Party were seduced by the 'fetishism of the state', building unwieldy state-owned enterprises to drag backward countries into the industrial age. The statist behemoths usually disappointed their creators (and their customers), rarely becoming the hoped-for 'Engine of Growth' for the rest of the economy.

At the other extreme lies neo-liberalism's trickle-down philosophy, which argues that the benefits of growth will eventually 'trickle down' to the poor, conveniently absolving planners of any responsibility for ensuring social and economic justice in their all-out rush for growth. In contrast, CEPAL believes that the promotion of equity is a precondition for sustainable growth, and goes well beyond mere poverty relief to include such measures as sweeping tax reform and redistribution of wealth.

According to CEPAL, growth with equity can only be achieved through a radically enhanced role for the state. But this does not mean a return to the octopus state of the 1960s, owning large chunks of the nation's industries and running a massive and inefficient state bureaucracy. CEPAL accepts that production should wherever possible be left in the hands of the private sector. Instead, it argues for a managerial state, in alliance with and regulating the private sector, intervening in the economy to move it towards higher levels of technology and industrialization, training and caring for its population.

CEPAL's programme does not convince all those looking for an alternative to neo-liberalism. For one thing, neo-structuralism is a decidedly broad church described by one think tank as 'a widely dispersed current of thought with no clear centre'.[24] Fernando Leiva, a radical Chilean economist, believes that 'neo-structuralism comes onto the scene once the dirty work has been done by neo-liberals'.[25] In his view, neo-structuralism is a logical and necessary second phase to follow the 'savage capitalism' of the Pinochet school, rebuilding consensus around a largely unchanged model of export-led growth.

While this view of neo-structuralism as merely 'neo-liberalism with a human face', rather than a true alternative, may ring true in Chile, CEPAL's policy framework goes farther than the Chilean government on crucial issues like the need for wealth redistribution, agrarian reform and increased rates of income tax. As a recipe for a fairer and more effective path to development, neo-structuralism is an impressive body of thought, drawing on the lessons of successful economies elsewhere and rejecting the dogma of both import substitution and the silent revolution.

The CEPAL model's main weakness is political – how to make it happen. At the global level, opponents of neo-liberalism must convince the IMF, World Bank, Washington, World Trade Organisation and international markets that neo-structuralism can work (and works for them). Unless these external forces can at least be persuaded to give an alternative development model a chance, the international obstacles to any move to a neo-structuralist model will be great and perhaps insuperable.

Within Latin America, the first problem is how to turn a traditionally inept, corrupt state into an efficient and honest regulator and strategic planner, an area in which most state bureaucracies have almost no experience. Even if the state machinery can acquire such skills, how can the region's business élite be persuaded to accept radical wealth redistribution without provoking massive capital flight and an immediate economic crisis? How can foreign investment be stopped from bolting once controls are imposed on it? What can be done to prevent retaliation from Washington or rows with the World Bank when protecting strategic industries? How does a government remain credit-worthy while negotiating a major write-off of the foreign debt?

CEPAL is also unconvincing on the issue of democratization. Its economic recipe calls for a technocratic state along East Asian lines, able to run the economy free from political pressures and demands. In countries such as Taiwan and South Korea, this was achieved through repression, as authoritarian regimes kept the workforce at arm's (or truncheon's) length from the decision-making process, yet CEPAL argues for increased participation and decentralization. But it does not explain how to prevent the acute needs and frustrations built up under neo-liberalism forcing the government into addressing immediate demands rather than the technocrats' long-term development objectives.

CEPAL has received strong backing from other UN agencies, notably the UN Development Programme, which in its 1993 *Human Development Report*[26] launched a swingeing attack on orthodox adjustment, calling for 'a searching re-examination of the Bretton Woods organisations'.[27] The report argued for a shift from orthodox structural adjustment towards 'people-friendly markets', involving the CEPAL agenda of a much higher profile for state regulation, greater investment in infrastructure, health and education, redistribution of wealth and a social safety net, along with the macro-economic stability, free trade and reduction in government red tape prescribed by the neo-liberals and neo-structuralists alike.

Despite the political weaknesses in CEPAL's proposals, a range of politicians, economists and intellectuals of different political stripes have clustered around this broad agenda, adding their own variations and emphases. One of the most ambitious is Jorge Castañeda, Professor of Economics and International Affairs at Mexico's National Autonomous University, who in *Utopia Unarmed: The Latin American Left after the Cold War* damns neo-liberalism's idolatry of the market, saying, 'Leaving the choice of winners and losers to the market, and acting as if the world market were truly free, is one of the great intellectual distortions of modern times.'[28] He then puts forward what he terms a 'hodgepodge solution' as the basis for a new left-wing agenda for the region.

Castañeda believes that the left should begin by abandoning any search for the utopia of socialist revolution and instead concentrate on the less glamorous, but more feasible, task of finding more equitable, successful alternatives to neo-liberalism within the current economic order. For this, he prescribes a 'pick and mix' approach to other forms of capitalism which he sees as superior to the Anglo-Saxon variety. The left should concentrate on 'blending the social corrections imposed upon the market by Western European capitalism, with the business-government complement to the market developed by Japanese capitalism'.[29] The left should fight for a genuine welfare state, and export-led, environmentally sustainable industrialization. In all this, 'the first item on the left's economic and social agenda must be tax reform.'[30]

Castañeda tries to deal with some of the political dilemmas avoided by CEPAL. Domestically, 'the business community must be convinced that a compromise of this sort is in its interests and the alternative is worse.'[31] Now communism is no longer around to force reforms on the businessmen, the left's only real argument is that the alternative is social breakdown of the kind already occurring in many of the region's cities. If the left fails to involve the private sector, it will exercise its option of 'picking up its marbles and going to Miami', where it can enjoy 'more of the same lifestyle, only nicer'.[32] The left's task is nothing less than to end the traditional get-rich-quick, short term thinking of Latin America's economic élite, converting it into a long-term partner of a technocratic state along Asian lines.

At an international level, Castañeda seems less convincing, even arguing that Latin American governments should seek an international agreement with tax havens to prevent capital flight. He also has little to say on how foreign investment can be regulated without frightening it off altogether. He believes that Latin America should offer Washington the sweetener of environmental and social reforms (to reduce migration pressures to the US), in return for the US granting it debt relief, a 'significant resource transfer' and access to US markets 'without draconian reciprocity'. Even Castañeda describes this highly implausible scenario as 'quite a package'.[33]

Is there a left alternative?

When discussing these issues, what can loosely be termed the political left tends to fall into two camps: those concerned with short-term improvements within the existing global and national economic frameworks, and those who think in the longer-term, and believe the existing order must be swept away and a new society built from scratch in order to achieve any lasting improvement in the lives of ordinary Latin Americans. Not surprisingly, short-term concerns are most in evidence among those parties and individuals with at least some interest in and real possibility of coming to power in the near future. Similarly, short-termists are more likely to believe that achieving state power is the essential first step to any social transformation, whereas many of the proponents of grassroots alternatives remain suspicious of the state whatever its political leadership, and look instead to a strategy of local organization and mobilization. Among the party political left, differences also emerge between their more rigorous intellectual supporters (such as Jorge Castañeda) and professional politicians, who often seem trapped in the rhetoric of the past, appearing nonplussed when asked to propose alternatives to neo-liberalism.

The gulf that separates the World Bank's view of development from that of the grassroots Latin American left is nowhere clearer than in the town of Marabá in the Brazilian Amazon.[34] Marabá lies at the heart of the Grande Carajás Programme, a giant mining and industrialization project funded by the Bank and the EU, among others. Opened in 1985, the Carajás iron ore mine now supplies half of the EU's annual iron ore demand and has reserves for another 500 years. The project has brought in export earnings with which to pay off Brazil's debt service, but at the cost of land conflict in which hundreds of small farmers have been murdered, coupled with widespread deforestation and the displacement of indigenous groups living nearby.

Marabá is also home to one of Latin America's myriad of small grassroots attempts to develop a less environmentally disastrous, people-centred development model which can provide an alternative both to

Carajás-style development, and the excessive use of slash-and-burn agriculture practised by the region's peasant farmers. Five local branches of the rural workers' union have joined together to form the Farming Foundation of Tocantins-Araguaia, FATA, an organization born out of their many years of organization against violence and intimidation at the hands of local landlords and their gunmen. To work with the farmers, academics specializing in subjects such as agronomy, sociology, economics and anthropology have formed a research group called the Socio-Agronomic Laboratory of Tocantins, LASAT.

The core of the work is investigating the cultivation of permanent crops, especially fruit trees, which may provide a livelihood more in harmony with the forest. Technicians distribute tree seedlings to village groups which cultivate tree nurseries under their supervision. The species being grown include exotic fruits such as passion fruit, papaya, mangosteen and others with no English names, including *cupuaçu, acerola, araça* and *biribá.*

Experiments are also going on combining traditional production techniques with modern ones. For example, the *genipapo* tree is a shade-giving tree whose fruit is used for making drinks. Amazonian Indians use its juices, mixed with charcoal, for body painting. It is being grown on steep slopes with pigeon pea, a leguminous ground cover traditionally grown in Asia which provides animal fodder and prevents soil erosion.

The *cupuaçu* fruit, which has yellow pulpy flesh and is used for ice cream and desserts in Brazil, has been the most successful. It was the farmers' idea to grow the shade-loving *cupuaçu* in combination with Brazil nut trees because they had traditionally been grown together. A *cupuaçu* produces 35 to 50 pieces of fruit per annum after four years, whereas a Brazil nut tree takes 20 years to produce nuts.

The most fundamental issue for this sustainable agricultural model is finding a market for the produce. In contrast to other Amazonian products such as the iron ore of Carajás or Brazil's mahogany, of which the UK is a major importer, the fruits of the forest are not in great demand. The farmers of FATA have therefore set up a co-operative to process, store and sell *cupuaçu* and the local market now buys all they can supply. Co-operative members have continued to cultivate rice as a cash crop and the co-operative provides credit, transport and storage for that too.

FATA's approach is the antithesis of the way in which the silent revolution has been conceived and implemented: it has been developed with the participants' involvement; it has family needs as the starting-point; the farmers themselves are implementers; a local market is actively being sought, and sustainability is a vital consideration in the project. Such approaches lie at the heart of many of the more radical proposals for a new Latin American development model to replace neo-liberalism. They are undoubtedly courageous and inspiring, but are they just utopian follies which ignore the global economic realities which must shape any national economic programme?

The call for a complete, long-term rethink is strongest among the NGOs who work closely with grassroots groups throughout the region in formulating a set of alternatives and a critique of orthodox adjustment which often goes far beyond that of CEPAL. One of the main differences is their starting-points. Through their daily experience, NGOs know that a large segment of the population struggles to survive while being excluded from the formal economy or traditional forms of political representation. The first step, they believe, should therefore be political rather than economic; to involve these people in the plethora of organizations lumped together under the heading 'civil society' and then to turn civil society into a third partner of the market and state. In the words of Marcos Arruda, a Brazilian economist, this would be the start of creating a 'people-centred adjustment' which would 'subordinate the equilibrium of macroeconomic indicators to macrosocial as well as ethical goals', thereby 'shifting the pole of development from the global economy to the popular communities'.[35] Such programmes stress the need to combat poverty by channelling credit and support to small producers and also tend to place far more emphasis on food security, the position of women under adjustment and environmental issues than the alternatives on offer from the more traditional left or the centre.[36]

Starting at the grassroots also tends to move the discussion away from the search for one 'big idea' with which to oppose neo-liberalism. One meeting of NGOs from all over the region concluded, 'There is no one alternative for all countries; there are many. One of the reasons for the failure of adjustment is that it was imposed in an undemocratic and secret manner, without taking into account the diversity of natural and human resources in different countries.'[37] The question becomes one of means as much as ends, of increasing people's involvement in drawing up national economic policy.

While it is undoubtedly absurd to prescribe the same economic medicine for a small rural economy such as Honduras as for an industrial giant like Brazil, the 'small is beautiful' approach does entail political costs for those seeking alternatives. The 'vision thing' which came to haunt George Bush is an essential means of rallying support around a particular economic or political model. As anyone who has lived through the Thatcher-Reagan years will know, the endless repetition of a simple, intelligible and apparently coherent 'big idea' is a far more powerful political weapon than saying 'There are no simple solutions, we'll have to look at everything case by case', even if in the end the comparison of the British economy with a Lincolnshire grocer's shop proves totally misleading.

The São Paulo Forum

One of the most important arenas in which Latin America's left-wing political parties can meet and exchange ideas is the São Paulo Forum, a series of regular seminars and conferences launched by the Brazilian Workers' Party (PT) in 1990. The Forum brings together the old and new left, from the Cuban Communist Party's traditional Marxist-Leninist approach to the PT's ramshackle coalition of grassroots movements, trade unions, and ultra-left political parties. In July 1992 the third meeting of the Forum, held in Managua, made discussion of an economic alternative to neo-liberalism its centrepiece, trying to establish common ground across the region's left.

Like political conventions everywhere, such meetings are not for the faint-hearted. Over 150 representatives from more than 50 'parties, organizations and movements' and 17 countries spent the first two days listening to 'an uninterrupted succession of speeches from the delegates of the main parties',[39] largely repeating each others' condemnations of the evils of capitalism/neo-liberalism. Those still conscious at the end of the first two days then got on with the main task of drafting a joint position paper on economic alternatives. Their conclusions give a useful insight into the state of the political left's search for a distinctive alternative to both neo-liberalism and the CEPAL model. The resulting Managua Declaration[39] stated:

1. The neo-liberal project 'cannot be amended' since it is part of an 'unjust world economic order'. A 'united world left' must instead change the world system towards one based on justice and peace.
2. The aim of any alternative model must be 'autonomous economic development aimed at satisfying the basic needs of the majority, replacing the present alliance of the national bourgeoisie and international capital with an alliance between all the forces interested in promoting national programmes for building social justice, democracy and national liberation'.
3. Genuine economic development must begin with 'a fair distribution of wealth and property, rule by the majority and the strengthening of civil society', as well as 'fighting structural adjustment policies, whether orthodox or heterodox, and favouring the development of productive forces'.
4. 'Popular individuals and organizations must assume the economic leadership in achieving the desired aims' of the economic programme.

5. 'The state ... must play a central role as regulator and promoter of social equity, without abandoning the leadership of the economy to market forces, which are nothing more than the wishes of large national and international capital and the multilateral financial organizations.'

6. Priority must be given to South-South trade and a 'joint renegotiation' of the foreign debt 'as a response to the unity of the creditors'.

Comparing the alternatives

Although the various proposals for alternatives to neo-liberalism share much common ground (for example, distrust of unregulated market forces, determination to revamp the international financial institutions, the need for an enhanced role for the state, support for tax reform and a degree of wealth distribution), there are several contentious issues which divide them.

Attitude to the market

The Managua Declaration is openly hostile to the market, foreign capital in general and the US in particular, whereas the centrist options aim to work within the existing system and balance of power.

The importance of growth

The delegates in Managua devoted themselves to deciding how to redistribute wealth and promote economic and social justice, while largely ignoring the vital question of how to generate it. The centrist options, on the other hand, make growth *and* equity the twin goals of any alternative.

Democratization

There are wide variations of opinion on the most desirable political system to devise and implement an alternative. CEPAL nods in the direction of greater participation, while actually proposing a largely technocratic, top-down solution, whereas the more radical programmes make grassroots democracy the centrepiece of the whole project and argue that the popular organizations, not the technocrats, should be running the economy. It is this commitment to grassroots democracy which most clearly distinguishes the Managua Declaration from the much more statist/élitist statements of the left of the 1960s or the policies of import substitution.

The new left believes in building networks and coalitions along US and Canadian lines, rather than relying on traditional left-wing political parties which are generally in decline in the region. New cross-border coalitions are seen as an essential response to the globalization of invest-ment, and supporters point to successful cooperation between unions in Mexico and the US:

> *In 1987 the Ohio-based Farm Labor Organizing Committee (FLOC) sought help from the National Union of Farm Workers (SNTOAC) in Mexico. A year earlier, during FLOC's negotiations with Campbell Soup, the company threatened to move tomato paste production to Mexico, where it already operated a cannery. Backed by a national boycott of Campbell's products, FLOC overcame this threat and won a unique three-way agreement between the union, Campbell and family farmers who grew under contract with Campbell.*
>
> *Anticipating Campbell's use of Mexico as a bargaining tool in future negotiations, the two unions [FLOC and SNTOAC] ... reached an agreement and ... launched the US-Mexico Exchange Program. They have continued to exchange information and develop bargaining strategies to work for 'wage vs living cost parity', full employment, protection of 'guest workers' in the United States, and the development of 'strong and democratic' unions in both countries. In 1989 FLOC's solidarity and the mobilization of its support network helped SNTOAC win a wage increase some 15 per cent higher than the government's legal cap for the year. In FLOC's negotiations with Campbell the same year, 'Not once did we hear any mention of Mexico', says [FLOC leader] Baldemar Velásquez.*[40]

Foreign capital and technology

Neo-liberalism's more cautious critics are willing to concede that inflows of foreign capital and technology will continue to be essential within any new socially responsible and environmentally sustainable alternative pro-gramme. Attempts to regulate capital, perhaps by encouraging long-term investment rather than short-term speculation, must be managed in such a way as to avoid frightening foreign investors away altogether. The more radical proposals see foreign capital as little more than a continua-tion of the plunder begun 500 years ago by the *conquistadores* and argue for a far greater degree of regulation. They are more willing to counten-ance a search for some kind of self-reliance as an alternative to exploita-tion from the North, despite the increasing integration of the world economy and the growing costs of being isolated from it. However, the left is generally silent when it comes to the thorny problem of how to generate sufficient internal savings to replace dependence on foreign capital for investment, and vague on how to achieve real technology transfer in a world where the transnationals hold the whip hand.

Trade

The CEPAL model clearly commits Latin America to free trade with the North, while promoting regional integration as a platform from which to export to the rest of the world. The more radical programmes also support regional integration, but more as an alternative to trade with the North, rather than as a stepping stone. If free-trade agreements with the North must happen, they argue for a European-style Social Charter to safeguard Latin American workers from exploitation by first world companies. In today's world, that is tantamount to opposing free-trade deals with the US, since Washington has made it clear it will never adopt a Social Charter as part of such a treaty. The radicals also argue that sweeping changes to the international economic order, including writing off much of the Third World's debt, acting to stop long-term deterioration in commodity prices and ending northern discrimination against southern products, are an essential component of any alternative.

Such differences stem from a very real dilemma for proponents of alternative economic models. How much can realistically be achieved within the current economic and political constraints in Latin America? As one Argentine participant in the São Paulo Forum process observed: 'It is very possible that once the left has got to government, it won't be able to do more than a fraction of what it promised to do, and will have to do many things it promised not to do, with the possibility that it will lose legitimacy and that the people will throw it out at the next elections.'[41] The same could easily be said of the CEPAL programme (or indeed of Bill Clinton's). The power of international capital, the international financial institutions, the industrialized nations and the local business community is genuinely great, but has also been exaggerated by a left which too often has dwelt on its own powerlessness. 'In Latin America we were better at establishing the way our action had been historically limited by outside forces, than in establishing our own abilities to run our own lives', admitted one group of radical economists.[42] The challenge is to determine what margin for manoeuvre truly exists, avoiding the twin pitfalls of defeatism or demanding the impossible which have historically plagued the left.

Notes

1 Eric Hobsbawm, *Guardian* (London), 30 November 1991.

2 Paul Krugman, 'The conservative vision became a mirage in US', *Guardian* (London), 23 August 1993.

3 *Financial Times* (London), 13 April 1994.

4 Frida Johansen, *Poverty Reduction in East Asia: The Silent Revolution*, World Bank Discussion Paper No.203 (Washington, DC, 1993), p.24.

5 This section is based on Gary Gereffi and Donald L. Wyman (eds), *Manufacturing Miracles: Paths of Industrialization in Latin America and East Asia* (Princeton, 1990).

6 *Ibid.*, Chapter 1.

7 Fernando Fajnzylber, *Unavoidable Industrial Restructuring in Latin America* (Durham, NC, 1990), p.170.

8 *The Economist* (London), 17 April 1990.

9 *Far Eastern Economic Review* (Hong Kong), 13 September 1990.

10 IMF, *International Financial Statistics* (Washington, DC, August 1994), p.37.

11 United Nations Development Programme, *Human Development Report 1993* (New York, 1993).

12 *Multinational Monitor* (Washington, DC, November 1991).

13 Carlos Fortín, 'Rise and decline of industrialisation in Latin America', in CEDLA, *Eight Essays on the Crisis of Development in Latin America* (Amsterdam, 1991), p.73.

14 Hubert Schmitz and Tom Hewitt, 'Learning to raise infants', in *States or Markets? Neo-liberalism and the Development Policy Debate* (Oxford, 1991), p.176.

15 IMF, *International Financial Statistics Yearbook 1993* (Washington, DC, 1993).

16 *Statistical Yearbook of the Republic of China 1993* (Taipei, 1993).

17 IMF, *International Financial Statistics Yearbook 1993* (Washington, DC, 1993).

18 CEPAL, *Anuario Estadístico de América Latina y el Caribe 1993* (Santiago, 1994),p.108.

19 World Bank, *World Development Report 1992* (New York, 1992), p.249.

20 Oxford Analytica, *Latin America in Perspective* (Boston, MA, 1991), p.182.

21 Walden Bello, *Dark Victory: The United States, Structural Adjustment and Global Poverty* (London, 1994).

22 *Financial Times* (London), 6 February 1995.

23 See Fajnzylber, *op. cit.*

24 Oxford Analytica, *op. cit.*, p.197.

25 Correspondence with author, 1 September 1994.

26 UNDP, *op. cit.*, Chapter 3.

27 *Ibid.*, overview.

28 Jorge Castañeda, *Utopia Unarmed: The Latin American Left after the Cold War* (New York, 1993), p.464.

29 *Ibid.*, p.434.

30 *Ibid.*, p.452.

31 *Ibid.*, p.446.

32 *Ibid.*, p.450.

33 *Ibid.*, p.446.

34 This section is drawn from 'Showing how nature's way can pay', by Catherine Matheson, *Christian Aid News* (London, October–December 1994).

35 Marcos Arruda, *Structural Adjustment: A Constructive Overview from the Perspective of Civil Society* (mimeo), NGO Working Group on the World Bank (Geneva, October 1993), p.16.

36 See, for example, John Madeley, Dee Sullivan and Jessica Woodruffe, *Who Runs the World?* Chapter 5 (Christian Aid, London, 1994).

37 Karen Hansen-Kuhn and Carlos Heredia (eds), *El marco de una alternativa al ajuste estructural* (draft), The Development Gap (Washington, DC, April 1994), p.2.

38 *Pensamiento Propio* (Managua, August 1992), p.22.

39 The Managua Declaration, reproduced in *Tierra Nuestra* No. 7 (Managua, 1992), (author's translation).

40 Harry Browne, *For Richer for Poorer: Shaping US-Mexican Integration* (London, 1994), p.48.

41 Interview with José Luis Coraggio, in Agencia Latinoamericana de Información (ALAI), *Servicio Informativo* No. 150 (Quito, 27 March 1992), (author's translation).

42 Síntesis de reflexiones y líneas alternativas (mimeo), Seminario Internacional César Jerez, (Zipaquirá, Colombia, July 1992), p.8

Conclusions

The debt crisis that broke in Mexico in August 1982 marked the end of the road for the import substitution model in Latin America. Despite its undoubted achievements in terms of industrialization and economic growth, it is hard to mourn import substitution's passing. It led to the impoverishment of the countryside and a massive increase in inequality throughout the region. The death throes of import substitution also saddled Latin America with an unpayable foreign debt.

The region had to adjust its economy, as indeed it should have done in the 1970s, when the ready availability of foreign capital would have eased the pain of adjustment. Latin America had to solve its persistent fiscal deficits and its industry's growing lack of competitiveness in a rapidly changing world economy. It also had to find solutions to its unjust and politically destabilizing levels of poverty and inequality. Yet the neo-liberal adjustment which has swept across the continent since the Mexican default is neither the only nor the best way of dealing with the region's problems. In its first 13 years, the silent revolution has acquired a record at least as mixed as that of import substitution.

When trying to assess neo-liberalism's record, it is essential to set out clear criteria for judging success or failure. The central question must be, success for whom? Most coverage of the issue is strangely impersonal, remaining in the safe world of national economic variables such as inflation or GDP growth, where the neo-liberal record tends to look rather more positive. Its image becomes rapidly tarnished once real people are made the focus of attention, for although the silent revolution has clearly created both winners and losers within each country and between different countries, the balance is overwhelmingly negative. A minority of the population in each country, comprising the economic and social élite, has benefited from being drawn into the global economy through the structural adjustment process, but the costs for the majority of poor Latin Americans have been extreme. In the eyes of the élite, adjustment has been a rip-roaring success; in the eyes of the poor, a disaster. As Susan

George, a leading critic of the World Bank, puts it:

> *Some critics make the mistake of proclaiming that development has failed.*
> *It hasn't. Development as historically conceived and officially practised has*
> *been a huge success. It sought to integrate the upper echelons, say ten to*
> *forty per cent, of a given third world population into the international,*
> *westernized, consuming classes and the global market economy. This it*
> *has accomplished brilliantly.*[1]

Another common feature of coverage of the silent revolution is its failure to differentiate between ends and means. The defenders of structural adjustment frequently confuse the two, arguing that a reform programme is successful simply because a dozen firms have been privatized or a free-trade agreement has been signed. Yet these can only be counted as successes if they further an expressed aim of adjustment, such as improving the quality of life of ordinary Latin Americans.

For both macro-economists and poor Latin Americans, the single greatest achievement of the silent revolution has been to get inflation under control. Excluding Brazil, the region's average inflation rate in 1994 fell to 16 per cent, compared to 49 per cent in 1991.[2] By early 1995, Brazil, too, appeared to be solving its inflation problem through the introduction of the *Real* plan, although the country has confounded so many shock programmes in the last decade that scepticism was still warranted over the Plan's long-term sustainability.

The region also saw in 1994 the fourth consecutive year of solid, if unspectacular, economic growth of the order of 3 per cent.[3] Growth may not be a panacea for the region's ills, but a growing economy is surely a necessary, if not sufficient, condition for improving the lot of the impoverished majority. The region's performance in the 1990s is a great improvement on the average annual growth rate of 1 per cent in the years from 1980 to 1990,[4] though a poor showing compared to pre-debt crisis days. Per head, however, Latin America's GDP in 1993 had still to regain its 1980 value.[5]

Other changes are harder to quantify, but no less far-reaching. Driven by the breakneck pace of trade liberalization, the region's industrial culture is well on the way to abandoning its protectionist past, where success depended as much on a firm's skill in lobbying (and bribing) government officials as on the quality or price of the product. Suddenly exposed to competition from cheap imports, many industries have gone bust, but the survivors are undoubtedly more efficient, and could provide a platform for growth led by manufactured exports.

Export growth is healthy, although nowhere near Asian levels. Improved world commodity prices in 1994, thanks largely to a rebounding US economy, helped lift Latin America's export income by 14 per cent compared to 1993.[6] Furthermore, the rising trend of regional integration is helping to diversify the region's exports away from an exclusive reliance on natural resources.

For the region's consumers, at least those of them still with money to spend, privatization has in some cases brought about improvements in services, while trade liberalization has brought in its wake cheaper, better-quality products, both imported and produced by newly competitive local factories. The availability of imported consumer goods has been enormously enhanced by the influx of foreign capital since the early 1990s, itself partly caused by the region's economic reforms.

Governments themselves have also shown some healthy changes, in many cases giving up their former penchant for acting as job-creation schemes for political supporters. Fiscal deficits are coming down, in part due to improved tax collection. Inefficient, loss-making state-run companies have been sold off (along with some perfectly good ones which could have continued to generate revenues for social spending and other purposes).

So much for the good news, for such gains have been achieved at enormous social and environmental cost. Structural adjustment has aggravated Latin America's existing economic failings. Just like import substitution, neo-liberalism has increased inequality in the region. However, import substitution at least managed to lower the proportion of the population living below the poverty line, even as it enlarged the rich minority's slice of the cake. Structural adjustment has not even achieved this. Instead, Adam Smith's benign market forces have in practice become an 'invisible fist', inflicting terrible damage on the poor. Just as during the Industrial Revolution, which spawned the classical school of economics, the unregulated play of market forces has favoured the rich and squeezed the poor, sweeping away the limited gains in terms of job security and a threadbare welfare state achieved by fifty years of import substitution and political pressure.

By 1993, 60 million more Latin Americans had slipped below the poverty line, bringing the total to 46 per cent of the population, nearly 200 million people.[7] Moreover, even the belated return to economic growth in the 1990s shows little sign of trickling down. 'Growth has largely bypassed the poor,' Oxfam concluded in 1994, as the region's recovery entered its fifth year.[8]

The deterioration in the quality of life is as much psychological as material, but no less painful for that. Adjustment-driven policies of 'flexibilization' have brought new levels of anxiety into millions of lives by generating more insecure, part-time or informal-sector jobs, yet neo-liberal governments from Argentina to Mexico are still arguing that 'labour deregulation' holds the key to growth and poverty reduction. Cuts in social services have left in their wake a less-educated population and have placed even greater burdens on women, who now have to juggle the increased demands of workplace and home, when the already inadequate level of state support has been further cut and a process of disintegration is threatening their families and communities. Already, family breakdown, deteriorating schools, spreading poverty and the rise in child labour are jeopardizing the well-being and productive potential of the next generation. Crime and social disintegration have become the principal cause for public concern in many Latin American societies.

In the countryside, peasant farmers find credit unobtainable and agrarian reform programmes thrown into reverse, as trade liberalization floods local markets with cheap food imports. Millions of farmers will in time be forced off the land to swell the ranks of the dispossessed in the shanty-towns. The advent of adjustment has ratcheted up Latin America's rate of deforestation and other pressures on an increasingly fragile environment.

In macro-economic terms, neo-liberalism's successes are mixed with failure. The debt crisis and ensuing adjustment have derailed Latin America's attempts to industrialize. From 1960 to 1980, manufacturing grew at over 6 per cent a year, becoming an increasingly important part of the regional economy.[9] The debt crisis, recession at home, the collapse of imported inputs and machinery for local industry, followed by an equally sudden trade liberalization and surge of cheap manufactured imports, have driven countless factories to the wall. Manufacturing in the 1980s bumped along with a growth rate of just 0.4 per cent a year,[10] well behind agriculture. Even its recovery in the first years of the 1990s has left it losing ground as a proportion of the overall economy.

Investment has been the chief casualty of the silent revolution, as governments have abandoned fifty years of development based on public investment, the local private sector has refused to invest in a recession, and foreign banks have washed their hands of a continent whose economy they had done so much to destroy with the easy credit of the 1970s. The sudden return of foreign capital in the early 1990s has filled the vacuum left by the state and the local private sector, taking investment back up to its admittedly inadequate pre-debt crisis levels. By then, however, the 1980s had taken a large bite out of Latin America's stock of investment, leaving a backlog of crumbling infrastructure and battered people which will take decades to make up. In 1993, the region invested just 18.5 per cent of its GDP, compared to investment levels of around 30 per cent in the Asian 'tigers'.[11] Furthermore, the debt crisis has shown the folly of relying so heavily on inflows of fickle foreign capital, a lesson that was repeated for the historically dull-witted with the Mexican crash of early 1995.

The shakiest area is the kind of money flooding into the booming stock and bond markets of the region. Latin America's sudden rehabilitation in the eyes of international investors was partly the result of thin pickings in the recession-hit US, European and Japanese markets in the early 1990s (only this could explain why non-adjusters like Brazil have cashed in just as much as Mexico or Argentina). When US interest rates started to bounce back in April 1994, 'emerging markets' lost their glitter and investors raced back to their traditional haunts, knocking holes in the Latin American bond market. The Latin American stock markets fell in value by 22 per cent in 1994,[12] while total bond issues, which had brought in $24bn in 1993, fell back to $17bn in 1994.[13]

In 1994, capital inflows fell $8bn from their 1993 peak of $65bn,[14] but were still just sufficient to cover debt and profits payments which the US interest rate rise had pushed up to $36bn and a trade deficit which had risen to $18bn.[15] A growing proportion of the remaining inflow is in the form of direct investment, which boomed in Mexico and Argentina in 1994 and was expected to pour into Brazil should the *Real* plan succeed in stabilizing the economy.

The availability of bountiful supplies of foreign capital has allowed late-adjusting governments like Argentina to engineer a relatively low-pain adjustment by running an overvalued exchange rate to hold down inflation, rather than by suppressing demand as in the fierce recessions of the early 1980s. However this 'easy option' carries the long-term cost of a loss of export competitiveness, undermining neo-liberalism's declared intention of achieving sustainable export-led growth. In Argentina and Mexico, the new model looks much like a re-run of the 1970s 'dance of the millions' which culminated in the debt crisis, a conclusion only strengthened by the run on the Mexican peso in early 1995, which caused panic in global capital markets from Bangkok to Buenos Aires.

Any interruption to the renewed inflow of dollars could indeed lead to a foreign exchange crisis like Mexico's crash in August 1982, but with some important differences. This time around, the debt is more diverse, both in terms of creditors, since it is no longer just banks which are doing the lending, and in terms of debtors, since Latin America's private sector is mopping up a far higher amount of incoming capital than in the 1970s. This added degree of complexity would obstruct any attempt at concerted action by debtors or creditors in the wake of a debt crisis. Moreover, the Brady Plan has also turned much of Latin America's debt into fixed-interest bonds, reducing the region's vulnerability to the kind of sudden hike in US interest rates which precipitated the debt crisis in 1982.

Before that happens, however, a squeeze in capital inflows is likely to force governments to raise their domestic interest rates to pull in dollars, thereby choking off domestic recovery. The Mexican government reacted in this way to its travails in 1995.

Much of the direct investment flowing into Latin America since the late 1980s has gone on buying state-owned companies in the great privatization sell-off. But once the family silver has all gone, will the foreign investors continue to invest and innovate, especially if slipshod privatization procedures have awarded them a virtual monopoly, devoid of government scrutiny? Transnational corporations are not philanthropic institutions; they are in business and will want their money back with interest. Profit remittances, currently ticking over at around $6bn a year,[16] are bound to climb once transnational companies' investments start to produce results, especially since restrictions on profit flows have been virtually eliminated by many governments in the scramble for investment.

Even in the area of neo-liberalism's greatest triumph, the fight against inflation, problems could lie ahead. Will governments be able to keep their deficits under control if foreign investors become wary of buying their bonds, or once the privatization bonanza ends? Furthermore, without greatly increasing public spending, how will they cope with the pent-up demands of a population who have so far seen so few of the benefits from the economic recovery?

Between them, the international financial institutions, western governments, commercial banks and foreign investors, in alliance with local policy-makers, have driven the region at high speed down a developmental blind alley. Abundant natural resources and cheap labour are no longer enough to guarantee sustained export-led growth in today's world (if indeed they ever were). Successfully industrializing countries like Taiwan and South Korea break into computers, not kiwi fruit, yet neo-liberalism has ignored the lessons offered by the Asian 'tigers'. Governments show little interest in R&D and have neglected their most important asset – their people – through a decade's deterioration of social services. The World Bank's revived awareness of the importance of education will be of little help, since it is confined to reducing poverty by concentrating on primary education and ignores the importance of long-term technological development.

The way forward
Ever since independence, Latin American governments and planners have veered between state and market in search of the elusive path to long-term development. The transformation of the world economy in

the last thirty years may have destroyed full-blown central planning as a viable economic model, but the crude recipes of the free marketeers also offer little hope for long-term success in the new world order. Rather, neo-liberalism is in danger of locking Latin America into a model of export-led growth based on raw materials and cheap labour, leading to growing impoverishment and irrelevance within the global economy.

If neo-liberalism has failed most Latin Americans, what realistic alternatives are there? Although supporters of the silent revolution routinely dismiss their critics as economic dinosaurs bereft of alternative ideas, there is already a rich debate over the ingredients for building a better economic model for the region. A clear-sighted study of the policies behind the success of the Asian NICs; the spectrum of ideas grouped together under the heading 'neo-structuralism' and the calls for a more visionary approach from grassroots organizations throughout the continent provide good initial starting-points for debating and constructing a more effective and just development model. The extent of the debate going on within the region is often ignored by even the most penetrating of the free market's critics in the North, who frequently fall into the trap of trying to prescribe solutions for the South, rather than listening to the ideas of those living at the sharp end of global restructuring. In the worst cases, adjustment's critics can resemble the IMF in their efforts to impose a single blueprint onto the diverse economies and cultures of the South.

There seems little doubt that if the region is to achieve long-term development, it must find a way of combining economic growth with a far higher degree of social and economic equality. This combination of 'growth with equity' has always eluded Latin America but other countries have shown not only that it is possible, but that the two are mutually reinforcing; equal societies tend to grow faster than unequal ones.[17] Growth with inequality leads to political instability, social breakdown and a substandard workforce, while seeking equity without ensuring growth is a recipe for political conflict and eventual collapse.

Success stories like Taiwan and South Korea show that governments can work with the market without subordinating national goals to the interests of private, especially foreign, capital. Given the failure of attempts to find alternatives to the market as a means of efficiently distributing goods and services, realistic alternatives must seek to use the market as the means to achieve national development.

Any attempt to depart from the neo-liberal path will be made more difficult by the growing globalization of the world economy. Agreements like NAFTA and GATT greatly reduce the ability of signatory governments to pursue a national industrial or development policy, obliging governments to hand out 'equal treatment' to supremely unequal players – local industries and giant transnational corporations. But even within such agreements, there is always room for manoeuvre if a government is determined and clear about what it is trying to achieve. Barring a sea-change in the world economic order, policy-makers in Latin America will have to work within the constraints imposed by the global economy.

Although the technological genie which drives economic globalization cannot be put back in its bottle, changes in the management of the global economy could ease the task of switching to a growth-with-equity development model. Calls for regulation of the global monetary system are growing after their predatory attacks on the European Monetary System proved how powerful and destabilizing international money markets have become. Any such regulation would help defend governments that wish to change economic direction from having their currencies instantly destroyed.

The debate over revamping the international financial institutions could also lead to positive changes for the region. One political side-effect of the debt crisis, the GATT Uruguay round and NAFTA has been that economic issues have acquired a far higher profile in the work of a broad spectrum of NGOs and pressure groups in the North. They could prove vital allies to those seeking to develop alternative models of development in Latin America and elsewhere, both through their efforts to mobilize public opinion to rein in or abolish the IMF and World Bank, and through their encouragement and funding for their counterparts in the South.

The arguments over the role of the Bretton Woods institutions stretches well beyond the left. Many mainstream economists are calling for the IMF to be removed from policing the Third World and put in charge of regulating the international monetary system. Whether they are abolished, reformed or diverted to more suitable and useful functions, the growing criticism of both Fund and Bank activities in the Third World is in any case likely to ease the pressure on Latin American governments blindly to follow the neo-liberal path whatever the social cost. Furthermore, the recent capital bonanza has allowed some governments to build up reserves to such an extent that they are less desperate for the largesse of the international financial institutions and are therefore in a better bargaining position when haggling over conditions on the next loan, although the speed with which the Mexican crisis of 1995 forced it back into the arms of the IMF showed how quickly global capital markets could wipe out a government's reserves.

One vital issue which has largely disappeared from the international political agenda is that of Latin America's debt burden. The Brady Plan has *not* solved the underlying problem, and as long as the region is required to pay tribute of over $30bn a year in debt service, it is highly unlikely that the crucial task of building up investment can ever get under way. Unfortunately, the return of capital inflows has masked Latin America's debt crisis to such an extent that most policy-makers think the problem has gone away altogether.

But Latin America needs much more than a new deal with outside forces, however important they are. Growth with equity demands little short of a cultural revolution within the continent. At the top, the new cosmopolitan élite of technocrats who increasingly identify more with their US college contemporaries than with the unwashed hordes of their own countrymen and women must be transformed into defenders of long-term national interests. The voice of the poor, which still goes largely unheard despite the return of liberal democracy to the region, must be given a central place in designing national development strategies, if their interests are not once again to be sidelined by the élites. The MIT graduates in the Finance Ministries must swallow their distaste and sit down with the peasant farmer of FATA and the small producers in the shanty towns to design national policies which benefit all the population.

Even more difficult, the middle and upper classes who place such importance on owning the latest consumer trinkets from their Miami shopping trips (and frequently work for local transnational corporation subsidiaries or other foreign interests) must be persuaded to change their ways and accept some degree of austerity, if they are to pay increased taxes *and* channel more of their wealth into domestic savings. Since the Latin American élite shows little evidence of philanthropy when it comes to giving up its privileges, it will have to be convinced that its long-term interests will be improved by short-term sacrifices (the kind of rhetoric the poor have had to swallow for the last thirteen years!). Jorge Castañeda believes the best means of doing this is by pointing to the level of social breakdown and crime which is one of the starkest legacies of neo-liberalism.[18] Yet the élite is used to walling itself off from the unsightly world of the poor, and appeals to place long-term goals before short-term greed are always likely to fall on deaf ears.

It may be that here lies the real challenge and historical role for the Latin American left; to construct an alternative that is sufficiently coherent either to replace the current model, or at least to frighten a section of the élite into accepting a Latin American New Deal that would give equal weight to economic growth and social equity. The leaders of the Brazilian left hoped this would be their legacy in the aftermath of their defeat in the 1994 elections.[19]

If the élite cannot be persuaded to change, there are enormous political obstacles to achieving a peaceful transition to a development model based on growth with equity, not least because the prospect of a reforming government coming to power will lead to an immediate bout of capital flight and a currency crisis before the new government even gets its hands on the levers of power. It may be that the Chilean transition under President Aylwin is the best that can be hoped for; a scenario in which the rich keep their slice of the cake, but are at least persuaded to accept some mild tax increases with which to improve social spending and engineer some real trickle-down to the poor. But this falls a long way short of growth with equity.

Another option is, of course, that the transition will not be peaceful, that the poor of Latin America, shortly to become the majority, will grow tired of waiting for wealth to trickle down to their slums and villages and will take matters into their own hands. They may be able to do so through democratic channels, but the balance of power is still weighted heavily in favour of the status quo, and frustrated opponents may seek more radical ways to change the system. Unfortunately, experiences such as Cuba and Nicaragua suggest that while violent revolution may lead to short-term improvements in the lives of the poor, it is not a long-term solution. Piecemeal reform may be less glamorous but it is usually more successful in the long run.

The Achilles' heel of all attempts to transform the neo-liberal model into one which works for growth with equity is the difficulty of building a sufficiently powerful political coalition behind the movement for change. Latin America's silent revolution required the catastrophe of the debt crisis and the unceasing arm-twisting of the international financial institutions to bring it about, and history suggests that another such trauma will be required to achieve the degree of change in economic and political thinking which is of life and death importance to the poor of Latin America. For them, the trauma is already happening, but they may have to wait until it touches the élites within the region and powerful interests abroad before a definitive shift can take place. But is it really too much to ask that those currently in charge of the region's destiny, whether they be Latin American, North American, European or Japanese, learn from history and make the necessary changes *before* the next disaster occurs?

Notes

1 Susan George and Fabrizio Sabelli, *Faith and Credit: The World Bank's Secular Empire*, (London, 1994), p.147.

2 CEPAL, *Panorama Económico de América Latina 1994*, (Santiago, September 1994).

3 *Ibid.*, p.5.

4 IDB, *Economic and Social Progress in Latin America 1993 Report* (Washington, DC, 1993), p.263.

5 CEPAL, *Balance Preliminar de la Económia de América Latina y el Caribe 1993* (Santiago, December 1993), p.31.

6 *Financial Times* (London), 21 December 1994.

7 CEPAL, *Panorama Social de América Latina 1993*, (Santiago, 1994), p.100.

8 Oxfam, *Structural Adjustment and Inequality in Latin America: How IMF and World Bank Policies have Failed the Poor* (mimeo) (Oxford, 1994), p.1.

9 IDB, *Economic and Social Progress in Latin America 1990 Report* (Washington, DC, 1990), p.266.

10 IDB, *Economic and Social Progress in Latin America 1993 Report*, p.264.

11 CEPAL, *Panorama Económico de América Latina 1994* (Santiago, September 1994), p.5.

12 Latin America Monitor, *Mexico*, (London, February 1995), p.7.

13 Stephanie Griffith-Jones, *European Private Flows to Latin America: The Facts and Issues* (mimeo) (London, 1994), p.4 ; *Financial Times* (London), 21 December 1994.

14 *Financial Times* (London), 21 December 1994.

15 CEPAL, *Balance Preliminar de la Económia de América Latina y el Caribe 1994* (Santiago, December 1994), pp. 52, 36.

16 CEPAL, *Anuario Estadístico de América Latina y el Caribe 1992* (Santiago, 1993), p.491.

17 D. Rodrick, *King Kong Meets Godzilla: The World Bank and the East Asian Miracle*, Centre for Economic Policy Research Working Paper (London, April 1994).

18 Jorge Castañeda, *Utopia Unarmed: The Latin American Left after the Cold War* (New York, 1993), p.446.

19 Sue Branford and Bernardo Kucinski, *Brazil: Carnival of the Oppressed. Lula and the Brazilian Workers' Party* (London, 1995), p.108.

Country-by-Country Guide to the Latin American Economy 1982–94

Sources for Statistical Tables: CEPAL (various publications and years); Economist Intelligence Unit

Sources for Country Profiles: CEPAL, Economist Intelligence Unit Country Profiles and Country Reports, Silent Revolution *text*

ARGENTINA

Population (1992): 33.1 million
GDP (1992): US$143.9 billion
Latin America ranking by GDP: 3

In Argentina the onset of the debt crisis coincided with the Falklands/Malvinas war and the subsequent fall of the military junta which had ruled the country since 1976.

The military's version of free-market reform had already devastated the economy. Trade liberalization combined with an overvalued peso led to an import boom funded by borrowing. Argentina's foreign debt quintupled during the military period. Unable to compete with artificially cheap imports, much of Argentina's industry was destroyed.

The new government of Raúl Alfonsín tried to avoid giving in to IMF pressure by launching the heterodox '*Austral* plan'. Its subsequent collapse drove Alfonsín back to negotiations with the Fund and World Bank, eventually resulting in substantial loans in 1992 and 1993.

In 1989 the Peronist candidate Carlos Saúl Menem won the presidency and undertook a profound neo-liberal adjustment programme involving privatization, trade liberalization and pegging the currency to the US dollar. The result has been the virtual eradication of inflation and an economic boom in the first years of the 1990s. Argentina's creation of the

Mercosur Regional Trade Agreement with Brazil, Uruguay and Paraguay has been an important source of export growth, especially to the large Brazilian market – total exports more than doubled from 1987 to 1994.

Economic recovery has not, however, created jobs; Argentina is perhaps Latin America's most depressing example of the 'jobless growth phenomenon'. As the economy grew by a third between 1991 and 1994, unemployment increased to over 11 per cent, while average wages were still less than their 1980 level.

The overvalued peso has harmed exports and led to a burgeoning trade deficit, increasing Argentina's dependence on constant injections of foreign capital. This has raised doubts over the medium-term sustainability of the model, which were borne out by the Mexican financial crisis of early 1995, stemming from a less extreme version of Argentina's programme. In the aftermath of the Mexican crisis, Argentina was forced to return to the IMF and World Bank in search of new capital.

	GDP/capita US$	Growth %	Exports US$m	Imports US$m	Debt US$bn	Inflation %	Wages
1982	3618	-6.8	7622	4859	43.6	209.7	80.1
1983	3644	0.7	7838	4120	45.1	433.7	100.5
1984	3669	0.7	8101	4119	46.9	688.0	127.1
1985	3445	-6.1	8396	3518	49.3	385.4	107.8
1986	3659	6.2	6852	4406	51.4	81.9	107.5
1987	3708	1.3	6360	5343	58.3	174.8	96.9
1988	3586	-3.3	9134	4892	58.5	387.7	93.7
1989	3322	-7.4	9573	3864	63.3	4923.3	75.8
1990	3278	-1.3	12354	3726	61.0	1343.9	79.4
1991	3527	7.6	11972	7400	63.7	84.0	80.5
1992	3787	7.4	12235	13685	65.0	17.5	81.6
1993	3969	4.8	13090	15545	68.0	7.7	80.3
1994*	4152	4.6	15200	19425	75.0	3.6	85.7

* estimate

Key: GDP per capita (1980 US dollars); growth of GDP per capita (%); exports fob (US$ millions); imports fob (US$ millions); total external debt (US$ billions); annual inflation (%); index of average real wages in manufacturing industry (1980 = 100)

BOLIVIA

Population (1992): 7.5 million
GDP (1992): US$6.7 billion
Latin America ranking by GDP: 12

After a century and a half of almost continuous political unrest and a record number of coups, Bolivia has had an elected government since 1982. The new civilian government came to power just as the debt crisis broke, presiding over a spectacular economic collapse from 1982 to 1985. In 1985 a new government took power and launched the 'New Economic Policy', a fierce structural adjustment programme to combat hyper-inflation (over 8000 per cent in 1985) designed with World Bank support.

The human cost of the NEP was deepened when the tin market crashed in October 1985 – tin had historically been Bolivia's main export. With state protection removed, the tin mines were largely shut down, causing great hardship in the towns of the Bolivian *altiplano*.

The NEP reduced inflation to 11% within two years, winning the Bolivian government international plaudits and a rapid reward in the shape of two IMF credits in 1986. These opened the door to debt renegotiation and new loans from banks and Western governments, as well as the World Bank and IDB.

Stabilization produced a further year of recession in 1986 before the economy returned to sustained, if slow, per capita growth. Nevertheless, by 1994 per capita GDP was still 15% less than in 1982. Export growth has been disappointing, and by 1994 was still less than pre-debt crisis levels. The main exports are natural gas and zinc.

Adjustment has also been achieved at enormous social cost (see p. 6). In 1991, according to the government, 80% of the population lived below the poverty line and half Bolivia's families were unable to feed themselves adequately.

In 1993 a new government took office, led by private sector entrepreneur Gonzalo Sánchez de Losada, and set about further adjustment, in particular a privatization programme which had previously failed to take off due to a combination of lack of foreign interest, government incompetence and corruption, and opposition from Bolivia's traditionally combative trade union movement.

	GDP/capita US$	Growth %	Exports US$m	Imports US$m	Debt US$bn	Inflation %	Wages
1982	753	-5.4	828	496	2.8	297	-
1983	685	-9.0	755	496	3.2	329	55.4
1984	661	-3.5	724	412	3.2	2177	45.6
1985	632	-4.4	623	463	3.3	8171	18.4
1986	598	-5.5	546	597	3.5	66	17.1
1987	597	-0.1	519	646	4.2	11	19.8
1988	600	0.5	543	591	4.1	22	20.9
1989	601	0.7	724	730	3.5	17	18.7
1990	614	2.1	831	776	3.8	18	17.3
1991	631	2.1	760	804	3.6	15	26.6
1992	628	-0.4	608	1041	3.8	10	-
1993	633	0.8	710	1078	3.9	9	-
1994*	643	1.7	905	1115	4.2	9	-

* estimate

Key: GDP per capita (1980 US dollars); growth of GDP per capita (%); exports fob (US$ millions); imports fob (US$ millions); total external debt (US$ billions); annual inflation (%); index of average real wages in manufacturing industry (1980 = 100)

BRAZIL

Population (1992): 154.1 million
GDP (1992): US$331.5 billion
Latin America ranking by GDP: 1

Brazil is the economic giant of Latin America, with a third of its people and GDP. In 1991 it was the world's tenth largest economy, and the Third World's largest. It has the Third World's largest foreign debt ($152 billion in 1994), is the most unequal society in Latin America (and second only to Botswana world-wide), has the region's highest rate of inflation (1294 per cent in 1994) and boasts the world's best football team.

As the main winner under import substitution, perhaps it is not surprising that Brazil has been most reluctant to join in the neo-liberal stampede. Import substitution has given Brazil a large and diversified industrial sector which is also a powerful exporter. It therefore has more to lose from blanket trade liberalization and has been more determined to find alternative ways out of the 1980s malaise. While undergoing a severe external adjustment to generate a massive trade surplus in the early years of the debt crisis, Brazil has until recently avoided the kind of orthodox domestic adjustment practised elsewhere.

Despite the collapse of the *Cruzado* plan, Brazil has persevered with a series of heterodox shock therapies involving a bewildering series of clever tricks and new currencies, yet none of them has proved able to curb the public sector deficit which drives inflation.

Severe political constraints have also helped tie the government's hands on inflation. The Brazilian élite has a long-standing aversion to paying taxes, while a series of weak governments has repeatedly placed short-term electoral considerations before long-term economic well-being. Furthermore, the new decentralizing constitution of 1988 obliges the central government to hand over a large part of its revenues to states and municipalities, making it far harder to reduce expenditure. Corruption in government is also a serious problem – President Fernando Collor de Mello was impeached on corruption charges in 1992 after being elected on an anti-corruption ticket.

In mid-1994 then Finance Minister Fernando Henrique Cardoso launched a new stabilization plan, the *Real* plan, which repeated Argentina's trick of running an overvalued currency to curb inflation, while trying to cut back on the fiscal deficit.

The plan was a spectacular initial success, winning international acclaim (and investment) by bringing inflation down from 50% a month to less than 2 per cent and winning Cardoso the presidency in October 1994. However, by early 1995 overvaluation had pushed Brazil into a trade deficit for the first time since the start of the debt crisis, raising fears that the model might increase Brazil's dependence on volatile international capital markets to plug the trade gap. In early 1995, Cardoso devalued the *Real* and restarted some import barriers to try and avert a Mexico-style crisis.

	GDP/capita	Growth	Exports	Imports	Debt	Inflation	Wages
	US$	%	US$m	US$m	US$bn	%	
1982	1812	-1.4	20172	19395	91.3	98	107.2
1983	1731	-4.5	21906	15434	97.9	179	94.0
1984	1790	3.4	27001	13915	102.0	203	96.7
1985	1895	5.9	25634	13168	105.1	239	120.4
1986	2007	5.9	22348	14044	111.1	59	137.3
1987	2038	1.6	26210	15052	121.2	395	127.7
1988	1998	-2.0	33773	14605	113.5	993	138.3
1989	2026	1.4	34375	18263	115.1	1864	149.1
1990	1903	-6.1	31408	20661	122.2	1585	130.8
1991	1889	-0.8	31620	21041	123.9	475	125.4
1992	1839	-2.5	36103	20578	130.2	1149	138.1
1993	1885	2.9	38783	25711	131.7	2489	151.9
1994*	1938	2.8	43300	32000	151.5	1294	162.7

* estimate

Key: GDP per capita (1980 US dollars); growth of GDP per capita (%); exports fob (US$ millions); imports fob (US$ millions); total external debt (US$ billions); annual inflation (%); index of average real wages in manufacturing in São Paulo (1980 = 100)

CHILE

Population (1992): 13.6 million
GDP (1992): US$38.9 billion
Latin America ranking by GDP: 6

Chile, which has become the jewel in neo-liberalism's crown, began the 1980s with Latin America's most spectacular collapse. Per capita GDP fell by over 14 per cent in 1982, precipitating a bank crash and forcing General Pinochet to renationalize a large part of the financial sector.

Thereafter it became a model IMF customer, successfully completing numerous Fund and World Bank structural adjustment programmes in the 1980s. After the crash of 1982, the regime moderated the extreme monetarism of the 'Chicago Boys' in favour of a more pragmatic pursuit of export-led growth. Trade liberalization, a high level of internal savings and investment and Chile's abundant natural wealth have enabled it to increase exports rapidly since 1985, diversifying away from its dependence on copper to a range of natural-resource based exports such as fishmeal, fresh fruit and forestry products. High levels of per capita growth from 1984 onwards have made Chile into the envy of other Latin American governments.

Chile was also one of the last Latin American countries to return to democracy. After 17 years of the Pinochet dictatorship, a Christian Democrat government took office in 1990. It largely continued the previous economic programme, but used the level of anti-Pinochet consensus and impressive growth rates to persuade the élite (which had become massively wealthy under Pinochet) to accept a limited increase in taxation.

This has enabled the governments of Patricio Aylwin and Eduardo Frei to run a fiscal surplus while increasing social spending on health, education and poverty relief with impressive results. Over a million Chileans were lifted out of poverty from 1987 to 1992.

Despite the macro-economic success story, adjustment under Pinochet radically increased inequality, something which the return to democracy has done little to redress. Although there are several other long-term weaknesses and numerous hidden costs to the model (see p. 131), Chile is the nearest thing to a Latin American neo-liberal success story and appears to have better medium-term prospects than most other countries in the region.

	GDP/capita US$	Growth %	Exports US$m	Imports US$m	Debt US$bn	Inflation %	Wages
1982	1946	-14.5	3706	3643	17.2	21	108.6
1983	1903	-2.2	3831	2845	18.0	24	97.1
1984	1985	4.3	3651	3288	19.7	23	97.2
1985	1999	0.7	3804	2920	20.4	26	93.5
1986	2073	3.7	4191	3099	20.9	17	95.1
1987	2160	3.9	5224	3994	20.7	21	94.7
1988	2272	5.7	7052	4833	19.0	13	101.0
1989	2446	8.0	8080	6502	17.5	21	102.9
1990	2483	0.3	8310	7037	18.6	27	104.8
1991	2577	4.1	8929	7354	17.4	19	109.9
1992	2774	8.5	9986	9238	18.9	13	114.9
1993	2896	4.4	9202	10181	19.9	12	119.2
1994*	2971	2.6	11500	10895	21.5	9	124.6

* estimate

Key: GDP per capita (1980 US dollars); growth of GDP per capita (%); exports fob (US$ millions); imports fob (US$ millions); total external debt (US$ billions); annual inflation (%); index of average real non-agricultural wages (1980 = 100)

COLOMBIA

Population (1992): 33.4 million
GDP (1992): US$49.8 billion
Latin America ranking by GDP: 5

The Colombian economy is something of a paradox. Whereas the country is best-known for its unstable political cocktail of drug barons, guerrilla wars and human rights abuses, the economy has been the most stable in Latin America since 1982, avoiding Chile's wild peaks and troughs in achieving a combination of steady per capita growth and low inflation.

Much of the reason lies in Colombia's conservative borrowing policy during the 1970s, which enabled it to avoid default on its foreign debt after 1982. As a result the government has been able to keep the IMF at arm's length, with more room for manoeuvre on the timing and nature of its adjustment process.

Like Chile, Colombia's growth has been based on natural-resource based exports. In recent years its previous dependence on coffee (it is the second largest world producer after Brazil) has been reduced thanks to spectacular finds of oil and coal. In 1990 oil replaced coffee as its major export.

Unlike Chile, Colombia also managed to reduce inequality in the 1980s, while pursuing export-led growth. The roots of these achievements lay in its more consistent effort at poverty eradication, involving regular increases in the real minimum wage. However, an accelerated adjustment process in the early 1990s has since reversed this tendency, leading to an increase in both inequality and urban poverty.

Colombia has taken a much more wary approach to trade liberalization than neo-liberal flagships such as Chile, although in recent years it has energetically pursued regional trade agreements, notably the G3 pact with Mexico and Venezuela.

	GDP/capita US$	Growth %	Exports US$m	Imports US$m	Debt US$bn	Inflation %	Wages
1982	1225	-1.1	3113	5358	10.3	24	104.8
1983	1221	-0.3	2970	4464	11.4	17	110.3
1984	1240	1.6	4273	4027	12.2	18	118.5
1985	1249	0.7	3650	3673	13.8	22	114.6
1986	1310	4.8	5331	3409	16.0	21	120.1
1987	1358	3.7	5661	3793	17.1	24	119.2
1988	1390	2.3	5343	4516	17.4	28	117.7
1989	1413	1.7	6031	4557	17.0	26	119.4
1990	1444	2.2	7079	5108	17.6	32	113.4
1991	1447	0.2	7507	4548	17.0	27	115.3
1992	1473	1.8	7263	6030	16.8	25	117.3
1993	1519	3.1	7429	9086	18.6	23	122.8
1994*	1569	3.3	8925	11085	21.5	23	122.2

* estimate

Key: GDP per capita (1980 US dollars); growth of GDP per capita (%); exports fob (US$ millions); imports fob (US$ millions); total external debt (US$ billions); annual inflation (%); average industrial real wages (1980 = 100)

COSTA RICA

Population (1992): 3.2 million
GDP (1992): US$5.6 billion
Latin America ranking by GDP: 15

Costa Rica is an island of calm in the turbulent seas of Central American politics. In 1949 it took the inspired step of abolishing the armed forces, opening the way to three decades of peace and growth, accompanied by the creation of the nearest thing to a welfare state in Central America. Yet when it comes to structural adjustment, Costa Rica has gone to greater extremes than any of its neighbours.

In the 1970s, heavy government borrowing ran up one of Latin America's largest foreign debts per capita, laying it open to the full neo-liberal treatment once the debt crisis broke in 1982. Costa Rica became one of the IMF and World Bank's most faithful customers, with numerous loans running right through to the mid-1990s, all pushing the country along the structural adjustment path of trade liberalization, privatization, and erosion of the welfare state. Costa Rica was also one of the first countries to be rewarded with a Brady Plan debt reduction scheme.

Since the mid-1980s, adjustment has produced an export-boom based on non-traditional exports such as fresh fruit and *maquiladora* products, as well as traditional commodities such as bananas and coffee. Exports doubled between 1985 and 1993, but at a significant environmental cost, as the excessive use of pesticides and other chemical inputs has damaged the country's ecosystem. As elsewhere, adjustment has been bad news for the poor, whose income has fallen remorselessly since 1980.

	GDP/capita US$	Growth %	Exports US$m	Imports US$m	Debt US$bn	Inflation %	Wages
1982	1318	-9.7	869	805	3.2	82	70.8
1983	1318	0.0	853	896	3.5	11	78.5
1984	1385	5.1	997	993	3.8	17	84.7
1985	1362	-1.7	939	1001	3.7	11	92.2
1986	1386	1.8	1085	1045	4.1	15	98.0
1987	1408	1.6	1107	1245	4.4	16	88.5
1988	1414	0.4	1181	1279	4.5	25	84.5
1989	1451	2.6	1333	1572	4.5	10	85.1
1990	1461	0.7	1354	1797	3.9	27	86.5
1991	1455	-0.4	1491	1698	4.0	25	82.5
1992	1516	4.2	1714	2212	4.0	17	85.9
1993	1569	3.5	1947	2610	4.1	9	94.7
1994*	1602	2.1	2165	2815	4.1	17	-

* estimate

Key: GDP per capita (1980 US dollars); growth of GDP per capita (%); exports fob (US$ millions); imports fob (US$ millions); total external debt (US$ billions); annual inflation (%); average real wages within social security system (1980 = 100)

CUBA

Population (1992): 10.8
GDP (1992): Ps 11.54 billion
Latin America ranking by GDP: ?

Cuba's economic travails in the 1980s and 1990s have been dominated far more by geopolitics than by the debt crisis or the IMF. Following the Cuban Revolution of 1959, Washington cut links before announcing a

trade embargo in 1962 which is still in place as of 1995. Cuba traditionally depended on trade with the US and the initial impact was severe.
Once isolated from the US, Cuba relied increasingly on Soviet support,
mainly in the form of cheap oil with which to run the economy and earn
hard currency – in the mid-1980s Cuban resale of Soviet oil generated
40 per cent of export earnings.

The crisis and subsequent collapse of the Soviet Union in the late
1980s have devastated the Cuban economy. Exports fell to one-third of
their former value between 1989-93. Deprived of Soviet aid to finance
the trade deficit, imports have been cut by three quarters. The economy
has halved in size and the effects of three decades of exemplary social
spending on Latin America's only national health service have started to
unravel among food shortages and rising unemployment.

The government has desperately courted foreign investors and tourists
and allowed dollars to circulate freely in the economy for the first time,
but the results have been mixed. Circulating dollars have increased
inequality and created growing frustration which broke out in mid-1994
into the first violent anti-Castro riots and an exodus of boat-people
towards the Florida coastline just 90 miles away. It looked as if the
endgame had begun in Washington's war of attrition with Fidel Castro.

	Growth %	Exports US$bn	Imports US$bn	Debt US$bn
1982	3.3	4.9	5.5	3.2
1983	4.3	5.5	6.2	3.2
1984	6.6	5.5	7.2	3.4
1985	3.8	6.0	8.0	3.6
1986	0.3	5.3	7.6	5.0
1987	-4.8	5.4	7.6	6.1
1988	1.2	5.5	7.6	6.5
1989	-0.2	5.4	8.1	6.2
1990	-4.0	4.9	6.7	7.0
1991	-25.7	3.6	3.7	8.4
1992	-14.7	2.2	2.5	10.0
1993	-10.7	1.7	2.2	10.8
1994*	-3.0	1.7	2.3	11.2

* estimate

Note: All economic statistics for Cuba should be treated with caution, since the Cuban
government has not issued official figures since 1990, and Cuba does not figure in the
annual reports of CEPAL or the Bretton Woods institutions. Instead of GDP, Cuba uses
its own measure of national output, Global Social Product. Figures are given in Cuban
pesos since the official exchange rate of one peso to the dollar is largely a fiction.

Key: Growth of Global Social Product per capita (%); exports fob (billions of pesos);
imports cif (billions of pesos); total external debt (US$ billions)

DOMINICAN REPUBLIC

Population (1992): 7.5 million
GDP (1992): US$5.2 billion
Latin America ranking by GDP: 17

The politics of the Dominican Republic have been dominated for the last three decades by Joaquín Balaguer, who in 1994 won a seventh term as president amid allegations of fraud. Since the mid-1980s, Balaguer has alternated austerity with short-lived economic booms, often timed to coincide with elections.

The initial impact of the debt crisis drove the Dominican Republic into the arms of the IMF. Subsequent austerity measures in 1984 provoked some of the bloodiest IMF riots in Latin America, leaving over a hundred dead.

The IMF and World Bank have promoted non-traditional exports to reduce the country's dependence on nickel and sugar, mainly via the free trade zones, using cheap Dominican labour to assemble clothing, shoes and electrical goods. By the end of 1992, 424 companies were employing 142,000 people in the zones, whose export revenues had increased five-fold since 1985, making them the country's single largest export earner. The government does not include income from the zones, or from tourism, in its export figures. Together, they cover much of the large apparent trade deficit.

	GDP/capita US$	Growth %	Exports US$m	Imports US$m	Debt US$bn	Inflation %	Wages
1982	1154	-1.1	768	1257	3.0	7	86.4
1983	1183	2.5	785	1279	3.3	7	80.8
1984	1159	-2.0	868	1257	3.5	8	82.2
1985	1106	-4.6	739	1286	3.7	28	80.2
1986	1100	-0.5	722	1352	3.8	7	86.0
1987	1169	6.3	711	1592	3.9	25	84.1
1988	1152	-1.4	890	1608	3.9	58	87.4
1989	1178	2.2	924	1964	4.1	41	77.7
1990	1097	-6.9	735	1793	4.5	101	65.2
1991	1064	-3.0	658	1729	4.6	4	66.2
1992	1113	4.6	566	2178	4.4	7	80.2
1993	1117	0.4	530	2118	4.5	3	-
1994*	1141	2.1	595	2250	4.0	11	-

* estimate

Key: GDP per capita (1980 US dollars); growth of GDP per capita (%); exports fob (US$ millions); imports fob (US$ millions); total external debt (US$ billions); annual inflation (%); index of real urban minimum wage (1980 = 100)

Companies setting up in the zones enjoy a 8- to 20-year tax holiday, duty-free raw material imports and low wage rates. Since 1984 they have also benefited from Washington's Caribbean Basin Initiative, under which a number of non-traditional exports have gained duty-free access to the US market.

In 1994 the government was rewarded for its good behaviour with a Brady Plan deal which wiped about 10 per cent off its foreign debt.

ECUADOR

Population (1992): 11.1 million
GDP (1992): US$14.4 billion
Latin America ranking by GDP: 8

Like Mexico, Ecuador struck oil in the 1970s and it has proved a mixed blessing. Oil production rose a hundred-fold between 1972 and 1992, as oil replaced bananas, shrimps and coffee as the main export. But as in Mexico, the oil boom helped mask the exhaustion of the import substitution process and led to a steep rise in indebtedness during the 1970s, laying Ecuador open to the full blast of the debt crisis after 1982.

This has involved the usual pattern of austerity and IMF agreements rewarded by new loans and debt rescheduling. However, Ecuador has shown itself more reluctant than most to go in for full-blown structural adjustment, for example over privatization and import liberalization, which it fears would destroy its heavily protected industrial sector. It has also persistently registered inflation of over 30 per cent. This has led to regular run-ins with the IMF and World Bank and periodic inability to keep up with debt service.

Internal division has also played a part in holding up adjustment; Ecuador spent much of 1994 locked in internal political in-fighting over President Sixto Duran Ballen's plans for free market reform, agreed with the IMF in April. Nevertheless, the government won a Brady Plan debt reduction deal in the same year, along with plentiful support from the World Bank and IDB.

Regional exports have been responding well to Ecuador's efforts to conclude free trade agreements with its neighbours. Exports to the Andean Group of Bolivia, Colombia, Peru and Venezuela quadrupled between 1986 and 1991. Since 1990 the government has undertaken limited trade liberalization after pressure from the IMF, announced its intention to join GATT and rewritten its foreign investment legislation to make itself more attractive to investors.

Other areas of adjustment, such as changes to the land-holding system, have provoked fierce resistance from Ecuador's highly organized indigenous groups, who have also protested at the environmental and cultural impact of the government's efforts to encourage foreign oil companies to drill for oil on traditional Indian lands.

	GDP/capita US$	Growth %	Exports US$m	Imports US$m	Debt US$bn	Inflation %	Wages
1982	1403	-1.8	2327	2187	6.2	24	75.9
1983	1347	-4.0	2348	1421	6.9	53	63.6
1984	1372	1.8	2622	1567	7.2	25	62.8
1985	1399	2.0	2905	1611	7.8	24	60.4
1986	1402	0.2	2186	1643	9.1	27	65.0
1987	1303	-7.0	2021	2054	10.3	33	61.4
1988	1384	6.2	2202	1583	10.6	86	53.4
1989	1353	-2.2	2354	1693	11.3	54	47.3
1990	1347	-0.4	2714	1711	11.9	50	39.6
1991	1379	2.4	2851	2207	12.3	49	33.5
1992	1393	1.0	3008	2048	12.1	60	32.5
1993	1393	0.0	2903	2325	12.8	31	-
1994★	1417	1.7	3600	2660	13.0	25	-

★ estimate

Key: GDP per capita (1980 US dollars); growth of GDP per capita (%); exports fob (US$ millions); imports fob (US$ millions); total external debt (US$ billions); annual inflation (%); index of real minimum wages (1980 = 100)

EL SALVADOR

Population (1992): 5.4 million
GDP (1992): US$6.0 billion
Latin America ranking by GDP: 13

The 1980s in El Salvador were dominated by the civil war between the government, backed by the US, and the guerrillas of the FMLN. Although this led to massive disruption of the economy, Washington's crusade against what it saw as the communist menace in Central America resulted in massive flows of military and economic aid – some $4.3bn by the time the war ended in 1992.

In addition, Salvadoreans living in the US sent an increasing number of dollars home until the annual figure reached around $700m a year in the early 1990s. This was approximately equal to the country's total export income.

US aid and remittances from Salvadoreans in the US have ensured that

El Salvador has never acquired the kind of debt burden experienced elsewhere in the region, and made only one visit to the IMF during the 1980s. However it has received regular IMF and World Bank support in the first half of the 1990s.

Even so, its economic trajectory has followed the regional trend. A slump in 1979 to 1982 was followed by stagnation during much of the 1980s and a recovery in the first half of the 1990s. As elsewhere, neo-liberals have come to dominate the political scene in the shape of the Nationalist Republican Alliance (ARENA) founded by death squad godfathers such as Major Roberto d'Aubuisson in the early 1980s. ARENA cleaned up its act in the late 1980s and won elections in 1989 and 1993.

The 1980s saw plenty of austerity, including a wage freeze between 1980 and 1984, but little structural change as the war took priority and US largesse cushioned the economy. Efforts to revive exports have had only limited results – export income in 1993 came to just $732m, compared to imports of $1723m. As US and other post-war reconstruction aid tails off, and Salvadoreans in the US start to forget their commitments back home, a painful crash-lending awaits the Salvadorean economy in the late 1990s.

	GDP/capita US$	Growth %	Exports US$m	Imports US$m	Debt US$bn	Inflation %	Wages
1982	656	-6.5	704	826	1.8	14	86.6
1983	654	-0.3	758	832	2.0	16	76.5
1984	663	1.3	726	915	2.1	10	76.8
1985	666	0.5	679	895	2.2	32	66.2
1986	661	-0.8	778	902	1.9	30	57.5
1987	667	1.0	590	939	1.9	20	46.0
1988	665	-0.3	611	967	1.9	18	43.6
1989	660	-0.8	498	1090	2.2	24	37.0
1990	669	1.4	580	1180	2.2	19	34.8
1991	677	1.2	588	1294	2.2	10	34.1
1992	697	3.0	587	1587	2.3	20	35.2
1993	714	2.4	732	1785	2.0	12	-
1994*	733	2.7	825	1950	2.0	9	-

* estimate

Key: GDP per capita (1980 US dollars); growth of GDP per capita (%); exports fob (US$ millions); imports fob (US$ millions); total external debt (US$ billions); annual inflation (%); index of urban real minimum wage (1980 = 100)

GUATEMALA

Population (1992): 9.8 million
GDP (1992): US$9.1 billion
Latin America ranking by GDP: 10

Guatemala has the largest economy and population in Central America. It has also suffered the longest and bloodiest civil war in the region. Guerrillas have been fighting the government since the 1950s, but the death toll took off in the early 1980s, when the Guatemalan military launched a pogrom against the country's majority indigenous population, killing around 70,000 people during the decade and wiping over 400 Indian villages off the map. By the mid-1990s hundreds of people every year were still dying in political violence.

The military oversaw a return to civilian rule in 1986, but still exercises enormous political and economic influence; it owns a large number of industries and other firms, including its own bank.

The barbarism of the military meant that the regime was cut off from Washington in the early 1980s, but unlike in nearby Nicaragua, Washington did not extend the boycott to the IMF, which agreed Standby Arrangements in 1981 and 1983.

The return to elected government in 1986 improved access to aid and credits, and helped Guatemala return to steady, if unspectacular, per capita growth.

Guatemalan governments are traditionally averse to raising taxes, but they also spend almost nothing on their people, especially the Indians. This allowed governments to avoid extreme indebtedness and inflationary spending in the 1980s, apart from a blip in 1990, and has obviated the need for some of the fierce shocks administered elsewhere. Nevertheless, real wages fell from 1983 to 1991.

The government has made some progress in diversifying into non-traditional exports such as textiles produced in free trade zones and fresh vegetables like mangetout and broccoli, but exports are still dominated by the traditional crops of coffee, bananas and sugar. Trade liberalization since 1990 has produced an import surge in the early 1990s, creating a large trade deficit since 1992. To date this has been covered by capital inflows, although the privatization programme shows little sign of getting going and remittances and aid from the US are far lower than in the case of El Salvador.

	GDP/capita US$	Growth %	Exports US$m	Imports US$m	Debt US$bn	Inflation %	Wages
1982	1041	-6.1	1170	1284	1.8	-2	124.7
1983	985	-5.4	1092	1056	2.2	15	126.2
1984	958	-2.8	1132	1182	2.5	5	114.8
1985	926	-3.3	1060	1077	2.6	28	99.2
1986	901	-2.7	1044	876	2.7	21	81.0
1987	907	0.7	978	1333	2.7	9	86.5
1988	916	1.0	1073	1413	2.6	12	91.0
1989	923	0.8	1126	1484	2.7	20	95.8
1990	923	0.0	1211	1428	2.6	60	78.5
1991	928	0.6	1230	1673	2.6	10	74.5
1992	946	1.9	1284	2328	2.5	14	85.6
1993	953	0.8	1356	2381	2.1	12	-
1994★	961	0.8	1620	2435	2.1	13	-

★ estimate

Key: GDP per capita (1980 US dollars); growth of GDP per capita (%); exports fob (US$ millions); imports fob (US$ millions); total external debt (US$ billions); annual inflation (%); index of average real wages for those enrolled in social security system (1980 = 100)

GUYANA

Population (1992): 0.8 million
GDP (1992): US$0.5 billion
Latin America ranking by GDP: 23

Formerly a British colony Guyana gained independence in 1966. It entered the 1980s run by Forbes Burnham, who committed the country to a 'transition to socialism' and strengthened links with Cuba and the Soviet Union. Large parts of the economy were in state hands.

Unfortunately, Burnham had also maintained sufficient links with the West to run up a large debt. In 1982 Guyana got the worst of both worlds – a debt crisis and no help from Western governments, banks or the international financial institutions, who objected to Burnham's politics. By 1984 the public sector deficit had reached 60 per cent of GDP, Guyana was in arrears on debt repayments and no rescheduling was in sight. Per capita GDP fell by over 12 per cent for two years in a row and then stagnated for the rest of the decade.

After Burnham's death in 1985, Desmond Hoyte became president and began to abandon statism and look to neo-liberalism for solutions to the country's crisis. In 1986 the government began to court foreign investors, bringing in a new investment code in 1988 which opened up virtually all the economy to private investors, especially foreign logging and mining companies, with disastrous consequences for its ecosystem (see p. 110). The same year it announced the Economic Recovery Programme, drawn up with IMF help, which included a crackdown on the deficit, privatization and other reforms.

In 1990 Guyana was duly rewarded with two IMF loans which opened the way to debt rescheduling and new loans from multilateral and bilateral sources. This enabled a swift return to impressive growth rates, but also meant increased debt service as new loans fell due. Debt service in 1992 already took up 45 per cent of the government's spending.

In 1992 former leftist Cheddi Jagan won the presidency and promptly continued along the neo-liberal lines of his predecessor. In 1994 the IMF kept up the pressure for reform with a further three year loan conditioned on reducing the fiscal deficit, further liberalization and tax reform to reduce direct taxes. However the IMF and World Bank were both critical of the slow pace of privatization and the government's decision to give wage rises to its employees.

	GDP/capita US$	Growth %	Exports US$m	Imports US$m	Debt US$bn	Inflation %
1982	603	-12.6	256	284	1.0	19
1983	531	-12.0	189	231	1.2	13
1984	552	3.9	210	213	1.3	25
1985	551	-0.1	206	226	1.5	15
1986	551	0.0	214	241	1.6	8
1987	557	1.1	242	266	1.7	29
1988	545	-2.3	230	216	1.7	40
1989	520	-4.6	238	258	1.9	89
1990	504	-3.1	218	269	2.0	65
1991	527	4.8	266	307	2.0	89
1992	561	6.4	341	380	1.9	14
1993	600	7.0	416	484	1.8	8
1994*	642	7.0	480	532	1.9	10

* estimate

Key: GDP per capita (1980 US dollars); growth of GDP per capita (%); exports fob (US$ millions); imports cif (US$ millions); total external debt (US$ billions); annual inflation (%)

HAITI

Population (1992): 6.8 million
GDP (1992): US$1.6 billion
Latin America ranking by GDP: 21

Haiti has the the worst economic record in the hemisphere; it started the 1980s with the lowest GDP per capita and this then fell every year, reaching a miserable $134 per person by 1994. By comparison the next poorest country, Nicaragua, had a per capita GDP of $424.

The government has traditionally run a small public sector, levying only minimal taxes on the Haitian élite. Remittances from Haitians in the US and elsewhere have traditionally provided vital foreign exchange, but balance of payments crises in the early 1980s forced it to go to the IMF for two one-year loans in 1982 and 1983, and then a longer term Structural Adjustment Facility in 1986. However, the chaos since then has destroyed just about the only sign of structural adjustment – Haitian free trade zones, which could undercut the labour costs anywhere else in the hemisphere and were producing 62 per cent of Haiti's export income in 1991–92, in the shape of everything from baseballs to electronic assembly.

The country's plight has been worsened by corruption, political unrest and the military's unwillingness to tolerate anyone other than a stooge as president. When free elections were finally held in 1990, leading to the election of a progressive priest, Father Jean-Bertrand Aristide, as president, the military overthrew him within six months.

After Aristide's overthrow, the economy was further battered by political unrest and a US trade and aid embargo, and shrank by a third from 1991 to 1994. In October 1994, Aristide was restored to office following a bloodless US occupation. In return for Washington's support, he accepted a World Bank structural adjustment programme, which included sacking 45,000 state employees, privatizating state companies, trade and investment liberalization, improved tax collection and the creation of a social security 'safety net' to offset the impact of the package.

	GDP/capita US$	Growth %	Exports US$m	Imports US$m	Debt US$bn	Inflation %	Wages
1982	231	-5.2	270	324	0.4	5	100.8
1983	228	-1.2	288	324	0.6	11	94.0
1984	225	-1.4	319	338	0.6	5	87.1
1985	222	-1.3	223	345	0.6	17	91.3
1986	219	-1.3	191	303	0.7	-11	84.8
1987	213	-2.6	210	311	0.8	-4	94.7
1988	210	-1.1	180	284	0.8	9	94.8
1989	208	-1.0	148	259	0.8	11	95.7
1990	204	-2.2	160	247	0.9	26	99.7
1991	194	-4.9	163	300	0.8	7	-
1992	163	-16.2	73	197	0.8	18	-
1993	152	-6.6	80	175	0.8	39	-
1994*	134	-11.8	45	140	0.9	-	-

* estimate

Key: GDP per capita (1980 US dollars); growth of GDP per capita (%); exports fob (US$ millions); imports fob (US$ millions); total external debt (US$ billions); annual inflation (%); index of minimum daily wage in manufacturing (1980 = 100)

HONDURAS

Population (1992): 5.5 million
GDP (1992): US$4.2 billion
Latin America ranking by GDP: 18

The original banana republic, Honduras has traditionally been the poorest country in Central America, depending on banana and coffee exports to bring in foreign exchange.

Since the onset of the debt crisis, Honduras has gone through a prolonged recession, followed by virtual stagnation. As in Nicaragua and El Salvador, Honduras' experiences in the 1980s were shaped by geopolitics. In return for allowing the US to station Contra rebels on its border with Nicaragua, Washington rewarded the Honduran government with large slices of aid, allowing it to resist the worst of IMF policies. After a Stand-By Arrangement in 1982, Honduras had no further IMF agreement until 1990.

From 1986 onwards, the Contra war began to decline and pressure for a full structural adjustment programme began to grow. In addition, US aid began to tail off, forcing Honduras to turn to the IMF and World Bank. The Bank approved a $50m Structural Adjustment Loan in 1988, but then suspended it when Honduras failed to reach agreement with the IMF the following year. USAID also froze its programme.

In 1989 a new government took office, led by the neo-liberal Rafael Callejas. He swiftly liberalized trade, devalued the *Lempira*, began a privatization programme and cleared the backlog of debt arrears. His government signed a second SAL with the World Bank, followed in 1992 by a three-year loan from the IMF.

In 1993 public hostility to structural adjustment was instrumental in electing Roberto Reina on an anti-neo-liberal platform. However, the escalating debt burden, rising fiscal deficit and falling US aid made his attempt to increase social spending and defy international pressure to toe the neo-liberal line look doomed from the start. As 1994 wore on, The World Bank and IMF increased their pressures for more privatization, cuts in transport subsidies and increases in sales taxes, provoking widespread strikes and other protests.

	GDP/capita US$	Growth %	Exports US$m	Imports US$m	Debt US$bn	Inflation %	Wages
1982	672	-5.2	677	681	2.0	9	104.5
1983	664	-1.2	699	756	2.2	7	96.5
1984	655	-1.4	737	885	2.4	4	92.1
1985	646	-1.3	790	879	2.8	4	89.1
1986	638	-1.3	891	874	3.4	3	85.3
1987	649	1.7	833	813	3.8	3	83.3
1988	660	1.7	875	870	3.8	7	79.7
1989	670	1.6	883	835	3.4	11	72.6
1990	647	-3.4	848	870	3.6	35	87.1
1991	643	-0.7	808	864	3.2	25	84.4
1992	662	3.0	843	983	3.5	7	97.0
1993	684	3.4	846	1080	3.8	13	-
1994*	656	-4.2	950	1115	3.9	28	-

* estimate

Key: GDP per capita (1980 US dollars); growth of GDP per capita (%); exports fob (US$ millions); imports fob (US$ millions); total external debt (US$ billions); annual inflation (%); index of minimum real manufacturing wage (1980 = 100)

JAMAICA

Population (1992): 2.5 million
GDP (1992): US$3.6 billion
Latin America ranking by GDP: 19

Jamaica has the dubious distinction of being the hemisphere's top IMF addict, signing eight separate agreements with the Fund from 1981 to 1994 as well as three World Bank Structural Adjustment Loans. These brought in their wake regular debt reschedulings with commercial banks and Western governments, as well as new loans. However the frequency is in part a sign of how often the agreements have broken down and had to be renegotiated, as Jamaica has regularly failed to meet its IMF targets.

For most of the 1980s, Jamaica was run by a soul-mate of President Reagan. Edward Seaga was elected in 1980, the same year as the US president, and brought to an end eight years of social democratic reform by Michael Manley, who had regularly challenged both Washington and the IMF. Seaga was rewarded with special treatment from Washington. In 1989 a chastened Manley was re-elected, but opted to continue with much of Seaga's economic adjustment programme.

Despite the efforts of both government and World Bank to diversify, the Jamaican economy is still based on mining and tourism. Alumina and bauxite (used in making aluminium) still account for around 60 per cent of merchandise trade, while tourism is instrumental in generating the dollars to make up the persistent deficit on trade. The booms and busts in world bauxite prices combined with periodic application of IMF austerity programmes to a large extent explain the behaviour of Jamaica's per capita GDP since 1982.

The adjustment process has succeeded in establishing a *maquiladora* sector, mainly based in free trade zones, where foreign companies can take advantage of some of the lowest wages in the Caribbean. The main product is clothing, which brought in around $300m in exports in 1991. Other factories produce chemicals and electrical equipment, or simply perform data input; Jamaican typists key in endless figures for US companies and the data is then beamed back to the parent organization by satellite.

	GDP/capita US$	Growth %	Exports US$m	Imports US$m	Debt US$bn	Inflation %
1982	1262	-1.5	767	1209	2.8	7
1983	1260	-0.2	686	1124	3.3	17
1984	1242	-1.4	702	1037	3.5	31
1985	1158	-6.7	569	1004	4.0	23
1986	1167	0.7	590	837	3.6	10
1987	1232	5.5	709	1061	4.0	8
1988	1258	2.1	883	1240	4.0	9
1989	1335	6.1	1000	1606	4.0	17
1990	1417	6.0	1158	1680	4.2	30
1991	1413	0.1	1145	1551	3.9	77
1992	1420	0.5	1053	1457	3.7	40
1993	1425	0.3	1045	1859	3.7	30
1994*	1426	0.1	1100	1910	3.7	25

* estimate

Key: GDP per capita (1980 US dollars); growth of GDP per capita (%); exports fob (US$ millions); imports fob (US$ millions); total external debt (US$ billions);6nual inflation (%)

MEXICO

Population (1992): 84.8 million
GDP (1992): US$196.4 billion
Latin America ranking by GDP: 2

Mexico has been the country in the news during the silent revolution, not always for positive reasons. In August 1982 it was Mexico that precipitated the debt crisis by announcing it could no longer pay its debt service. Tough stabilization policies were demanded in return for being bailed out by the Western nations and the banks. Real wages fell by 25 per cent in 1983 alone.

Mexico first suppressed imports, generating a multi-billion dollar trade surplus with which to pay off the debt. Then, following the fraudulent election of Carlos Salinas in 1988, the ruling Institutional Revolutionary Party (PRI) embarked on a sweeping market transformation of the traditionally state-dominated Mexican economy.

Salinas privatized hundreds of state enterprises, including the telecommunications companies and national airlines. He deregulated trade (Mexico had joined the GATT in 1986) and began negotiating a free trade treaty with the US which came into force in 1994 as the North American Free Trade Agreement (NAFTA). NAFTA tied Mexico's future permanently to that of the US economy and generalized the *maquiladora* experience to the whole Mexican economy – in the early 1980s the fall in Mexican wages attracted hundreds of US companies to set up assembly plants just over the US-Mexican border.

Once the economy had been stabilized, privatization and deregulation attracted billions of dollars in foreign capital, both in investment and loans (in 1993 Mexico overtook India as the World Bank's largest borrower). Simultaneously, Salinas lowered tariffs and removed other barriers to imports. The result was a massive import boom; imports almost quintupled from 1987 to 1994, turning the trade surplus of the early 1980s into a $23bn deficit. Mexico won the first Brady Plan debt reduction deal, but its debt continued to rise due to its reliance on bond issues to finance its trade deficit. By 1995, it was threatening to overhaul Brazil as the Third World's largest debtor.

The human cost of this transformation was severe. Real wages in 1994 had yet to recover their 1980 value, while inequality had massively increased – Mexico's stock of dollar billionaires rose from 2 to 24 during the course of Salinas's presidency. The PRI's decision to reverse its traditional support for communal land-ownership by Mexico's large indigenous population sparked an Indian rebellion in Chiapas in 1994, souring the advent of NAFTA. However the PRI, now the oldest one party state in the world, is nothing if not durable, and came back to win the elections in 1994 without even needing to resort to widespread fraud.

The new government of Ernesto Zedillo got off to a nightmare start. Finding itself rapidly running out of foreign reserves, which had been drained throughout 1994 to prop up the peso, the government devalued, provoking a stampede of foreign investors. Washington was forced to step in to refloat its neo-liberal flagship, putting together a huge $50bn rescue package, involving US, IMF and other funds, but by then Mexico's image with foreign investors was badly tarnished. In return for the bail-out, sky-high interest rates and renewed government austerity forced Mexico back into recession, and real wages seemed set for another sharp fall. The government predicted half a million jobs would be lost within a three-month period.

	GDP/capita US$	Growth %	Exports US$m	Imports US$m	Debt US$bn	Inflation %	Wages
1982	2505	-3.2	21230	14434	87.6	99	104.4
1983	2339	-6.6	22320	8553	93.8	81	80.7
1984	2363	1.0	24196	11256	96.7	59	75.4
1985	2363	0.0	21663	13212	97.8	64	75.9
1986	2213	-6.3	16031	11432	100.5	106	71.5
1987	2205	-0.4	20655	12222	102.4	159	72.0
1988	2180	-1.0	20566	18898	100.9	52	71.3
1989	2129	-1.1	22765	23410	95.1	20	77.8
1990	2181	2.2	26838	31271	101.9	30	79.4
1991	2211	1.4	26855	38184	114.9	19	84.7
1992	2222	0.5	27516	48193	114.0	12	92.9
1993	2195	-1.2	30033	48924	127.4	8	100.2
1994*	2224	1.3	34190	57835	136.0	7	99.4

* estimate

Key: GDP per capita (1980 US dollars); growth of GDP per capita (%); exports fob (US$ millions); imports fob (US$ millions); total external debt (US$ billions); annual inflation (%); index of average real industrial wages (1980 = 100)

NICARAGUA

Population (1992): 4.0 million
GDP (1992): US$2.0 billion
Latin America ranking by GDP: 20

After Haiti, Nicaragua is Latin America's most tragic economic disaster story. In the 1980s, its fate was determined by its conflict with the US. Following the Sandinista Revolution of 1979, Washington isolated the new government, preventing lending by the IMF and World Bank, ending US aid and in 1985 announcing a total embargo on trade. At the same time it launched a counter-insurgency war against the Sandinistas, building up the Contra army who launched raids across the border from Honduras.

The embargo and war effort undid most of the initial achievements of the revolution, diverting government spending away from health and education and generating an escalating fiscal deficit which brought hyper-inflation in its wake. In 1988 Nicaragua recorded a Latin American record of 33,548 per cent inflation in a single year.

The Sandinistas launched their own stabilization efforts, but with limited success, and in 1990 were voted out of office. By then real wages were down to less than 15 per cent of their 1980 value.

Once the Sandinistas were out, the IMF took over where the US had left off. The new government of Violeta Chamorro was promptly rewarded with an influx of US aid and the ending of the trade embargo, culminating in a three year IMF loan in 1994 which in turn opened the way to debt rescheduling and new loans. In return the US, and subsequently the IMF, demanded the usual measures: privatization, stabilization, cutbacks in state spending and mass lay-offs of public employees.

The government complied with most of the measures, and its March 1991 stabilization package succeeded in bringing inflation down from 13,500 per cent to just 4 per cent in the space of two years. However, it failed to produce economic recovery; by 1994 GDP per capita was down to $424, compared to $743 in 1982; export revenues were less than half of those from imports and Nicaragua had hardly begun to diversify away from the traditional export crops of coffee, bananas, sugar, meat and cotton.

In 1994, the government signed a three-year IMF structural adjustment package committing it to yet more austerity, job cuts and deregulation (see p. 56). The government also obtained a World Bank Structural Adjustment Loan in the same year.

	GDP/capita US$	Growth %	Exports US$m	Imports US$m	Debt US$bn	Inflation %	Wages
1982	743	-4.0	406	723	3.1	22	95.8
1983	752	1.2	429	778	3.8	33	97.4
1984	716	-4.8	386	800	4.4	50	78.5
1985	664	-7.3	305	794	4.9	334	5.0
1986	639	-3.7	258	677	5.8	747	19.8
1987	619	-3.0	295	734	6.3	1347	13.6
1988	522	-15.6	236	718	7.2	33548	4.8
1989	500	-4.3	319	547	9.7	1689	9.2
1990	485	-3.1	332	570	10.5	13490	14.8
1991	467	-3.6	268	688	10.2	775	15.3
1992	452	-3.4	223	771	10.8	4	17.7
1993	430	-4.7	267	659	11.0	20	-
1994★	424	-1.3	330	720	11.6	12	-

★ estimate

Key: GDP per capita (1980 US dollars); growth of GDP per capita (%); exports fob (US$ millions); imports fob (US$ millions); total external debt (US$ billions); annual inflation (%); index of average real wages of those enrolled in the social security system (1980 = 100)

PANAMA

Population (1992): 2.5 million
GDP (1992): US$5.7 billion
Latin America ranking by GDP: 14

Panama is a special case, its economy dominated by the Canal Zone running through its heart and the fact that its currency is effectively the US dollar, giving the government far less leeway in economic management.

In the early 1980s, problems with debt service forced Panama to go to the IMF. In exchange, some structural adjustment got under way but rapidly fell victim to the escalating conflict between Washington and Manuel Noriega. The crisis in US-Panamanian relations led to US sanctions, while political instability drove investors away from Panama and the enormous Colón Free Zone, the biggest free zone in the world after Hong Kong. Colón is used to re-export industrial goods all over Latin America and generates large amounts of income for the Panamanian government.

Instability and US actions forced per capita GDP into a 17.6 per cent nose-dive in 1988, paving the way for the US invasion the following year.

After the installation of Guillermo Endara as president, sanctions were lifted and the economy recovered much of the lost ground, growing rapidly until 1995. Exports more than doubled between 1989 and 1994.

	GDP/capita US$	Growth %	Exports US$m	Imports US$m	Debt US$bn	Inflation %	Wages
1982	1911	2.7	2411	3045	3.9	4	94.1
1983	1869	-2.2	1676	2321	4.4	2	98.2
1984	1820	-2.6	1686	2509	4.4	1	105.0
1985	1855	1.9	1974	2731	4.8	0	105.6
1986	1859	0.8	2366	2907	4.9	0	108.4
1987	1862	0.2	2492	3058	3.7[a]	1	109.9
1988	1535	-17.6	2347	2531	3.8	0	101.2
1989	1500	-2.2	2681	3084	3.8	0	108.9
1990	1547	3.1	3316	3805	3.7	1	102.1
1991	1658	7.2	4181	4983	3.7	1	106.0
1992	1764	6.4	5012	5894	3.6	2	106.0
1993	1827	3.6	5259	6244	3.5	1	-
1994*	1880	2.9	5645	6685	3.5	2	-

* estimate

Key: GDP per capita (1980 US dollars); growth of GDP per capita (%); exports fob (US$ millions); imports fob (US$ millions); total external debt (US$ billions); annual inflation (%); index of average industrial real wages in Panama City (1980 = 100)
[a] From 1987 onwards debt figures are for public debt only.

An IMF agreement followed in 1992, although Endara rapidly fell out of favour with the Fund over the speed of reform. In 1994 the new government of President Pérez Balladares drew up a five year plan to open up the economy by liberalizing trade and foreign investment and deregulating the labour market.

PARAGUAY

Population (1992): 4.5 million
GDP (1992): US$6.9 billion
Latin America ranking by GDP: 11

When Argentina or Brazil sneezes, Paraguay catches cold. The economic fortunes of the small, land-locked South American nation are largely determined by events in its giant neighbours. Both are more important than the US as trading partners for Paraguay, something of a rarity in Latin America. That relationship deepened still further when Mercosur came into force in 1995.

In the 1970s the country enjoyed a boom based on the construction of the giant Itaipú hydroelectric dam on the borders of the three countries. Construction ended just as the West went into recession and the debt crisis broke in Argentina and Brazil. In Paraguay 1982 to 1983 were years of recession.

However Paraguay's own debt burden was not sufficient to create a foreign exchange crisis and Paraguay, along with Colombia and Suriname, was one of the only countries in the region never to need an IMF Stand-by Arrangement. However the debt burden rose inexorably during the 1980s and Paraguay fell into arrears in 1987–88.

In 1989 the old tyrant Alfredo Stroessner was ousted after 35 years in power, and economic policy began to change. The new president, General Andrés Rodríguez, moved to begin a privatization programme and signed the Mercosur agreement. Yet Paraguay has continued to treat the IMF and adjustment in general with caution.

In 1994 the Senate voted to ban the pending privatization of five state companies, while talks on a Stand-by Arrangement began in 1989 but were still deadlocked in 1994 over Paraguay's refusal to accept severe austerity policies as a condition for the loan. The government meanwhile, successfully broke with debt crisis protocol and renegotiated its debt with the Paris Club nations in the absence of an IMF agreement.

	GDP/capita US$	Growth %	Exports US$m	Imports US$m	Debt US$bn	Inflation %	Wages
1982	1309	-4.0	396	711	1.2	4	102.4
1983	1230	-6.0	326	551	1.5	14	95.2
1984	1230	0.0	361	649	1.7	30	91.8
1985	1241	0.9	466	659	1.8	23	89.8
1986	1199	-3.4	576	864	1.9	24	85.9
1987	1216	1.4	597	919	2.0	32	96.5
1988	1257	3.4	871	1030	2.0	17	103.9
1989	1291	2.7	1242	1016	2.0	29	109.8
1990	1293	0.1	1376	1473	1.7	44	103.5
1991	1285	-0.6	1106	1691	1.7	12	102.3
1992	1271	-1.1	1032	1827	1.3	18	98.8
1993	1285	1.1	1216	1876	1.2	20	-
1994*	1287	0.2	1240	2000	1.3	19	-

* estimate

Key: GDP per capita (1980 US dollars); growth of GDP per capita (%); exports fob (US$ millions); imports fob (US$ millions); total external debt (US$ billions); annual inflation (%); index of average real industrial wages in Asunción (1980 = 100)

PERU

Population (1992): 22.5 million
GDP (1992): US$29.1 billion
Latin America ranking by GDP: 7

Peru took the full IMF medicine in 1982, signing a three-year IMF loan in exchange for the usual stabilization package. The result was disastrous, with per capita GDP falling 14.1 per cent in 1983, and the IMF suspending the loan over missed targets. By then 400,000 jobs had been lost in the recession.

In 1985 a new government headed by Alan García changed tack and opted for a heterodox stabilization programme, known as the *Inti* plan. García raised and then froze prices and wages, devalued the Inti before fixing the exchange rate, and imposed import controls. He also publicly defied the banks and IMF, declaring that Peru would unilaterally impose a ceiling on its debt repayments equivalent to 10 per cent of export income. Peru was severely punished for its temerity, a virtual financial boycott being used to turn it into an international pariah. The *Inti* plan produced two years of strong growth and rising wages, but then collapsed in a welter of inflation and uncontrollable fiscal deficits. By 1988 economic policy was back on the orthodox straight and narrow.

In 1990 Peruvians elected as president the least neo-liberal presidential candidate, Alberto Fujimori, but upon taking office he executed a spectacular U-turn and announced a programme which became known as 'Fujishock'. All subsidies were eliminated – the price of petrol went up 3000 per cent overnight – public spending was cut, a tax reform increased tax revenues and a longer-term adjustment programme of trade (Peru has announced it wants to join GATT) and privatization introduced. Fujishock also had an immediate social impact: in Lima average protein intake fell by 30 per cent between July and November.

Fujimori also privatized pension funds along Chilean lines to try and create a strong local capital market. In 1992 Fujimori dissolved a troublesome Congress in a 'self-coup' to become a virtual dictator, backed by the army. In 1993 Fujishock received its inevitable reward – a three-year IMF loan.

IMF approval, falling inflation, and privatization have guaranteed large inflows of foreign capital since 1991, creating a stock market boom and a sudden growth spurt in 1993 and 1994, turning Peru into the region's fastest-growing economy. As elsewhere, capital inflows and import liberalization have swung the trade balance into deficit.

While the macro-economic record is impressive, Fujishock has had a devastating effect on real wages, which in 1994 were still just 47 per cent of their 1980 level.

	GDP/capita US$	Growth %	Exports US$m	Imports US$m	Debt US$bn	Inflation %	Wages
1982	1205	-2.3	3294	3721	11.5	73	100.5
1983	1035	-14.1	3017	2723	12.5	125	83.7
1984	1057	2.1	3149	2141	13.3	112	70.1
1985	1056	-0.1	2978	1806	13.7	158	77.6
1986	1112	5.3	2531	2596	14.5	63	101.1
1987	1177	5.8	2661	3182	15.4	115	108.9
1988	1057	-10.2	2691	2790	16.5	1723	82.1
1989	917	-13.2	3488	2291	18.5	2775	44.8
1990	849	-7.5	3231	2891	20.0	7650	39.1
1991	854	0.6	3329	3494	21.0	139	42.1
1992	819	-4.1	3485	4050	21.7	57	41.6
1993	855	4.4	3463	4043	22.1	40	41.3
1994*	931	8.9	4250	5500	23.1	18	47.4

* estimate

Key: GDP per capita (1980 US dollars); growth of GDP per capita (%); exports fob (US$ millions); imports fob (US$ millions); total external debt (US$ billions); annual inflation (%); index of average real private sector wages in Lima (1980 = 100)

SURINAME

Population (1992): 0.4 million
GDP (1992): US$1.3 billion
Latin America ranking by GDP: 22

Suriname, formerly Dutch Guiana, is an oddity in many ways. The Dutch government forgave all Suriname's debts at independence in 1975, and then continued to fund most of the public investment programme. As a result Suriname has managed to avoid incurring a large foreign debt. Even so, rising government fiscal deficits (reaching 29 per cent of GDP in 1986), have driven the country into debt arrears.

Suriname has also refused to contemplate IMF-style stabilization and adjustment. As of 1993, it still had widespread import controls and demanded that all foreign companies reinvest their profits locally. Despite these restrictions, foreign companies have been lured in by Suriname's mineral wealth, principally bauxite and gold. Bauxite and its processed form, alumina, make up 85 per cent of exports.

Suriname's growth is largely determined by a combination of the world bauxite price and the degree of political chaos at home (the country was involved in a civil war in the late 1980s). The Dutch government cut off aid in 1982 in protest at political repression by the regime of Lt. Col. Desi Bouterse, triggering several years of economic decline. In 1988 Suriname returned to civilian government, but the military continued to exert a high level of control, replacing the president in 1990 and calling new elections.

	Growth %	Exports US$m	Imports US$m	Debt US$bn	Inflation %
1982	-	429	514	-	-
1983	-	367	472	-	4
1984	-3.2	356	346	-	5
1985	0.7	329	299	.057	16
1986	-0.6	335	327	.060	30
1987	-8.0	306	294	.073	52
1988	6.1	409	351	.071	7
1989	2.2	549	331	.08	15
1990	-3.6	466	374	.58	20
1991	-4.3	346	347	-	26
1992	-6.8	341	273	-	44
1993	-	351	250	-	144
1994*	-	-	-	-	140

* estimate

Key: Growth of GDP per capita (%); exports fob (US$ millions); imports cif (US$ millions); total external debt (US$ billions); annual inflation (%)

TRINIDAD AND TOBAGO

Population (1992): 1.3 million
GDP (1992): US$5.3 billion
Latin America ranking by GDP: 15

The Trinidadian economy has been built on oil, which replaced its colonial dependence on sugar. By 1980 oil made up 92 per cent of exports. The global recession and interest rate surge of the early 1980s coincided with the end of the oil boom as Trinidad's oil fields started to run dry. For most of the decade, the government could rely on the reserves built up in the boom years to finance its deficit and debt repayments. But by 1988 the cupboard was bare, and Trinidad had no choice but to fall into line, approve austerity measures and approach the IMF for help.

In early 1989 the IMF agreed a Stand-by Arrangement in return for public spending cuts, the removal of protection for local industries and restrictions on credit. A similar agreement was reached the following year. The government has also signed a World Bank Structural Adjustment Loan, commenced a privatization programme and begun rescheduling debt repayments to its creditors.

By 1995 the boom years were well and truly gone. Per capita GDP has fallen to $3628 from $5578 in 1982 and a return to sustained growth is proving elusive.

	GDP/capita US$	Growth %	Exports US$m	Imports US$m	Debt US$bn	Inflation %
1982	5578	-0.5	2289	2487	1.2	11
1983	4986	-10.6	2027	2233	1.4	15
1984	4602	-7.7	2111	1705	1.2	14
1985	4409	-4.2	2111	1355	1.4	7
1986	4246	-3.7	1363	1209	1.9	10
1987	3985	-5.9	1397	1058	2.1	8
1988	3814	-4.3	1453	1064	2.0	12
1989	3768	-1.2	1535	1045	2.4	9
1990	3775	0.2	1935	948	2.5	10
1991	3802	0.7	1751	1210	2.4	2
1992	3673	-3.4	1662	996	2.2	9
1993	3526	-4.0	1560	1020	2.1	14
1994*	3628	2.9	1610	1060	2.3	6

* estimate

Key: GDP per capita (1980 US dollars); growth of GDP per capita (%); exports fob (US$ millions); imports fob (US$ millions); total external debt (US$ billions); annual inflation (%)

URUGUAY

Population (1992): 3.1 million
GDP (1992): US$9.5 billion
Latin America ranking by GDP: 9

Sandwiched between its two giant neighbours, Argentina and Brazil, Uruguay is heavily dependent on their economic fortunes. Both countries are its main trading partners, outweighing the importance of the US or EU, and this dependence only increased when Mercosur, the Southern Cone Common Market, came into force in 1995. Uruguay is highly reliant on its traditional *gaucho* exports of meat and wool, which still bring in about 50 per cent of export income.

Uruguay has been a regular customer of the IMF and World Bank since 1981, but the relationship has not been an easy one. Uruguay is proud of its welfare state, one of the most developed in Latin America, and has resisted IMF pressure to dismantle it. Several IMF loans have been suspended as a result, and Uruguay has failed to get inflation below 50 per cent since 1983, leaving it with one of the highest rates in the region.

Economic policy since the onset of the debt crisis has largely followed Argentina's. Initial stabilization led to a fierce recession in the early 1980s. In 1985 the new civilian government opted to reflate the economy and produced a short-lived boom, but in 1990 a neo-liberal presi-

	GDP/capita	Growth	Exports	Imports	Debt	Inflation	Wages
	US$	%	US$m	US$m	US$bn	%	
1982	2156	-10.7	1256	1038	4.2	21	107.1
1983	2012	-6.7	1156	740	4.6	52	84.9
1984	1973	-1.9	925	732	4.7	66	77.1
1985	1956	-0.9	854	675	4.9	83	67.3
1986	2071	5.9	1088	815	5.2	71	71.7
1987	2218	7.1	1182	1080	5.9	57	75.0
1988	2204	-0.6	1405	1112	6.3	69	76.0
1989	2220	0.7	1599	1136	7.0	89	75.8
1990	2226	0.3	1693	1267	7.4	129	70.4
1991	2285	2.6	1605	1544	7.2	81	73.0
1992	2447	7.1	1703	1941	7.7	59	74.6
1993	2469	0.9	1645	2190	7.9	53	78.2
1994*	2565	3.9	1850	2700	8.1	45	79.2

* estimate

Key: GDP per capita (1980 US dollars); growth of GDP per capita (%); exports fob (US$ millions); imports fob (US$ millions); total external debt (US$ billions); annual inflation (%); index of average real wages (1980 = 100)

dent, Luis Alberto Lacalle, took office pledged to fight inflation and privatize state companies. However his plans had to be shelved when the privatization programme was rejected in a referendum in December 1992.

Uruguay reduced its debt and debt service with a Brady Plan agreement with the banks in late 1990. In the early 1990s, Uruguay followed the Argentine example, with high rates of per capita growth and capital inflows financing an import boom. However by 1994 wages were still under 80 per cent of their 1980 value.

VENEZUELA

Population (1992): 20.2 million
GDP (1992): US$72.7 billion
Latin America ranking by GDP: 4

Venezuela is a petroleum junkie whose economy rises and falls in line with the international price of oil. Oil still made up over 80 per cent of exports in 1991. In the 1970s, Venezuela borrowed billions of dollars on the strength of its future oil wealth, but most of them went out the back door as capital flight – a Venezuelan speciality.

The early 1980s brought a severe recession as rising debt service coincided with falling oil prices. Import suppression generated a trade surplus which rose as oil prices recovered, before being wiped out in 1986 when oil prices collapsed again. The US-Iraqi war of 1990 brought another oil windfall, allowing Venezuela to stockpile over $4bn in reserves that year.

Throughout the first part of the 1980s, Venezuela used its trade surplus and reserves to keep up with debt repayments and avoid recourse to the IMF. However by 1988 its reserves were exhausted and it embarked on a painful adjustment in 1989, backed by loans from the IMF and World Bank. Real wages collapsed to less than half their 1980 level, prices rose as subsidies were cut, and anywhere between 300 and 1500 people died as IMF riots broke out in the major cities.

The government has been lukewarm about privatization of the massive state sector (which accounts for over 90 per cent of exports through the state's oil, aluminium, steel and other industries). Instead, it has encouraged joint ventures to acquire foreign capital and technology without ceding control. It has also introduced some partial trade liberalization and signed a number of Regional Trade Agreements, notably the G3 treaty with Colombia and Mexico.

The adjustment programme remained extremely unpopular and in 1994 Rafael Caldera took office after running a fiercely anti-neo-liberal campaign. He was confronted by an immediate run on the currency as capital flight took off, and a bank collapse which forced the government to partially nationalize the banking sector and impose exchange controls. Within weeks, Venezuela was back to its traditionally statist regime of price and import controls and state intervention throughout the economy. Not surprisingly, Caldera and the IMF are barely on speaking terms.

	GDP/capita US$	Growth %	Exports US$m	Imports US$m	Debt US$bn	Inflation %	Wages
1982	3839	-4.1	16332	13584	35.1	7	100
1983	3525	-8.2	14570	6409	36.0	7	98.4
1984	3394	-3.7	15481	7260	34.7	18	93.5
1985	3286	-3.2	14283	7501	33.8	7	84.2
1986	3371	2.6	8535	7866	33.8	13	85.4
1987	3416	1.3	10437	8870	34.8	40	74.5
1988	3522	3.1	10082	12080	34.7	36	66.0
1989	3163	-10.2	12915	7283	33.2	81	48.4
1990	3296	4.2	17444	6807	33.1	37	46.2
1991	3530	7.1	14892	10101	34.0	31	42.4
1992	3650	3.4	13988	12714	37.0	32	46.8
1993	3562	-2.4	14222	11013	38.0	46	-
1994*	3352	-5.9	15695	7710	38.8	71	-

* estimate

Key: GDP per capita (1980 US dollars); growth of GDP per capita (%); exports fob (US$ millions); imports fob (US$ millions); total external debt (US$ billions); annual inflation (%); index of average real wages in Caracas (1980 = 100)

Rival Economic Models

Comparison of Neo-structuralism, Import Substitution and Neo-liberalism

Note: The reader should be aware that the appendix compares the failure in practice of import substitution and neo-liberalism with the proposals of an as-yet-untried neo-structuralism. Since such proposals are usually over-optimistic, it is hardly surprising if neo-structuralism emerges looking the strongest option.

Role of the state

Import substitution
Over-intrusive, especially in production, leading to bloated, inefficient state-owned enterprises (SOEs) which drove up fiscal deficits and inflation. In other areas, state was usually inefficient, bureaucratic and corrupt.

Neo-liberalism
In economic terms, the state is part of the problem, not the solution. Market mechanisms seen always as preferable to the state. Assault on state involvement throughout the economy involves cuts in spending, deregulation and privatization. However, state as *political* actor seen as vital in establishing the rules of the game for private investment and in disciplining labour.

Neo-structuralism
Problem is not one of size, but quality. State must be overhauled, strengthened and turned into an efficient regulator and manager, while keeping direct involvement in production to a minimum. Apart from managing macro-economic policy, the state's main tasks should be in providing basic services (transport, health and education) and intervening through R&D and infrastructure programmes, to improve competitiveness of economy as a whole.

Poverty and equity

Import substitution
Welfare state gave only partial coverage, largely to urban working class, allowing poverty and inequality to grow, especially in deprived rural areas.

Neo-liberalism
Growth will eventually 'trickle down' to the poor. During adjustment, however, the government should actively pursue poverty alleviation through targeted social compensation programmes. Poverty relief is more important than equality or changes in income distribution, which can endanger the prospects for growth.

Neo-structuralism
Equity and growth are not mutually exclusive, but complementary. They should become the twin goals of adjustment, instead of an exclusive focus on growth. This requires greater emphasis on job creation, human capital formation (health, education, housing) and wealth redistribution, including agrarian reform.

Democracy

Import substitution
Associated with populist regimes like those of Perón (Argentina) and Vargas (Brazil) which brought the urban working class into the political fray, but largely excluded the peasantry. In later years, was also linked to military dictatorship (Brazil after 1964), but rarely with participative democracy.

Neo-liberalism
Supports restricted concept of liberal democracy and the rule of law, but in practice has often been associated with authoritarian rule, as in Pinochet's Chile. The erosion of equity resulting from neo-liberal adjustment endangers the democratic transition by increasing social and political instability.

Neo-structuralism
Participation and consensus-building are essential to increase equity and create the political basis for sustained growth. Decentralization of government to the regions should be part of this process.

Public finances

Import substitution

Inefficient SOEs, the commitment to subsidies, large state payroll, a limited welfare state and inability/unwillingness to collect taxes led to regular fiscal deficits and inflationary pressures. Governments prefer milking profitable SOEs (such as oil companies) instead of unpopular tax increases.

Neo-liberalism

Fiscal deficits cut by sharply reducing public spending. Subsidies and public employment cut back. Some improvement in tax collection. One-off income from privatizations helps balance books and gets rid of some loss-making companies (but also some profitable ones).

Neo-structuralism

Accepts need to avoid fiscal deficits, but argues for increase in revenue through tax reform, allowing increased public spending.

Taxation

Import substitution

Taxes low and largely unpaid. State revenues are largely income from SOEs, import and export tariffs, foreign borrowing or the printing press.

Neo-liberalism

Tax revenues increased and shifted from income tax to sales taxes, hitting the poor. Collection also improved.

Neo-structuralism

Tax burden should be increased still further, since still lags a long way behind other areas of the world. Tax reform should be made progressive by shifting towards direct (income and wealth) taxes and away from sales taxes like VAT.

Technology and training

Import substitution

Ineffectual level of government support, due to lack of demand. Most modern technology imported by transnational companies.

Neo-liberalism
State funding for R&D and training schemes cut, technological innovation and training left to private sector/transnational companies.

Neo-structuralism
Essential area of state activity and key to long-term development. State should fund R&D, national training schemes and promote awareness of importance of technological innovation in achieving global competitiveness.

State-owned v private-sector enterprises

Import substitution
Large SOEs and private sector companies created, operating as monopolies/oligopolies in protected markets. Prestige projects of public works given priority over quality of service.

Neo-liberalism
SOEs privatized and competition encouraged by withdrawal of protection. However, small and medium-sized companies decline as unregulated market forces favour monopolies.

Neo-structuralism
Concentrate on reforming remaining SOEs to make them efficient, rather than privatizing them. State should intervene to encourage the creation of new enterprises by the private sector, especially in strategic areas. More support for small and medium-sized enterprises, especially co-operatives.

Natural resources

Import substitution
Seen as infinitely exploitable, often by SOEs.

Neo-liberalism
Intensified exploitation for export, privatization of SOEs.

Neo-structuralism
Increased state regulation of market to ensure 'proper exploitation'. Tax and regulate private sector, rather than nationalize.

Infrastructure

Import substitution
Massive state investment in roads, dams, electrification, etc.

Neo-liberalism
Shift to private sector, encourage charging users for infrastructure.

Neo-structuralism
Priority for telecommunications expansion. Emphasize quality and maintenance over new works.

Capital formation and the financial system

Import substitution
State development banks, massive state projects geared to industrialization for domestic market, financed by overseas borrowing, leading to the debt crisis.

Neo-liberalism
Encourage private commercial banks to take over investment in productive sectors. Lack of regulation of private sector leads to numerous banking crises. Downplays problem of how to increase domestic savings and capital formation.

Neo-structuralism
Priority is to shift credit to small and medium-sized enterprises. Major effort to boost domestic savings, rather than borrowing abroad, through improved pension fund legislation. Legislate to shift the domestic financial market away from short-term speculation towards long-term, productive investment.

Trade and integration

Import substitution
A high degree of permanent protection, both through tariffs and quotas. Anti-export bias, putting domestic market first. Regional integration to expand domestic market.

Neo-liberalism
Trade and financial deregulation and liberalization. Suppress domestic

consumption to achieve short-term trade surplus, but otherwise do little on specific export promotion. Free international trade.

Neo-structuralism
Low levels of protection, temporary protection for new sectors contributing to technical progress. Aim for competitiveness based on productivity, not low wages. State intervention to promote manufactured exports. Regional integration aimed to help Latin America compete in world markets by pooling R&D, marketing, communications etc.

Foreign capital flows

Import substitution
After initial period of hostility towards transnational corporations, foreign capital inflows encouraged both as direct investment and, increasingly, as bank loans during the 1970s. Accumulated debts sparked the Mexican crisis of August 1982 and ensuing capital famine.

Neo-liberalism
Restrictions on capital movements eliminated. Along with privatization, bond issues by governments and private companies, and stock market expansion, this encourages a renewed inflow of capital. However, most of the incoming capital does not go into productive investment and also makes many currencies overvalued, thereby reducing the competitivity of exports and building large trade deficits.

Neo-structuralism
Foreign capital should be managed to prevent it distorting the economy and make it contribute to growth with equity. Long-term investment should be given preferential treatment over short-term 'hot money'.

---

1. Sources: CEPAL, *Changing Production Patterns with Social Equity*, Santiago, 1990, pp. 98, 99 and 100; O. Sunkel and G. Zuleta, 'Neo-structuralism v Neo-liberalism in the 1990s', in *Cepal Review* No.42, Santiago, December 1990; CEPAL, *Social Equity and Changing Production Patterns: An Integrated Approach*, Santiago, 1992; CEPAL, *Latin America and the Caribbean: Policies to Improve Linkages with the Global Economy*, Santiago, 1994.

Glossary of Terms on Structural Adjustment/Neo-liberalism

Amortization Repayment of principal of a loan over a period of years (as opposed to interest payment).

Asian Tigers The rapidly industrializing economies of East Asia, such as Taiwan and South Korea, often held up as an example to other Third World countries. Also known as NICs.

Baker Plan Debt initiative announced by US Treasury Secretary James Baker in 1985. The plan unsuccessfully attempted to force commercial banks to loan new money, while giving the World Bank an enhanced role in overseeing the adjustment process.

Balance of Payments Deficit/Surplus A country is said to have a balance of payments deficit when its income (credits from exports, cash inflows, loans etc) is less than its payments (debits such as imports, cash outflows, debt repayments etc.).

Brady Bond Government bonds issued by debtor countries as part of the Brady Plan debt reduction scheme, in exchange for part of their foreign debt.

Brady Plan Debt reduction scheme launched in March 1989 by US Treasury Secretary Nicholas Brady.

Bretton Woods Town in New Hampshire, the site of an international conference in 1944 which set up the World Bank and the IMF to regulate the international monetary system after the Second World War.

Capital Flight Transfer of money abroad, usually in dollars; often illegal, or irregular, in Latin America.

Capital Goods Heavy machinery such as turbines, cranes etc used by industry to produce consumer goods.

Capital-intensive The kind of production which involves a high ratio of capital investment, e.g. in machinery, compared to labour costs. Generates few jobs for a given amount of investment.

CEPAL Spanish acronym of the UN's Economic Commission for Latin America and the Caribbean, based in Santiago, Chile.

Cepalismo Economic model promoted by CEPAL in the 1950s and 1960s, which provided the theoretical underpinning for import substitution.

Comparative Advantage Concept developed in the 18th century by

David Ricardo. Argues that the best way to increase overall welfare is for each nation to stick to the activity at which it is best, and to trade with others working on the same principle. Frequently cited as a reason why Latin American countries should stick to exports based on natural resources and cheap labour.

Current Account Deficit   That part of a country's international balance of payments which refers to current, rather than capital, transactons. Includes foreign trade, payments of interest and dividends.

Debt for Equity Swap   The exchange, at a discount, of developing country foreign debt for equity (i.e. shares) in local companies.

Debt Service   The payment of interest and repayment of the original loan on national debt, whether domestic or foreign.

Default   Non-payment of debt service.

Devaluation   A deliberate reduction of the official exchange rate at which one country's currency is exchanged for others. Short term effect is to make imports dearer and reduce the dollar value of local currency holdings. In longer term should improve export competitivity.

Disbursements   Actual payments of promised loans, debt service etc.

Diversification   Increasing the range of goods produced, usually for export. Reduces a country's vulnerability to sudden price swings for a particular product.

ECLAC   The UN's Economic Commission for Latin America and the Caribbean, based in Santiago, Chile.

Economies of Scale   Phenomenon by which unit costs for a particular product fall as the total number produced increases, since initial investment in research, technology, machinery etc. is now spread over a greater quantity of goods.

Eurodollars   Dollars held by individuals and institutions outside the US.

Export–led Growth   GDP growth driven by increasing exports, rather than by increasing domestic consumption or investment.

Fiscal Deficit   Caused when a government's expenditure exceeds its tax income. The government is forced to cover its deficit by borrowing (increasing its debt) or by printing money (increasing inflation).

Fordism   Form of mass production based on assembly lines which dominated the world economy after the Second World War, until it was superceded by more flexible Japanese working practices such as JIT.

Foreign Direct Investment (FDI)   Investment abroad, usually by transnational corporations, involving an element of control by the investor over the corporation in which the investment is made.

FTA   Free Trade Agreement, such as NAFTA or GATT.

Fujishock   Peruvian stabilization programme launched by President Fujimori in 1990.

GATT General Agreement on Tariffs and Trade. The major global forum for negotiations aimed at reducing tariffs and other barriers to free trade, controlled by the industrialized countries. Superceded by World Trade Organisation in 1995.

GDP Gross Domestic Product. The total annual value of domestic production of goods and services in a national economy.

GNP Gross National Product. The GDP corrected for the net flow of capital into or out of the country.

Gold Standard A system which prevents exchange rate fluctuations by obliging a country's central bank to give gold, at a fixed exchange rate, in return for its currency.

Heterodox Name given to a number of Latin American stabilization programmes in the mid and late 1980s. These combined orthodox IMF measures with others involving a higher degree of state intervention, such as price freezes. Often involved the introduction of a new currency.

IDB InterAmerican Development Bank. Washington-based regional development bank.

Inflation The rate of increase (usually measured over a year) in the general level of prices, reflecting the decreasing purchasing power of a national currency.

IMF International Monetary Fund. Established in 1944 at the Bretton Woods conference. Its purpose is to provide short to medium-term financial assistance to countries with balance of payments problems. In exchange, countries are expected to adopt structural adjustment policies.

IFC International Finance Corporation. Arm of the World Bank which lends to private sector bodies.

IFIs International Financial Institutions, such as the World Bank, International Monetary Fund or InterAmerican Development Bank.

Import Substitution Economic model pursued by much of Latin America from 1930 to 1980, whereby the state intervened in the economy to speed up the process of industrialization and reduce a country's reliance on imports. Usually involved protection for local industry against imported goods.

IPRs Intellectual Property Rights. Copyright and patent laws applied to designs, inventions and trademarks. Also known as TRIPs (trade-related intellectual property rights).

JIT Just in Time. Name given to Japanese practice of running very low stocks so that each component in a finished product arrives 'just in time' from a network of subcontractors. Allows cheaper, more flexible systems of production.

Keynesianism Economic doctrine inspired by the British economist John Maynard Keynes. In the aftermath of the great depression, Keynes pioneered government intervention in the economy to manage demand and reduce unemployment.

Labour Intensive The kind of production which involves a low ratio of capital investment e.g. in machinery, compared to labour costs. Generates many jobs for a given amount of investment. One example of labour intensive investment is the *maquiladora* sector.

Letter of Intent Document in which a government sets out its policy targets for the IMF as a basis for the IMF agreeing a Stand-by Arrangement or other loan.

Maquiladoras Assembly plants set up along the US-Mexican border, using cheap Mexican labour to assemble parts imported from the US and elsewhere, which are then re-exported to the US market for sale.

Mercosur Latin America's largest Regional Trade Agreement, signed in 1991 by Brazil, Argentina, Uruguay and Paraguay. Came into force in 1995, with longer timescales for protection to be phased out in some sectors e.g. computers.

Monetarism Economic theory which holds that inflation is caused by excessive growth in the money supply. Based on the work of economists such as Milton Friedman.

Moratorium Cessation of debt-service payments.

NAFTA North American Free Trade Agreement, between the US, Mexico and Canada. Came into force on 1 January 1994.

Neo-liberalism *Laissez-faire* economic theory underlying structural adjustment, which has revived belief in the central role of the market, and opposes state intervention in the economy.

Neo-structuralism Attempt by CEPAL and others to define a new body of thought to challenge neo-liberalism. Involves increased role for the state.

New Deal US President Roosevelt's economic recovery package, launched to rebuild the US after the great depression of the 1930s. Involved increased government spending and state intervention in the economy to reduce unemployment and prevent repeats of the 1930s slump.

NGO Non-Governmental Organization.

NIC Newly Industrialized Country. Third World countries such as South Korea or Taiwan which have successfully industrialized in recent years. Sometimes also applied to Latin America's main industrial powers, such as Brazil and Mexico.

Non-traditionals New kinds of exports, seen as a key part of the export-led growth strategy promoted by structural adjustment. May be agricultural (e.g. flowers or vegetables) or manufactures, such as textiles.

OPEC Organization of Petroleum Exporting Countries.

Paris Club An informal gathering of creditor nations which meet to discuss rescheduling requests from debtor nations of the loans outstanding to official agencies and governments.

PRI Spanish acronym of Mexico's governing party, the Institutional Revolutionary Party, which has ruled the country since 1929 in what is now the world's oldest one-party state.

Principal The capital sum of a loan, as opposed to interest which is then added on.

Protectionism Practice whereby a government uses tariff barriers, quotas or other means to protect domestic producers against competition from cheaper imports.

PT Portuguese acronym for the Brazilian Workers' Party, the continent's largest left-wing political grouping.

R&D Research and Development. Usually applied to government and private sector spending on developing and adapting new forms of technology to improve productivity or produce new kinds of product. Increasingly seen as the key to economic success.

***Real* plan** Brazilian stabilization plan announced in 1994 by then Finance Minister Fernando Henrique Cardoso.

Reschedule To revise or postpone dates on which capital or interest payments are due.

RTAs Regional Trade Agreements, such as Mercosur or the Andean Pact, involving more than two nations in mutual tariff reductions and other measures.

SDRs Special Drawing Rights were created in July 1969 as a form of international reserve asset to replace the dollar as the IMF's official unit of account. The IMF makes loans in SDRs to member countries, which can be used to buy dollars to resolve balance of payments problems.

Secondary Market A market for the resale of foreign debt, at a discount, outside the official market.

SOE State-owned enterprise.

Stabilization Programme Government policy package aimed at curbing inflation and stabilizing the economy. Seen by neo-liberals in the IMF, World Bank and elsewhere as the first stage in a broader structural adjustment programme.

Supply Side The forces considered by some economists to determine output; the availability or supply of capital and labour, and the state of technology.

Stand-By Arrangement The name given to the agreement between a government and the IMF, under which funds can be drawn by the government over a period of time subject to the government meeting performance targets agreed in advance and enshrined in a letter of intent.

Structural Adjustment Set of policies designed to move the economy of a Third World country onto the path of export-led growth. This involves deregulating trade and commerce, cutting back the role of the state and encouraging foreign investment. Structural adjustment is the neo-liberal panacea for most Third World ills.

Technocrat New generation of academically qualified, high-ranking civil servants or, increasingly, elected politicians who are taking over many powerful positions in Latin American governments from the older traditional politicians.

Temporeros Temporary agricultural workers, often involved in producing non-traditional exports such as grapes or kiwi fruit.

Terms of Trade The ratio of the index of export prices to the index of import prices. If export prices rise more quickly than import prices, the terms of trade improve.

Trade Deficit Negative balance created when a country imports more than it exports.

Transnational Corporations International companies which have grown so large that they have effectively ceased to be based in any one country, moving factories and investments around the world according to business criteria such as access to market and local government legislation. Also known as multinational companies.

TRIMs Trade Related Investment Measures. Measures relating to investment which affect trade, for example tax incentives or subsidies offered to foreign companies in return for locating their factories in a particular place.

TRIPs See IPRs.

UNICEF United Nations Children's Fund.

Value Added The value added to a commodity at each stage of its manufacture.

World Bank Otherwise known as the International Bank for Reconstruction and Development (IBRD). Created in 1944 at the Bretton Woods conference. Originally designed to help with post-war reconstruction in Europe, then shifted its attention to the Third World, where it has taken on an increasingly central role in pushing through neo-liberal reforms.

World Trade Organisation International body set up by the Uruguay Round of GATT to increase pressure for tariff reductions and other free trade measures. Began operation in 1995.

Zapatista Member of the Zapatista National Liberation Army, a guerrilla group based in the southern Mexican state of Chiapas.

Further Reading

There is a vast and constantly expanding literature on each of the subjects covered in this book, but to help readers keen for further information, I have selected some of the most useful sources in English.

General introductions

There is no one easily accessible introduction to the Latin American economy. Economics students should try Victor Bulmer Thomas' excellent and comprehensive *The Economic History of Latin America since Independence* (Cambridge, 1994). One of the best general introductions to the region's economic history and current challenges is Eliana Cardoso & Ann Helwege, *Latin America's Economy: Diversity, Trends and Conflicts* (Cambridge, MA, 1992).

More general political and economic introductions are available from Oxford Analytica, *Latin America in Perspective* (Boston, MA, 1991) and Duncan Green, *Faces of Latin America* (London, 1991). For a damning case study of the neo-liberals' favourite economy, try Joseph Collins and John Lear, *Chile's Free Market Miracle: A Second Look* (Oakland, CA, 1995).

For those wishing to consult the original neo-liberal gurus, there is Friedrich von Hayek's *The Road to Serfdom* (London, 1944) or *Constitution of Liberty* (Chicago, 1960) while Milton Friedman's vast output includes *A Monetary History of the United States* (Princeton, NJ, 1963), *Inflation: Causes and Consequences* (New York, 1963) and *Free to Choose. A Personal Statement* (New York, 1980). Readers who prefer their economic history ready-packaged could instead browse in John Kenneth Galbraith, *A History of Economics: The Past as the Present* (London, 1987).

To help you keep up to date with Latin America's fast-changing economy, there are several annual economic surveys of the region. The Inter-American Development Bank publishes *Economic and Social Progress in Latin America* (Washington, DC), while the World Bank produces the influential *World Development Report* (New York). More critical reviews are contained in UNCTAD's *Trade and Development Report* (New York) or in CEPAL's two annual overviews, *Economic Panorama of Latin America* and the more comprehensive *Preliminary Overview of the Economy of Latin America and the Caribbean* (both Santiago).

Origins and consequences of the debt crisis

The debt crisis has spawned a massive literature, largely consisting of highly critical studies of the role of Northern institutions and the harsh social impact of their policies in the South. The most readable and evocative general overviews are those of Susan George, notably *Fate Worse than Debt* (London, 1988). For particular studies of Latin America, try Jackie Roddick, *Dance of the Millions: Latin America and the Debt Crisis* (London, 1988) or Sue Branford and Bernardo Kucinski, *The Debt Squads: The US, the Banks and Latin America* (London, 1988).

The role of the World Bank and IMF
The debt crisis and the Bretton Woods institutions' 50th birthday in 1994 have generated a number of critical studies. For a general polemic, try Graham Hancock, *Lords of Poverty* (London, 1989), while Susan George and Fabrizio Sabelli have written an unbeatable study of the World Bank in *Faith and Credit: The World Bank's Secular Empire* (London, 1994). For a more academic critique of the Bank's approach, see Paul Mosley *et al.*, *Aid and Power: The World Bank and Policy-based Lending* (2 vols) (London, 1991), while the voice of a disenchanted insider can be heard in Davison Budhoo, *Enough is Enough Mr Camdessus: Open Letter of Resignation to the Managing Director of the International Monetary Fund* (New York, 1990).

In the highly readable *Dark Victory: The United States, Structural Adjustment and Global Poverty* (London, 1994), Filipino economist Walden Bello portrays structural adjustment and the role of the international institutions as part of a general US strategy of 'global rollback'.

Social and environmental impact of adjustment
Again, this area has generated a substantial literature, often as part of broader studies of the debt crisis and the role of the international institutions. For the views of a number of authors from the South, see Dharam Ghai (ed.), *The IMF and the South: The Social Impact of Crisis and Adjustment* (London, 1991), while David Woodward has written two comprehensive analyses for the British development agency, Save the Children Fund, *National and International Dimensions of Debt and Adjustment in Developing Countries* and *The Impact of Debt and Adjustment at the Household Level in Developing Countries* (both London, 1992).

Susan George, in *The Debt Boomerang: How Third World Debt Harms Us All* (London, 1992), tries to broaden the debate by showing how the debt crisis harms the North, as well as the South. For specific studies of the environmental impact of adjustment, see Morris Miller, *Debt and the Environment: Converging Crises* (New York, 1991) and David Reed, *Structural Adjustment and the Environment* (London, 1992). One example of the World Bank's huge paper-mill on these issues is George Psachoropoulos *et al.*, *Poverty and Income Distribution in Latin America: The Story of the 1980s* (Washington, DC, 1992), while for a more critical look from within the UN, see UNICEF's landmark publication by G. Cornia *et al.*, *Adjustment With a Human Face* (Oxford, 1987) or *The Invisible Adjustment* (New York, 1989).

Useful annual surveys can be obtained from the UN Development Program, which publishes *The Human Development Report* (New York) or CEPAL, which has started an annual publication, *Social Panorama of Latin America* (Santiago). The impact of adjustment on the labour force can be followed through the International Labour Organisation's annual *World Labour Report* (Geneva).

Foreign investment and capital markets

Most of the day-to-day information on such fast-changing areas comes in the shape of periodicals, newspapers and, if you can afford them, on-line services. See, for example, the IMF's *International Capital Markets* (Washington, DC) or the World Bank's International Finance Corporation publication, *Investment Review* (Washington, DC). For a more long-term look at the role of transnational companies, there is Robert Grosse, *Multinational Companies in Latin America* (London, 1989) or the fascinating *World Investment Report* (New York), an annual overview of the role of transnationals published by UNCTAD's Program on Transnational Corporations. *Multinational Monitor* (Washington, DC) publishes a monthly magazine highly critical of the activities of transnational corporations around the world.

Readers wishing to try and grapple with the increasingly important and elusive role of international capital markets should obtain Howard M. Wachtel, *The Politics of Supranational Money* (Amsterdam, 1987).

Trade and free trade agreements

For critical analyses of the South's role in world trade, see Michael Barratt Brown, *Fair Trade: Reform and Realities in the International Trading System* (London, 1993) or Belinda Coote, *The Trade Trap: Poverty and the Global Commodity Markets* (Oxford, 1992). In the case of the GATT agreement, Kevin Watkins provides a lucid critique in *Fixing the Rules: North-South Issues in International Trade and the GATT Uruguay Round* (London, 1992). More dispassionate views of the GATT agreement can be found in Phillip Evans, *Unpacking the GATT: A Step by Step Guide to the Uruguay Round* (London, 1994) or (for the well-heeled) Phillip Evans and James Walsh, *The EIU Guide to the New GATT* (London, 1994).

For a well-argued assault on NAFTA, try Harry Browne, *For Richer for Poorer: Shaping US-Mexican Integration* (London, 1994). A more pro-NAFTA view can be found in William A. Orme Jr, *Continental Shift: Free Trade and the New North America* (Washington, DC, 1993). Augusta Dwyer has written a powerful condemnation of the social impact of US-Mexican integration in *On the Line: Life on the US-Mexican Border* (London, 1994).

Alternatives to neo-liberalism

Books on alternatives tend to be restricted to the field of academic debate, since the more popular books often concentrate on condemning the iniquities of the present system while failing to offer convincing alternatives. For well-argued academic presentations, see Christopher Colclough and James Manor, *States or Markets? Neo-liberalism and the Development Policy Debate* (Oxford, 1991) or Patricio Meller (ed.), *The Latin American Development Debate: Neo-structuralism, Neo-monetarism and Adjustment Processes* (Boulder, CO, 1991).

To date, the most convincing (and certainly the most readable) overall alternative proposal from a Latin American is probably Jorge Castañeda's *Utopia Unarmed: The Latin American Left after the Cold War* (New York, 1993).

Fernando Fajnzylber has written an excellent analysis of the challenge of industrialization in the off-puttingly titled, *Unavoidable Industrial Restructuring in Latin America* (Durham, NC, 1990), while Gary Gereffi and Donald L. Wyman (eds) provide a brilliant and engrossing comparison with the East Asian 'tigers' in *Manufacturing Miracles: Paths of Industrialization in Latin America and East Asia*, (Princeton, NJ, 1990).

A more accessible look at the alternatives is contained in John Cavanagh, Daphne Wysham and Marcos Arruda (eds), *Beyond Bretton Woods: Alternatives to the Global Economic Order* (London, 1994), while Kies Biekart and Martin Jelsma (eds) have pulled together work on alternatives in agriculture in *Beyond Protest: Peasants in Central America* (Amsterdam, 1994).

CEPAL publishes regular calls for a change of approach, playing a pioneering role in developing the neo-structuralist school of thought in such works as *Changing Production Patterns with Social Equity* (Santiago, 1990); *Social Equity and Changing Production Patterns: An Integrated Approach* (Santiago, 1992) and *Latin America and the Caribbean: Policies to Improve Linkages with the Global Economy* (Santiago, 1994)

More fundamental critiques of the assumptions and impact of neo-classical economics, coupled with calls for a radical rethink of the discipline, are contained in Herman E. Daly and John B. Cobb Jr, *For the Common Good: Redirecting the Economy towards Community, the Environment and a Sustainable Future* (London, 1990) and Paul Ekins, *Wealth Beyond Measure: An Atlas of New Economics* (London, 1992).

Newspapers and periodicals

In the UK, *The Economist* and the *Financial Times* have the most comprehensive coverage of economic events in the region, although readers should take *The Economist*'s excessive self-confidence with a large pinch of salt. There are numerous weekly and monthly summaries aimed at foreign investors, such as *Latin American Newsletters* (London), *Business Latin America*, (New York) and *Latin America Monitor* (London), as well as the excellent country-by-country quarterly reports and annual profiles of the Economist Intelligence Unit (London).

More critical coverage can be found in a few periodicals published in the South, such as the fortnightly *Third World Economics* (Penang, Malaysia). CEPAL's biannual *CEPAL Review* is not for the fainthearted, but contains good analytical articles on many issues surrounding the development debate. Of the many academic journals on development and related issues, *World Development* (Oxford) is one of the most authoritative.

Index